Merthyr Tydfil

The Tempus History of Wales

Series Editor
Professor Gareth Williams, University of Glamorgan

Our curiosity about the past remains insatiable. Interest in the Welsh past is no exception, and exists not only among the Welsh themselves. Partly as the consequence of a general resurgence of interest in the Celts, partly because of the rapidly changing nature of the social and physical landscape of Wales itself, the history of a Wales that was or may have been continually attracts new audiences. While scholarly research finds outlets in academic publishing and leaned journals, its specialist findings are not always accessible to the general reader, who could often benefit from a broader synoptic view. Valuable and often innovative studies in community, family and special-interest history are enthusiastically pursued outside the academy, too. Established scholars and younger researchers will contribute to this new series aimed at illuminating aspects of the Welsh past for a wide readership.

Published
David Moore, *The Welsh Wars of Independence: c.410-c.1415*
'Beautifully written, subtle and remarkably perceptive... a major re-examination of a thousand years of Welsh history' John Davies, author of *The History of Wales*

Commissioned
Matthew Griffiths, *Tudor Wales 1440-1640*
Ioan Matthews, *The Welsh Valleys: A Social & Industrial History*
Nia Powell, *The Renaissance in Wales*
Richard Suggett, *Welsh Witches & Wizards: A History of Magic and Witchcraft in Wales*
Eryn White, *The Welsh Bible*

Further titles are in preparation

If you are interested in purchasing other books published by Tempus,
or in case you have difficulty finding any Tempus books in your local bookshop,
you can also place orders directly through our website
www.tempus-publishing.com

Merthyr Tydfil
Iron Metropolis

LIFE IN A WELSH INDUSTRIAL TOWN

KEITH STRANGE

TEMPUS

For Alexander

First published 2005

Tempus Publishing Limited
The Mill, Brimscombe Port,
Stroud, Gloucestershire, GL5 2QG
www.tempus-publishing.com

British Library Cataloguing in Publication Data.
A catalogue record for this book is available from the British Library.

ISBN 0 7524 3451 9

Typesetting and origination by Tempus Publishing Limited
Printed in Great Britain

CONTENTS

ABOUT THE AUTHOR

Keith Strange is a Senior Lecturer in History at the Cardiff School of Education, University of Wales Institute, Cardiff.

INTRODUCTION

This book is a study of Merthyr Tydfil in the middle decades of the nineteenth century. Merthyr has been chosen for three reasons: in the first instance it was the undisputed centre of the Welsh iron trade and it was the iron industry which catapulted Wales into the industrial economy. Its growth was phenomenal: between 1796 and 1846 Merthyr's export production soared from some 16,000 to over 200,000 tons and of this over 40% was produced by the Dowlais Iron Company, then the largest single ironworks in the world. Secondly, as the Iron Metropolis, Merthyr was the first Welsh town of any size. For the first time significant numbers of Welsh people experienced urban industrial life and, as the great majority of its inhabitants were working people, Merthyr provided Wales with its first urban proletariat. This provides the third justification, as the town was chosen by contemporaries eager to find fault with, or praise, the economic and social innovations brought by industrialisation. No tour of Wales was complete without a visit to the town and no other community drew forth so much debate on the values of the new order. Just as Manchester came to epitomise industrialisation in England, so Merthyr rapidly came to symbolise the transformation in Wales. As the *Morning Chronicle* put it in March 1850:

> In no other part of the mineral district of South Wales are the peculiar characteristics
> of the population engaged in mining and the manufacture of iron so strikingly devel-
> oped as at Merthyr; nor is there any other place which affords so favourable a point for
> observing the merits and defects of what may be comprehensively termed the economy
> of the iron works.

Given its pre-eminence, much has already been written about the town and in particular the rise of the iron industry, the appalling housing and public health provision, the tradition of political radicalism and the rise of the chapel, but there is more to the story of nineteenth-century Merthyr than belching furnaces, cholera epidemics, Chartist petitions and nonconformity. This book marks an attempt to broaden the picture by looking too at the paupers and thieves, thimble-riggers and prostitutes, Catholics and Mormons, Oddfellows and Ivorites, drunks, fighters and freaks of what was once the iron capital of the world.

PART 1

REALITIES

1

THE PEOPLING OF MERTHYR

Despite having something of a tradition of iron-making, with a scattering of small charcoal-burning furnaces since at least the reign of the Tudors, during the first half of the eighteenth century there was little sign that south Wales would emerge as one of Britain's major iron-manufacturing centres, and Merthyr Tydfil, which was to become the largest iron production centre in the world, was said to have no better use for its iron ore than 'the repair of the parochial road... when it became impassable for the farmer's car'.

Three factors were, in less than a century, to bring about a transformation: increased demand for iron, technological developments and improved communications. In the first instance, increased demand for iron for munitions, coupled with the interruption of supplies from abroad during the Seven Years War of 1756–63, meant that the conflict marked a watershed in the development of the Welsh iron industry. Previously regarded as far too remote to produce iron in any quantity at a profit, the region now came to be seen in a different light.

That south Wales contained all the necessary minerals was already known. Explorative surveys had revealed the extent of its coalfield, and associated with the coal reserves were clay ironstones, iron oxide ores, limestone and silica, all of which were necessary for iron production. Furthermore, the rivers and streams of the area, fed by a rainfall which reaches as much as 100 inches a year in places, provided abundant water power in an age prior to steam. As a result, outside interest grew into practical development and the establishment of all four of Merthyr's works: Dowlais in 1759, Plymouth in 1763, Cyfarthfa in 1765 and Penydarren in 1784. In each case the entrepreneurial acumen came from existing English iron centres backed by the financial capabilities of London and Bristol merchants, as well as indigenous wealth from well-established market towns like Brecon.

The fledgling industry was given a further boost by the American War of Independence and the long wars with France while, simultaneously, technological and transport developments enabled the works to expand beyond anything previously envisaged. Watt's perfection of the steam engine not only provided a new motive power, and one based on coal, but also increased the demand for iron. Of far greater significance, however, was the invention of the puddling process. Although usually attributed to Henry Cort in 1784, puddling was independently discovered by Peter Onions, a foreman at Cyfarthfa, and it was so widely adopted in south Wales that it became known throughout Britain as 'the Welsh method'. According to the historian Gwyn Alf Williams, it was Onions' discovery which really marked 'the point of break-through. It enabled coal to be employed to make malleable iron and in the context of massive demand... large, technically-advanced firms mushroomed'.

If the early years were characterised by expansion, it could only of necessity be limited, since the deplorable state of regional communications ensured that Merthyr would continue to be isolated and remote. Realising this, and having failed to overcome the problem by using packhorses and improving the turnpike road, the ironmasters turned to canals. Work began on the Glamorganshire Canal in 1790 and by 1794 it provided a link between Merthyr and Cardiff which was finally extended to the sea lock in 1798. The canal's contribution to Merthyr's development was immense and almost immediate: 'It was found that each barge with its load of 24 tons, drawn by one horse and attended by a man and a boy, brought down just as much [iron] as had previously occupied 12 wagons, 48 horses, 12 men and 12 boys'. It was the canal which enabled Merthyr's ironworks to prosper during the long Napoleonic Wars.[1]

Following Waterloo, and the post-war slump, Merthyr turned to the production of iron for a rapidly growing peacetime market. Ballast iron for shipping, plating for high-pressure boilers, cables and pipes were all manufactured to satisfy the ris-ing demand from both the domestic and foreign markets, but by far the greatest stimulus was provided by the coming of the railways. The first Welsh rail was rolled at Penydarren for Stephenson's Liverpool to Manchester line, and before long there was hardly a railway company in Britain which had not obtained at least a proportion of its rails from south Wales. However, if Merthyr was to capitalise fully on the grow-ing railway mania it was apparent that still better transport links were needed with Cardiff. Although Trevithick's steam locomotive – the first in the world – had made its historic run from Penydarren as early as 1804, it was not until 1841 that Brunel's Taff Vale Railway connected Merthyr with Cardiff, it being extended to Dowlais some ten years later. In 1853 the opening of the Aberdare tunnel meant that Merthyr's works could also use the Vale of Neath line to export their iron. Thus, at a time when Merthyr was providing the raw materials for the railway industry, the latter ensured her continued expansion by providing cheap and reliable access to the sea.

Once the domestic railway market had stabilised, Merthyr increasingly began to meet the demands posed by the North American, Austro-Hungarian and Russian markets. In 1844, for example, Dowlais had one order from Russia for 50,000 tons of rails. Because of such orders and the ever-expanding demand for iron both at home and abroad, the years between Waterloo and the Great Exhibition witnessed a massive growth in production. The same region which had been dismissed as an iron-producing centre in 1750 was manufacturing 40% of Britain's pig iron by 1823 and, though capacity increased faster in some other districts, with an annual output of 720,000 tons in 1847, south Wales still accounted for 35% of the national total. By common consent, the main impetus for such dramatic growth came from abroad, and as early as 1827 the region was supplying half of Britain's iron exports. This dependence on foreign markets was of crucial importance as it exposed Merthyr and the other Welsh iron centres to the vagaries of the trade cycle at a time of considerable continental unrest and upheaval. Consequently, by the 1840s Merthyr's economy was characterised by an all-too-familiar pattern of boom and depression, a pattern which was to pervade every facet of life in the town.

Despite the periodic setbacks and slumps, in general the first half of the nineteenth century was an age of expansion for Merthyr's works and this was reflected in the size and the scale of the plant involved. In 1819, for example, the average yield per furnace at Cyfarthfa was sixty-five tons; by 1845 this had risen to eighty tons and in 1857 it was 120 tons. By 1845 the Dowlais works was the biggest in the world, covering forty acres, ten of which were built on. Its eighteen furnaces produced over 1,700 tons of iron a week; its mills produced 2,000 tons of rails and 200 tons of bars each month; and in all, its miners and colliers dug 80,000 tons of iron ore and 140,000 tons of coal that year. Collectively, the ironworks were the wonders of the age; their 'towering furnaces' inspired observers, while their miles of piping and tramroads and their acres of mills and forges, refineries and engine houses lent credence to Britain's status as the 'Workshop of the World'.

For all their scale and technology, however, and despite the inventiveness of her engineers, Merthyr's ironworks were labour-intensive. Without a ready supply of labour there could be no iron made, and so once the ironmasters had formed their partnerships and secured enough land and mineral rights to establish their concerns, their most pressing problem was the recruitment of labour and especially skilled labour. As regards the success of their actions, when, much later, the *Western Mail* published an article on the history of south Wales, it wrote of Merthyr: 'The youth of Wales directed their footsteps to that El Dorado among the hills... It was as if a conscription had called away the strongest and most daring from the families of the poor'. There can be little doubt that such was the case, for the great mass of evidence points to a massive and quite unprecedented influx of people into the town in the first half of the nineteenth century.

Looking at the figures for the Parish of Merthyr, which, unfortunately, did not include significant areas of the town such as Cefn Coed and Vaynor, the population was 7,705 in 1801. By 1821 this had risen to 17,404; by 1841 it stood at 34,977; and by 1851 it was 46,382. In overall terms, the half-century saw a six-fold increase. From being a small and insignificant rural hamlet in 1750, Merthyr had easily become the largest town in Wales, over twice the size of its nearest rival, Swansea (with 21,533), and greater than the combined populations of both Swansea and Cardiff (which had a population of 18,351). That this rise was brought about by immigration rather than any significant natural increase was universally acknowledged, and nor could there be any questioning the fact that these immigrants were drawn by the ironworks. In 1849, Inspector Rammell reported to Westminster:

> The population consists entirely of:-
>
> 1. Ironmasters (four in number), their agents and workmen; and -
>
> 2. Such professional men and tradesmen as are necessary for supplying the wants of the former.

Turning now to an examination of these immigrants, in the case of Merthyr's elite (with the notable exception of the Dowlais works, which was launched by a partly local consortium) the ironworks were all founded by Englishmen, and within a generation or two each was a family concern. Having leased land at nominal rents, the works grew under the management of the Crawshays, Guests, Hills and Homfrays, men who came from the iron centres of Shropshire, Yorkshire and the north-east and who displayed all the characteristic traits of the new industrial pioneers.

Just as the masters originated from England, so too did their managers and agents, although by the middle of the nineteenth century a proportion of this managerial class was local in the sense that Merthyr, as a centre of technological innovation, tended to produce its own engineers – some of whom, like Watkin George and Adrian Stephens, became world-famous. As for the town's professional and trading class, once again the great majority were of English extraction, and particularly from the south-west. Historically, much of south Wales had come to regard Bristol as its financial and retailing centre; Bristol merchants and bankers awash with cash generated by the slave trade had been among the very first to operate in the emerging iron districts of south Wales, and the link was still important almost a century later. Not all such people originated from England, however, and Brecon also contributed to the supply. Furthermore, the existence of a Caledonian Society in the 1840s draws attention to the number of Scottish traders in the town. By no means all of Merthyr's middle-class residents were outsiders, however, and among its most influential inhabitants 'very striking is the survival... of many of the older, pre-industrial families of the district'. Despite such affiliations, however, so anglicised had these become by the 1840s that as a class, Merthyr's 'shopocracy' was, in an economic, social, cultural, religious and linguistic sense, poles apart from the great majority of the town's inhabitants, the working classes.

As far as the latter were concerned, despite the evidence that reveals American, Italian and even Indian workers in the 1840s, and Charles Wilkins' assertion that 'A greater diversity of speech you could not hear in any other place in the land', it would be a mistake to stress the cosmopolitan nature of Merthyr, for it was overwhelmingly a Welsh town. One observer at the turn of the nineteenth century maintained 'The workmen of all description at these immense works are Welshmen. Their language is entirely Welsh. The number of English amongst them is very inconsiderable.' By September 1846 little had changed, with the *Merthyr Guardian* reporting 'Welsh is the spoken language of nine-tenths of the operatives', while according to a paper delivered the year before at Cambridge to the British Association, 84% of the population of Merthyr Parish in 1841 were Welsh, 13% were English and the remaining 3% were Irish.

An analysis of the 1851 census revealed that, of those aged twenty or over, 26% were Merthyr-born, another 12% had been born elsewhere in Glamorgan, 40% came from Carmarthenshire, Pembrokeshire, Cardiganshire and Breconshire, 15% from north Wales, England, Scotland and elsewhere and 7% from Ireland. Thus 78% of the adult population had originated from south and west Wales while more had moved from mid- and north Wales. Such figures are misleading, however, as not only do they ignore those aged under twenty but they refer to Merthyr as a whole and do not differentiate between different localities within the town. Though the question of settlement will be dealt with later, it needs to be pointed out here that, if the business area of central Merthyr and its immediate environs was ignored, the working-class communities surrounding the four works would emerge as being far more Welsh than the overall returns suggest. A study by Carter and Wheatley, for example, analysed the 1851 returns for three enumeration districts, namely North Georgetown (Cyfarthfa), New South Wales (Dowlais) and Pentrebach (Plymouth), and revealed that the percentage of Welsh-born inhabitants in each was 91.8%, 91.9% and 92.4% respectively.[2]

As far as the pattern of immigration to Merthyr was concerned, the picture which emerges is one of almost concentric appearance, whereby, as the works expanded, so people from further and further away were attracted to the town. Evidence suggests that the steady growth of the works prior to 1800 enabled them to meet most of their demands for skilled workers locally, 'while the tardy adoption of… [the puddling process] in England prior to 1797 hardly created there a reservoir of skilled workmen upon which the Welsh industry could draw'. By the 1840s, the clear impression is one of skilled workers being generally born and bred in Merthyr with one generation passing on its skills to the next, frequently from father to son. One should not suppose that skill was not imported, however, especially in the early days. When Samuel Homfray moved down from Shropshire he brought some men from the Callcot works with him. Similarly, the first Guest, in order to attract skilled workers to such a 'remote' and 'extreme' area, offered free housing as an incentive, and even as late as 1834, when the Dowlais works engaged a John Buddle from Newcastle, he was 'to be provided with a dwelling house and fire coal, and with pit flannels by the Company'.

When they were unable to recruit from other iron centres, Merthyr men were sent to English works to gain the necessary skills or the masters resorted to tempting skilled men away from other local works. Such poaching was a constant irritant to the masters of south Wales and allegations of it continued well into the middle of the century. Generally speaking, however, it was associated with the early days of development, when the masters were determined to recruit the labour they required and 'every effort was made to provide a nucleus of skilled operatives to lay the foundation of an indigenous supply for the future'. By the 1840s it appears this policy had been very largely successful, and once this tradition of skill had been established the migrants were increasingly employed in those tasks classed as semi-skilled or unskilled.

Before addressing why it was that Breconshire and the counties of south-west Wales provided the bulk of such labour, some attention should be paid to the relative absence of migrants from other areas. The statistics reveal that only a small minority of Merthyr people originated from north Wales and that of the similar proportion to have come from England the majority had been born in Herefordshire, Gloucestershire or Somerset. That this should have been the case comes as no surprise. In the first instance, lines of communication between north and south Wales were abysmal, as indeed were those between upland south Wales and anywhere in England other than those counties immediately adjacent to the Welsh border. Though the advent of railways enabled people to travel over much longer distances, it was not until the second half of the nineteenth century that they came to influence the character of immigration into south Wales.

Secondly, north Wales had traditional links with Lancashire and the West Midlands, and so the industrial centres of those regions exerted a far more attractive force to would-be migrants from north Wales than did south Wales. It should also be remembered that north Wales was itself experiencing industrialisation, with the development of copper, tin, coal and lead mines, slate-quarrying and, at Brymbo and Bersham, iron-making. There was simply no need, therefore, for migration south. A third factor was the fact that no matter how busy Merthyr's works became, their capacity to absorb unskilled labour was finite, and as the neighbouring counties and south-west Wales continued to produce a ready supply of labourers willing to journey to the town, there was little need for the masters to look further afield.

The exception to this pattern was provided by the Irish. No strangers to south Wales, for many years prior to industrialisation they had tramped the countryside in search of harvest work, but the expansion of the iron, tin and copper works led to a growing demand for unskilled labour, especially in the 1790s when the construction of the canals called for large numbers of navvies. In the early decades of the nineteenth century, continued industrial growth coupled with a series of harvest failures in Ireland saw more and more Irish journeying to and settling in south Wales. It was only in the 1840s, however, that the steady trickle became a flood, as unprecedented famine and distress in Ireland led to the greatest exodus in that country's history. Thus while an analysis of the 1841 census revealed that just 3% of Merthyr's inhabitants were Irish-born, ten years later it was 7%.

That the majority of immigrants came from Breconshire, Pembrokeshire, Carmarthenshire and Cardiganshire is not surprising. In the first place, census returns reveal that between 1801 and 1851 the populations of these counties rose by an average of over 70%. This growth occurred in an area characterised by its poverty and where the prevailing agricultural system was one of the most primitive in the British Isles. The hill-farming economy, based on subsistence agriculture, was comparable to that of Ireland, and there can be no doubt that in a climate of poverty and hardship Merthyr exerted a considerable pull, which was first and foremost financial in nature. 'News of wondrous wealth in the primitive town and neighbourhood tempted men from all parts', wrote Charles Wilkins, the town's historian in 1867, while the *Merthyr Guardian* reported in March 1843 'Many at a distance infer that the generality of the people at Merthyr "get money like sand" as they say...'.

Thanks to the seasonal nature of much of the migration, discussed later, and the regularity with which postal orders were despatched from the town, Merthyr soon gained a reputation for wealth which ensured immigration would continue. Precisely how much more could be earned labouring in and around the works as opposed to the farm is problematic, given the trade cycle and the fact that remuneration in the countryside was not strictly on a cash basis, but the statistics for immigration speak for themselves and the fact was that 'in reasonable times... [wages] were several times those of farm workers in the west'.

Not surprisingly, immigration corresponded with the fortunes of the iron industry. During slumps, few bothered to travel to Merthyr, but as soon as news came of an upturn so fresh waves of migrants descended on the town. Within weeks of publishing details of wage increases in the spring of 1845, the *Merthyr Guardian* told of 'large numbers' of labourers heading for the ironworks from Pembrokeshire and south Carmarthenshire, while in the same year Education Commissioners were told at Llandingat, Carmarthenshire, that 'agricultural labourers are less numerous now than they formerly were owing to their being drained off to Merthyr and the manufacturing districts'.

Nor was the attraction simply financial. Girls and young women came looking for a wider choice of marriage partners and a better chance of marriage; the young of both sexes rejected the countryside in favour of greater independence and autonomy, while 'the adventurous and restless of all ages' were also drawn to the town. There was something intangible in the lure of Merthyr: the bright lights of urban life, the wonder of its size and strangeness, the lure of 'China' with its bars and beautiful women – the very name of the town must have sent a shiver of expectation through those whose lives, ordinarily drab and monotonous, centred around the all-too-familiar parameters of farm or village existence. As Gwyn Williams noted, 'They were coming for the money of course... but they were also coming for a fuller if chronically insecure life; they were coming for what many of them called "freedom"'.[3]

If Merthyr and the other industrial towns exerted a magnetic attraction, immigration also occurred as a direct result of what has since been described as a crisis in the Welsh countryside. As David Howell explains:

> To a certain extent the agricultural wage earner was 'pushed' out of the... countryside by adverse conditions. This was obviously so during the difficult farming years after the French Wars, when the supply of farm wage earners far exceeded the demand. These years witnessed a fast growth in the population, and the growing numbers could neither be absorbed by alternative employment nor by the traditional subsistent agricultural economy.[4]

Unemployment was no stranger to agricultural labourers, many of whom either migrated to the ironworks or fell back onto the parish. However, with the coming of the Poor Law Amendment Act of 1834 with its compulsory clauses consigning the able-bodied to the workhouse, the *fear* of poverty intensified and thousands sought either seasonal or more permanent escape from the countryside. Such seasonal migrations in order to make ends meet were by no means a new phenomenon in upland Wales:

> The more prominent Celtic seasonal migrations of the Irish and Scottish had their counterpart in the bands of Welsh labourers who harvested the crops of the Midland counties. With the development of industrialisation, the summer migration was often replaced, or added to, by a winter migration to the iron works. 'There are many', noted an ironmaster... 'who come from Cardiganshire to the iron works for five or seven months in the winter season, live economically while here and take home £15 or £20 to their families which pays the rent of their farm, and purchases for them clothing and a few luxuries'.[5]

The exodus was also prompted by other considerations. Hours of labour in the countryside were strenuously long, with indoor servants working indefinitely 'from early morning till late at night, while the married labourer's average day was from 5 am to 8.30 pm.' Accommodation too was appalling, with indoor labourers sleeping above stables and in barns while their married counterparts lived in cottages whose design and construction had not changed in centuries. Earth floors, windowless mud walls and low thatched roofs provided a degree of shelter from the elements but little by way of comfort. As elsewhere, poverty led directly to malnutrition, and the diet of the labourer and his family was both meagre and monotonous. Fresh meat, apart from at weddings and other festivities, was a rare luxury, and until the second half of the nineteenth century the Welsh agricultural labourer 'virtually subsisted on oaten or barley bread, potatoes and milk'. Without further elaboration, therefore, immigration into Merthyr was the result of both push and pull factors.

Quite apart from those who came to Merthyr on a seasonal basis, there were those who continually tramped around in search of employment. According to Royal Commissions in 1847, many of Merthyr's workers were 'wanderers who frequently change their place of abode and never remain more than a few months with any employer', while two years later the *Westminster Review* argued that as many as 10,000–11,000 people circulated through the town every year. These were unskilled and casual labourers and their dependants, who found work wherever they could, be it building docks or railways, harvesting, or labouring in and around the various works. Constantly on the move, they formed the least stable and most impoverished section of Merthyr's population.

Regarding settlement patterns within the town, the geological and morphological factors which, together with leasing arrangements, dictated the positioning of the ironworks also shaped the character of the town's development, in as much as the latter owed far more to the needs of industry than to any truly urban factor. Beginning with the masters, the English entrepreneurs who moved into the district in the 1750s and 1760s leased or bought farmhouses to accommodate themselves and their families. As the works expanded, so their successors brought in their architects and landscape gardeners to build mansions more befitting their status, although, characteristically, these were always near – and in the case of Dowlais actually among – their works. This process was to culminate in the erection by the second William Crawshay of Cyfarthfa Castle in 1825. Designed by Robert Lugar, it boasted battlements, fifteen towers and no fewer than seventy-two rooms. Overlooking the Cyfarthfa ironworks and set in a large estate, it was a symbol of the power, prestige and independence that he had long sought. In time, the humbler houses forsaken by the masters were occupied by their managers and agents. Once again, these were never far from the works, and thus each of Merthyr's four industrial nuclei had its social elite, living in oases of affluence and surrounded by their workforces.

As the town developed, so its professional people and tradesmen adopted the territory immediately to the north of the old village centre as their operational base. This was the natural focus for the four works and enabled bankers and greengrocers alike to profit from the needs of the separate workforces. Thus, although each community had its shops and service industries, the most important of which in terms of size and significance was not surprisingly in Dowlais, it was the area around the High Street in Merthyr which was the central business district.

Merthyr's workers lived in neighbourhoods immediately adjacent to the four works in which the basic socio-economic characteristics were common: each was overwhelmingly Welsh and in each employment was dominated by iron manufacture. Thus in Pentrebach, associated with the Plymouth works, 92.4% of household heads were Welsh-born and 74% were employed in iron-making. It is only when one compares the districts surrounding the works that interesting differences emerge associated with the place of birth of residents. Thus in Pentrebach, for example, almost three times as many of the household heads had been born locally than was the case in Dowlais, while in the latter over 30% had been born in Carmarthenshire compared to less than 13% in Pentrebach. Contemporaries were certainly aware of such differences. 'The workmen' asserted Royal Commissioners in 1847, 'who are perpetually immigrating, live together very much in clans, eg. the Pembrokeshire men in one quarter, the Carmarthenshire men in another, and so on'.

When the immigrants first reached the town many would have sought out those with whom they had kinship or community ties, in an attempt to facilitate accommodation and employment. This process would have been strengthened by the strangeness of Merthyr to those fresh from small and isolated rural settlements, by intermarriage and the development of other recognisable neighbourhood links, and also by the traditional suspicions and enmities which characterised relationships between the different counties and regions of Wales. Whatever the case, distinctions based on place of birth were not the only ones to affect settlement within Merthyr – so too did ones based on occupation and status. Both Cefn Coed and Twynyrhodyn, for example, were characterised by concentrations of miners and colliers, and it would seem that underground workers often lived side by side.

When examining settlement in terms of status, the major divisions were not between the different grades of skilled and semi-skilled workers but between these groups and the unskilled sections of the workforce. The former inevitably lived in localities immediately adjacent to the works, frequently in streets built by their employers and generally on land owned by the iron companies, while the latter congregated in peripheral areas. Put simply, the skilled and semi-skilled could afford company housing while unskilled labourers could not, and whereas the masters used housing as a means of attracting and maintaining the skilled and stable elements essential for production, there was no such compulsion to accommodate the unskilled because a ready supply was always at hand. In practice, this meant that the localities immediately to the north and south of Merthyr's central business district, China and Caedraw, as well as a smaller one in Brecon Street in Dowlais, housed the unskilled and transitory and were characterised by, among other things, relatively low percentages of people employed in iron-making and high ratios of people born outside Wales, especially the Irish.

Before concluding, some analysis of the social divisions within the town is warranted, and the most important feature here was the fact that the gulf between the masters and their workers was stark and almost total, for, apart from a small number of managers and agents, Rammell found 'There are no men of middle station, none of the ordinary class of "residents" who are to be found, more or less in number, in every other town in England, however they may be disconnected from the ordinary commerce of the place'. His 1849 report included an examination of the rateable value of housing in the town – always a good index of middle-class strength – and he found that of a total of 6,616 houses 'the number... rated between £15 and £60 p.a. was only 372. There were only eight between £60 and £80 and three between £80 and £100', with the vast majority not being rated at all.

In the 1840s the four most important men in Merthyr were the ironmasters, Sir John Guest of Dowlais, William Crawshay of Cyfarthfa, Anthony Hill of Plymouth and, indirectly, due to his decision never to live in the town, Alderman Thompson of Penydarren. The first three and their families constituted the town's upper class, and in economic and social terms their dominance was complete. When Lady Charlotte Guest referred to her husband as 'Merthyr' she could never have been accused of exaggerating. Next came the works' managers and agents, drawn by the salaries they were offered, for as one report in 1854 put it: 'There are few or no residents who have made it their abode from choice, uninfluenced by pecuniary considerations, or family circumstances'. Among the middle class Rammell found 'whenever a man made a little fortune or even a sufficiency for the supply of his future days, he took leave of the town of Merthyr and settled in some other more agreeable or more healthy place', prompting one historian to argue that 'what could be called a middle class element amounted to only 1% of the population'.

In practical terms, the vacuum created by the lack of a middle class was filled by the town's 'shopocracy'. Providing a buffer between the masters and their workmen, it was from this group that the impetus for local government came. In numbers if not influence, traders and shopkeepers dominated the organs of parish affairs in an age prior to central control. Between 1843 and 1853, for example, of the 220 elected Parish Constables no fewer than 127 were shopkeepers, merchants and tradesmen, and sixty-seven of these were grocers. Of the remainder, only forty-four could have truly been described as middle-class, and even then almost half were farmers and 'yeomen'.

Then came the working classes. Deprived of the vote, all they had was their skill and their labour. The power of the masters was awesome: controlling as they did employment and wage levels and to a considerable extent housing and rents, they dominated whole communities, not only at individual levels but 'also at the profounder social level of the family'. Though the impression may be given that those who migrated to Merthyr did so in the hope of enhancing their economic and social status, one should not forget that, in the words of historian Ieuan Gwynedd Jones, 'Families which passed from the rural scene to the industrial did not change their relative positions in society. A new field was opened to them, but it was not wider'. Such was the masters' control that, as far as working-class Merthyr was concerned, 'In a very real sense... it would seem that [the four] individual communities were the industrial analogues of the rural estates from which their inhabitants, for the most part, had come and continued to come'.[6]

2

EMPLOYMENT

To 'win' and 'get' the minerals at prodigious depths in the bowels of the earth, surrounded by a sulphurous and explosive atmosphere, and subject to accidents which no human sagacity can forsee nor any precaution avert; to convey the rough treasures to the surface; to break, cleanse, and calcine, to smelt, refine, and manufacture them – are the duties of the workman. For the successful accomplishment of these tasks, the requirements are – physical courage, strength and endurance, and, above all, a fair degree of practical skill: these qualities are combined in him. Although capital is the motive power, it is upon the rude virtues of the workman that the entire system of the manufacture of iron practically relies.

The Morning Chronicle, 18 March 1850

Beginning with the size of the workforce and its distribution, probably the most frustrating aspect of any study of employment during this period is our inability to state with certainty just how many people worked for each of the iron companies and in what capacity at any given time. Nevertheless, based on what information is available, the following estimates are arrived at for the 1840s:

Year	Dowlais	Cyfarthfa	Plymouth	Penydarren	Total
1842	5,000	3,043	2,225	1,666	11,934
1845	7,300	4,443	3,248	2,432	17,423
1848	6,000	3,652	2,670	2,000	14,322

Despite being crude estimates and no more, the figures clearly illustrate the size of the works. Dowlais and Cyfarthfa in particular were large-scale enterprises and all four concerns employed thousands, at a time when operations involving hundreds or even scores of workers were considered large. As regards the make-up of the workforce, the only detailed breakdown was given in 1840:

Classification	As a Percentage
Furnace and Mill Men	25
Miners and Colliers	35.7
Artisans	14.3
Labourers	12.5
Boys, Women, Old and Inferior Workmen	12.5

Fortunately, we know far more about the nature of the jobs Merthyr's workers undertook, and our survey of these begins with the extraction of the necessary raw materials. Underground, no truly typical pit existed in the 1840s and 1850s and the coal and iron ore was reached in a number of ways. Some mines were inclines driven into the hillsides surrounding the town; others were shafts operated either by winches or water-balances, and then there were the patches which were opencast operations at locations where the coal and iron seams came close to the surface. Most of the minerals came from mines in the accepted sense, however, and each of the companies employed several hundred underground workers to satisfy the constant demands of their furnaces. In 1850, for example, at a time of deep depression, it was estimated that the Dowlais works alone consumed 1,000 tons of coal a day.

To save confusion, the point needs to be made straight away that the terms miner and collier were by no means synonymous but described two distinct jobs: miners extracted iron ore, or 'mine' as it was known, and colliers worked the coal seams. Sometimes both groups worked at different levels within the same mine, while in other instances production was dedicated to either coal or iron. Regarding the working of these minerals, the method universally adopted by miners and colliers alike in south Wales was the 'post and stall' system, best realised by imagining a draught-board on which the white areas are the stalls and the black the pillars. Pushing outwards from pit bottom, miners and colliers would leave untouched barriers of minerals and rock to support the roof.

Both groups worked in cramped, often wet and dangerous conditions, exposed to extremes of temperature and constant dust. In March 1850 the *Morning Chronicle* found that of the two jobs mining was the harder, though the pay was lower: 'the great liability to explosions of fire-damp being, in a degree, compensated to the collier by increased pay'.

Miners, dressed in flannel shirts, fustian trousers and with handkerchiefs tightly bound around their heads, used hammers and large iron chisels to bore a yard or so into the rock at an upward angle. Into the borehole was placed a cartridge containing half a pound of cheap but 'very strong' gunpowder, which was sealed in place by clay made from the displaced rock dust. Fuses were then inserted which were lit by means of short trails of gunpowder, before the miners retreated to a safe distance:

> In a few seconds the explosion happened; there was a half stifled roar, a gush of smoke and flame, the rattling of a few missiles... and the miner then stepped briskly forward, pronouncing it a successful blast. About a ton of stone rubbish had been displaced, leaving the vein of iron-stone above clean, smooth, and flat, as though it had been levelled by a carpenter's plane. He had now only, with his crowbars and wedges, to break this down, and place it in the trams for removal.

The colliers, dressed again in flannel shirts, fustian trousers and with handkerchief headscarves:

> ...use picks for cutting, and wedges for separating the coal. Sometimes they work seated – at others sideways – and occasionally lying, as necessity requires. They cut the coal to an acute angle, and then wedge off the mass to the square. The grain of the coal dips north and south... a circumstance which favours the collier, who, thus enabled to calculate with certainty the line in which the mineral will split, directs his operations accordingly. The colliers call these lines 'slips'. In one stall after clambering over some trams, I saw a mass thus detached with a single wrench of a crowbar, which weighed upwards of a ton...

Nor were the miners and colliers the only underground workers, as they were supported by a small army of ancillary workers such as the roadway cutters, who drove new headings, and the hauliers, who worked the horses which pulled the journeys of trams to the pit bottom.

Moving onto the ironworks themselves, above the blast furnaces which were inevitably built into the hillsides, workers broke up and then calcinated the coal, iron and limestone in kilns to remove impurities before it was tipped into the furnaces. Some forty-five feet below the charging platform was the hearth, where a constant stream of molten slag ran out of purpose-built apertures into iron trams, which the cinder-fillers dragged away. When the time came to tap the furnace, the furnaceman and his underhand used a sledgehammer and long iron bar to drive a hole through the vitrified sand used to seal the dam-plate, when:

> A stream of liquid iron, almost as fluid as water, and of the most beautiful yellow... gushed forth and followed the course of the channel in the sand, down to the refinery... This stream of liquid iron is called 'a runner': at night its light is so intense that the eye cannot endure it. In the present instance the stream was... directed to the refinery, which is

comparatively a new process; in the generality of cases it is run into moulds on the casting floor, where it takes the form of the 'pig-iron' of commerce… A large floor of such castings is called 'a sow'.

At the refinery, 'an open square furnace, like a deep pan', coal was added and the mass subjected to a further two hours of blast to remove superfluous carbon and oxygen before the metal was run off into pig-moulds by the refiner. Then: 'Having cooled, or nearly so, the pig moulds are broken into fragments of a convenient size for the puddling furnaces. This is done with huge and heavy sledge-hammers, each having two handles and wielded by two men…'. From there the iron was wheeled to the puddling furnaces, located in buildings which consisted 'simply of roofs perforated by a great number of chimneys… and supported on all sides by pillars of masonry. The floor is paved with cast iron, and not an inch of space is lost…'. At these furnaces, the puddler and his underhand subjected the refined iron to great heat to further remove impurities, and:

> During this long process the puddler is either stirring with his lever the iron in the furnace, or regulating the fire, which he is enabled to do at convenience; consequently he is in a bath of perspiration from the heat alone, not to speak of that which follows such heavy labour…

Once satisfied, the puddler divided the iron and rolled it up into 'puddlers' balls', which were taken by a 'second hand' to the 'shingler', 'who grasps the white-hot mass with a pair of huge pincers, and drags it, at a run to the "squeezers", where, with a dextrous twist of the arm, he swings it, though nearly a hundredweight, without apparent effort, on the anvil where it is to be compressed…' to a rough bar 'about 20 inches long and 4 wide'. These bars were then introduced to huge rollers, where pairs of men and boys fed them rapidly through successively smaller grooves until the required length and width was achieved; they were then dragged to heavy shears:

> …which cut them into lengths of about two feet… These are carried to the 'piler', who puts together as many of them as the future bar (whether it be railway iron or otherwise) will require, and each pile is next placed separately in the balling furnaces which are similar in size and structure to the puddling furnaces.

Following further refining, the piles of iron, now known as 'blooms', were wheeled at speed to further rollers where, in the case of railway rails, the iron was passed through nine times before the rail was dragged to a circular saw which cut off the ends, then to the 'rougher down' to file off the jagged edges left by the saw and finally to 'the "straightener" by whom it is finished. The entire operation, from the presentation of the "bloom" to the roller down to the perfection of the rail, takes a minute and a quarter'. In all some forty recognised trades existed in the ironworks and it was here that the labour aristocrats were exclusively employed.

Turning now to the hours worked in the mines, most of the evidence points to a twelve- to thirteen-hour day six days a week, although towards the end of the month, when workers attempted to boost production and thus their pay, eighteen-hour stints were not unknown. As far as meals were concerned, then no facilities existed underground for either cooking or eating, and nor were there any fixed meal breaks. Miners and colliers went to work carrying 'their dinner of bread and cheese, [and] a closed tin jug filled with tea' and took their meals whenever it was convenient:

> They sat like North American Indians, squatting upon their hams – a position they are
> much accustomed to by the nature of their work… They were eating bread and cheese
> – their only aliment in the pit; their drink was cold tea, milk or water…

In the ironworks a twelve-hour shift was the norm, although when deadlines had to be met or when furnaces and machinery were being erected or repaired then longer hours were worked. Shift systems operated in all four works, the most common being from 6a.m. to 6p.m., and from 6p.m. through to 6a.m. Some worked days one week and nights another, others worked days or nights 'regular', but some, because of the arduous nature of the work and the concentration involved, worked just eight-hour shifts, as was the case with the puddlers. Unlike in the pits, many in the works also laboured on Sundays, as the blast furnaces demanded constant attention. It appears that at Dowlais restricted Sunday hours were introduced early in the 1830s, whereby 'We stop the furnaces after the morning tapping at 7 o'clock, and cease to blow until 4 o'clock in the afternoon, when the engine is again set at work, and the men come on…'. Elsewhere, however, iron-making was an uninterrupted process which saw the longest shifts being worked on the sabbath. At Penydarren, for example, 'The Long Turn' saw workers begin at six o'clock on Sunday morning and did not finish until twenty-four hours later.

Meals, as underground, were taken as and when, and there were no canteens, or set meal breaks. For all workers, only two holidays were officially recognised: Good Friday and Christmas Day, and when, in the 1860s, the 'half-day Saturday' movement threatened to change the old order, it was scornfully dismissed by the management at Dowlais who argued that any extension to existing holidays was 'quite unnecessary. As a rule the workmen have many holidays, they frequently absent themselves from the works, and owing to accidents to machinery and from other causes… they are off quite often enough as it is'.

Women worked as well as men, though so sensitive was the issue that the masters were reluctant to disclose the numbers involved. Thus, in 1841, the official figure for women employed by the ironworks was given as 332 for the whole of Wales, and yet in the following year a breakdown provided by the Plymouth works revealed 140 women aged over eighteen and a total female workforce of 355 – and this at a time of deepening depression when casual labour was increasingly being laid off.

From the figures that are available, we know that at least several hundred adult women were employed in Merthyr and that of these around 70% were employed in and around the ironworks, with the remainder working at the pits and patches. In the works it is possible to classify their jobs as those undertaken exclusively by women, those done principally by them and those undertaken by both sexes. As far as the first classification is concerned, then perhaps the best examples concerned the brick-girls whose job it was to manufacture firebricks for the numerous kilns and furnaces, and the coke-girls, who stacked coal for coking prior to its being tipped into the furnaces, a process which involved some skill as otherwise the mass would not burn evenly and produce good coke. According to the *Morning Chronicle*'s reporter:

> The pitiful condition of these girls once very forcibly struck me, when, on a day of heavy rain and high wind, I saw them at work on the mountain side, with the rain liter- ally running off their coal-bedaubed petticoats over their boots, in black streams, to the ground.

One coke-girl, aged twenty-four, who had worked at the Penydarren works for three and a half years, stated:

> My business is to stack the coal for coking... I have often to lift from the trams pieces of coal which weigh over a hundredweight, and carry them to the [coking] pit... I work in all weathers – rain, snow, or frost. I stand the rain and wind often all day long, because we must work...

As for jobs principally undertaken by women, perhaps the two best examples involved the limestone-breakers and the pilers. The former were employed to aid the men whose responsibility it was to ensure the flow of raw materials to the blast furnaces. They worked near the tunnel heads of the furnaces, in the open air, smashing the limestone into fragments with heavy hammers. Pilers worked at stacking and arrang- ing the puddled bars ready for the balling furnaces. One nineteen-year-old piler told the *Morning Chronicle*:

> I work by day one week, and by night another. When the works are working 'rails' two other girls and myself pile, on an average, 35 tons a day between us. We have to lift up the pieces from the ground as far as my middle. Sometimes the iron is very hot, and we can't

take hold of it without thick leathers. I have burnt my hands shockingly, and so have the other girls.

Despite the heavy nature of such work, the masters argued that 'girls have a particular aptitude for piling, being more active than men or lads' and in 1866, fearing that the introduction of new legislation would prevent all women from working, the Dowlais management insisted:

> It would be difficult to supply the place of these girls with men and boys, partly from the great scarcity of labour, but mostly from the fact that the men are not suited to the work. The frequent stooping and rising wearies them, whereas the girls being shorter and more active, get through with comparative ease.

Most women worked side by side with the men and undertook a variety of jobs. Near the furnace heads, for example, pollers emptied iron ore from trams, separated it from the stone shale and then piled it ready for the furnaces. One twenty-one-year-old poll-girl told of how 'I clean and stack about 4 tons of "mine" a day. The mine is often so flinty that it cuts my hands…'. Male and female labourers loaded and then emptied trams of burning slag and cinder:

> There is a coarse occupation, in which girls are employed… in the removal of the cinders from the furnaces… These… are generally transported to some neighbouring aclivity… [They] are called tip-girls. Their dress is peculiar, their labour hard, and their appearance indicates personal strength.

Prohibited since 1842 from working in the mines themselves, there was no law to prevent women working about the pit head, and they were employed to operate the winches and water-balances which lowered and raised the coal and iron ore. These were, according to the *Morning Chronicle*, the highest-paid women, earning some £2 a month. Next came the limestone-breakers, who laboured twelve hours a day, seven days a week, for 7s, a rate of just one penny an hour; the fillers earned between 6 and 7s; the brick-girls, who also earned a penny an hour, took home 6s while the tippers averaged around 5s 6d a week. Below these came the coke-girls who, though they worked a seven-day week, earned only 5s; the pilers, who made between 4 and 5s; the tip-girls with 4s and the pollers, whose earnings did not exceed 3s 9d.

Moving on to the employment of children, despite the statistical problems outlined earlier and the sensitive nature of the issue, we know that somewhere in the region of a quarter of all Merthyr's workers were under eighteen. Of these, around 60% were aged thirteen to eighteen and 40% were twelve and under, with males outnumbering females by three to one. We also know that a disproportionate number were employed in the mines, as opposed to the works generally. Indeed, according to the 1842 Royal Commission on child labour, 'in the coalfield of South Wales... more cases are recorded of the employment of children in the pits at very early ages than in any other district...'. Children of a very tender age were taken underground. In 1842, for example, Frederick Evans, clerk to the Dowlais Collieries and Mines, recounted 'I have known instances of a father carrying his child of 4 years of age on his back to work, and keeping him with him in the stall all day for the purpose of obtaining an additional tram allowed him', while the Commissioners found that most young children were employed as air-door keepers and they were 'generally from 5 to 11 years of age'. Following the publication of the 1842 Report, legislation banned the employment of all women and boys under ten underground, but it was to take many years before effective policing came about and all the evidence suggests that children under ten continued to be employed.

As for the jobs undertaken by children, we start with the mines and the air-door keepers. The primitive ventilation systems employed underground necessitated using a series of air-locks, and in order to ensure the free and unhindered passage of workers and materials, youngsters were employed to open and close them. Their:

> ...post is in the mine at the side of the air-door, and their business is to open it for the haulier, with his horse and tram, to pass, and then to close the door after them. In some pits the situation of these poor things is distressing. With his solitary candle, cramped with cold, wet and not half fed, the poor child, deprived of light and air, passes his silent day.

The lot of the air-door keeper was indeed a sorry one. In one of the Cyfarthfa mines in 1842 Commissioners found seven-year-old Mary Davies:

> A very pretty little girl... fast asleep under a piece of rock near the air-door... Her lamp had gone out for want of oil; and, upon waking her, she said the rats or someone had run away with her bread and cheese, so she went to sleep.

Perhaps the most poignant observation, however, came from the *Morning Chronicle*'s reporter when he visited the Glynderris pit and was astonished to discover a superb drawing of a prancing horse:

> I may state that the boys in the coal pits have in general a taste for drawing. The poor boy who has to attend all day one of the doors... takes in his pocket – for the purpose

of whiling away the tedium of his situation – a farthing's worth of happiness in the form of a piece of chalk. The doors are inevitably covered with such productions, and I could detect the peculiar likings of each by his performances – one, drawing horses and animals; another men fishing; and a third, architectural objects, such as churches and houses...

If the greatest hardship such children had to endure was long hours of uncomfortable and solitary boredom, this paled besides the exhausting labour of the girl drammers:

The employment the females are put to is the filling and drawing the drams... of coal or iron-stone; it requires great strength. The main roads are made as easy as the work will allow, by iron rails being run to the ends of the workings; but this does not alter the nature of the employment, which is certainly unfit for women.

One thirteen-year-old girl said 'the work is very hard... the mine is wet where we work, as the water passes through the roof, and the workings are only 30 to 33 inches high'. Her eleven-year-old sister told of how 'when well I draw the drams, which contain 4 to 5 hundredweight of coal from the heads to the main road, I make 48 to 50 journeys'. These girls were, therefore, by means of chains secured to their waists, each dragging an average of eleven tons of coal per shift.

Similarly arduous was the work of the windlass girls, who were employed in the levels to haul drams up slopes. In 1842 Hannah Bowen, a sixteen-year-old in one of the Plymouth mines, told how she had spent the previous two years drawing up 400 loads daily, each weighing between 1½ and 4 hundredweight. Ann Thomas, also sixteen, told of how she worked a windlass with another girl and that some days they hauled 800 loads.

Also working in the levels were boys whose job it was to dig narrow ventilation shafts:

The 'windways'... are entirely cut by boys. They are 3 feet wide by 2 feet 6 inches high; within these narrow limits, without the means of working out the coal in masses, these boys work, doubled up of necessity into the most painful and inconvenient postures.

In and around the ironworks, children were employed to assist the casual labourers and also the skilled craftsmen. The furnacemen employed boys as underhands who, after serving an apprenticeship, would hope to take on their own furnace by their early twenties. At the puddling and balling furnaces the position was the same, though puddlers also employed another boy or girl aged seven to ten to open and close their furnace doors.

At the rollers:

The compressed bar, as it passes through each groove, is received by a youth on the other side, sometimes with a lever and sometimes with tongs, and handed over the rolls to the roller... Now the youth who catches the compressed bar... is called a *catcher*... [and] there is another younger lad also employed as *hooker-on*, whose station is before the rolls with a suspended lever to support the bar of iron before it enters the groove.

From the rollers, children of both sexes dragged the red-hot bars to the shears after which other children carried the smaller lengths in small iron barrows to the balling furnaces, following which the iron was again rolled, with children doing the same jobs as before. Finally, under the supervision of the straightener, boys 'with tongs, drag the thin bars... into a separate heap, and, while they are still hot, knock them *straight* with a hammer'.

As far as hours and conditions of work were concerned, exactly the same shifts applied to children as to adults. When it came to wages, in the works some children were paid by those they assisted while others were hired directly by the companies. Thus thirteen-year-old Thomas Rees was given a shilling a day by the furnace-filler he helped and the catchers and hookers-on were paid 7s and 4s a week respectively by the roller-men, while at Dowlais shearers were paid 9s a week by the Company Manager. In 1850 the boys who worked around the Plymouth mills and forges earned between 3s and 15s a week depending on the position they occupied, while the girls took home between 3s and 6s 6d. In the mines in 1850, hauliers were paid 12s a week by the owners while air-door keepers earned 2s 6d. The masters also directly employed the windway-boys, who were not paid a weekly rate but received a piece-rate of 1s 2d a yard, while those boys who aided the miners and colliers in their stalls earned between 4s and 6s a week. Not that the children themselves saw the money for, as the 1842 Commissioners explained:

The collier boy is, to all intents and purposes, the property of his father (as to wages) until he attains the age of 17 years, or marries; his father receives his wages, whether he be an air-door boy of 5 years of age or a haulier of 15.

What was true for boys was also the case for girls, though in their case the money continued to be given to the father until such time as they married, while according to the *Morning Chronicle* all the very young children could hope for was little more than 4-6d a week pocket money from their parents.

Child labour had some very tangible economic effects. For the masters these children represented a constant pool of cheap labour which could be drawn on at will, and their earnings, however slight, were of significance to individual families. That children were an important section of the workforce was emphasised in 1866 when the Dowlais Trustees admitted: 'The machinery of the mills has been specially adapted for boys, where they are strong enough to do the work'. However, it was probably the long-term effects which were viewed most appreciatively by the masters, for the young labour of the mills and mines would, in time, and barring accidents and ill-health, become the skilled and semi-skilled labour of the future.

Turning to wages, it has to be admitted at the outset that these are very difficult to pin down precisely, as some employees were paid on a piece-work basis and others by the shift. Both rates varied from job to job and from works to works and from time to time. Most workers directly concerned with the extraction of coal and iron ore or the production of iron were paid by the ton, and this led to considerable fluctuations in earnings depending on demand. As one Penydarren roller reported in 1850:

> I get from 25/- to 30/- a week. I have... earned as much as 75/- a week. That was in 1846, when there was a great demand for rails... The reason why I earn so much less now is, that I cannot get rail work... When we work 'merchants bars' we make only from 15 to 20 tons... but when working rails we make from 30 to 35, therefore we then get much more.

Indeed, the difference between producing rails and bars could be staggering. At Cyfarthfa in 1850, for example, working rails as opposed to bars meant increases in earnings of between 25% and 33% a week for ballers, 100% and 166% for rollers and no less than 150% and 178% for roughers. To further complicate the issue, differentials between different grades of workers were a well-established feature in all four works. In the mills and foundries, experience and skill were at a premium and wage rates varied accordingly. For example, at the Penydarren works in 1850, master puddlers were reported to earn 20s a week and second-rate puddlers 15-16s, while first-rate 'second hands' earned 14s and second-rate ones 12s.

Not all workers were paid on piece-rates and many workers not directly involved in mineral or iron production were paid on a shift basis. Thus at Dowlais in 1857, labourers were earning 2s a day, mine-burners 2s 10d, carpenters 2s 10d, cinder-tippers 2s 2d and masons 5s.

Wages were also affected by the systems of stoppages and bonuses employed by all the works. Stoppages were made to provide benefits to workers, to ensure good-quality work and to discourage 'unreliable' behaviour. By the 1840s all the works had established medical schemes to provide doctors, medicines and sick pay for ill or injured employees, although there was no uniformity about the charges imposed for such services. In 1850, for example, a miner working for the Plymouth Company paid 1½d in the pound for the services of a company doctor, while Dowlais charged just ¾d and at Penydarren it was no less than 6d. Until 1849 such stoppages had been considerably lower, but the disastrous effects of the cholera epidemic that year forced the masters to increase payments in order to replenish their exhausted 'funds'. Other benefits paid for by stoppages included the provision of coal, housing and schooling.

Stoppages were also imposed to replenish stocks of working tools and to repair plant. Miners and colliers, for example, were made to pay for new or broken tools as well as for their candles and gunpowder. In 1841 it was calculated that at the Plymouth pits such stoppages amounted to over 13% of colliers' wages. Above-ground workers paid for new or broken tools, as well as for such things as clay to repair furnaces – 4d a week for founders, puddlers and ballers at Dowlais in 1850. Quite apart from such regular stoppages, fines were imposed by each company to discourage shoddy workmanship, short weights and measures and absenteeism. Colliers, for example, were fined for including any 'small-coal' in their drams and puddlers adjudged to have produced 'inferior' iron were similarly dealt with.

As far as bonuses were concerned, when order books were full or production deadlines had been delayed workers were given food and drink in an attempt to secure their full co-operation and maximum effort. The Dowlais Company also used a system of cash incentives to encourage good timekeeping and regular attendance.

Without any doubt, the most important factor controlling wages in Merthyr was the demand for iron. High demand led to wage increases as the price for iron rose, and vice versa. Thus, in April 1850, the *Morning Chronicle* found wage levels to be 'less by full 40% than two or three years ago'. This adjustment of wages to iron prices was more often than not retarded by delaying actions on the part of both masters and men. Workers would react quickly to wage reductions, taking strike action if they considered them unnecessary or if a rise in the price of iron was not accompanied by a suitable advance, while the masters tended to place much emphasis on the 'unprofitable' nature of their concerns, arguing that losses had to be recouped before they could afford to raise wages. Despite such delaying tactics, the adjustment of wages to the price of iron was definite and inevitable, although the very size and scale of the works at Cyfarthfa and Dowlais ensured that they could cushion reductions to an extent, in order to stockpile and retain skilled labour.

In human terms, the vicissitudes of the trade cycle are easily demonstrated. For example, as far as master puddlers were concerned in 1838 they were earning up to 50s a week; two years later this was down to 20s, and by 1849 their wages had fallen to 19s and probably less. Thus, in a little over ten years their wages had fallen by over 60%.

Reductions, delays and disparities in wages were not the only sources of friction between the masters and their workers, and in many cases antagonism arose out of the methods used both to calculate and distribute earnings. Piece-rates, for instance, consistently caused trouble in the mines and collieries, where the system of payment partly by measure and partly by weight was seen as oppressive by the men, since production could be and was affected by adverse geological conditions beyond their control. In 1850 a road-cutter in one of the Cyfarthfa pits told the *Morning Chronicle*:

> I like this work well enough if I could get more of it. The rock is so hard that I make only 6 yards way in a month, and that by the use of 40lbs. of powder in blasting. I get from 6 to 7 tons of 'mine' in that distance, for which I am paid 6/10 a ton; for cutting the rock, I earn 6/2 a yard; but the cost of gunpowder must be deducted.

The methods employed to calculate production also caused resentment. Not only were colliers fined for including 'small-coal' in their drams, but only 'full' drams were counted by the company weighers and until 1860, when legislation allowed for a workers' checkweighman, underground workers had no control whatsoever over the recording of their output and accusations of under-weighing frequently arose.

The distribution of wages was perhaps the cause of most bitterness. In the early days of industrialisation, a number of financial factors combined to make the provision of money to meet short-term expenses a considerable problem. The masters overcame this by introducing their own coinage and banknotes, establishing truck shops and developing a 'long pay' system. In Merthyr the company tokens and banknotes, together with the notorious truck shops, had disappeared by the 1840s, but the long pays were still very much a feature of life in the town. Employees were paid every six or seven weeks, and in every quarter two paydays existed for final settlements, though they were supplemented by 'draws' or subs which, in the case of the Dowlais works, occured weekly and involved advances of around two-thirds of the actual wages. According to the masters, weekly pays were prevented by the shortage of available coin and the fact that so many workers were paid by measure or weight or distance, involving calculations which needed time to be worthwhile. However, the real reason for their reluctance to abandon tradition was the absenteeism which followed every payday. It should be remembered that this was a time when 'Saint Monday', the practice of absenting oneself from work on that day, was the curse of employers throughout Britain, though in Wales the problem was exacerbated, as far as the masters were concerned, by the 'flaws' in the Welsh character:

> …we mean their national indolence and want of perseverance – the absence of that indomitable energy and spirit of improvement which has raised the Anglo-Saxon race… A Welsh peasant, amidst his own mountains, if he can get a shilling a day, will prefer starving upon that to labouring for another twelve pence.

Yet another cause of considerable antagonism was the way in which wages were paid by gaffers rather than the companies themselves. In 1840 Tremenheere explained:

> The 'master-miner' receives the money for the detachment working under him either in £5 notes or in gold. He meets his men at a public house or beer shop, where change is procured by the publican. About 6d in the £ is paid for the accommodation, and is spent in beer.

As far as job security was concerned, the iron companies' colliers were paid at a lower rate than their sale-coal counterparts on the basis of their greater regularity of employment. Thus, in 1850, colliers working for the Plymouth Company were earning 10½d per ton, while sale-coal colliers working exactly the same seam at Aberdare recieved 1s 4d per ton. This greater regularity of employment for Merthyr's colliers and miners occurred because even when orders for iron declined production only decreased gradually, as the masters usually chose to produce for stock, at lower wage rates, at the start of any depression, 'so that they could meet orders swiftly when the upswing ensued' and charge the higher prices increased demand brought in its wake.

Despite this, job security was never guaranteed in Merthyr even for the most skilled of operatives. In the mines frequent accidents not only prevented those involved from working but also slowed down or stopped others, and firedamp and other gases could close complete sections of the workings for weeks. Above ground, employment was not only subject to the ready supply of raw materials but was also dependent on the weather, at least as far as the Cyfarthfa and Plymouth works were concerned, as both still relied on water to power their mills and forges. Hence in September 1843 the *Merthyr Guardian* reported hundreds of firemen being idle or taking work as mere labourers because of the shortage of water: 'Even at Cyfarthfa, where the two Taffs meet, and where engines of such power are... [employed] for using the same water twice, scores of firemen were labouring at the quarry last week, and glad to get anything to do'.

When depressions were prolonged and redundancies affected even the most skilled workers, what were the chances of alternative employment? Merthyr was a one-industry town and, other than the service industries which were equally dependent on the iron trade, little other work existed. Having said as much, the demands of local agriculture – hard pressed for labour because of the migration to the works – could also meet the needs of some jobless workmen at certain times of the year. In July 1843, for instance, the *Merthyr Guardian* reported that at the Plymouth works several men were being discharged each week and 'Fortunately many of them will be employed during harvest time, either here or elsewhere'. Local farms could only absorb so much labour, however, and the 'elsewhere' points to the fact that during the worst of times many of the unemployed simply packed up and returned to the farms and villages from where they had come in the first place. Merthyr was no place to be without a job.

3

HOUSING AND SANITATION

They were not so much towns as barracks, not the refuge of a civilisation, but the barracks of industry.

J.L. & B. Hammond, *The Town Labourer, 1760–1832*, London, 1949

Just as immigration and employment prospects were tied to the demand for iron, so too there was an inextricable link between the fortunes of the iron industry and the housing market. Thus in February 1840, at a time when the high demand associated with the first period of railway mania had yet to abate, the *Cambrian* could report 'a great many houses are now building in Merthyr, and more would be commenced but for the scarcity of masons'. Six years and another railway boom later, the *Merthyr Guardian* noted in March 1846: 'Contemporaneous with the flourishing state of the iron trade, many workmen's cottages are being erected in and around the town…'. In August 1851, however, during one of the worst depressions ever to hit Merthyr, the same newspaper reported that some 300 houses were vacant, and nine months later that figure had trebled.

The demand for iron was not the only factor to affect the housing market, however, and topographical considerations and the needs of the works themselves also restricted the amount of land which was available to accommodate the workforce. Steep gradients did not lend themselves to housing and much land was taken up by the ironworks themselves and their tips, mines, tramroads and railways. Still other land, seen by the masters as potentially valuable as a source of future mineral extraction, was also denied to housing. Consequently, accommodation for the labour force was quite severely restricted and so, almost from the outset, housing was characterised by congestion. The one notable exception to this pattern was at Troedyrhiw where the Plymouth works were situated. Prevented from expansion to the north by the town itself, the settlement spread down the valley unimpaired by conflicting demands on land use. As one health inspector noted in 1845:

> The cottages belonging to the Plymouth Works are widely scattered, some in rows, usu-
> ally having gardens attached to them. These habitations, therefore, are of a rural character,
> and, as it were, constitute straggling building down the valley of the Taff...

Elsewhere the situation was very different. With the continued, if erratic, expansion of the industry during the 1840s came fresh demands for space for new furnaces, forges, mills and foundries, tramroads, railways, mines and tips, and so the pressures on land that was available for housing increased accordingly. As the *Merthyr Guardian* noted in November 1846:

> The rage for building in Merthyr is so far from having exhausted itself, that it continues
> with unabated vigour... sly little bits of ground concealed from public view by a som-
> bre wall, and accessible from the public streets only by narrow alleys, are introduced to
> notice, and forthwith become the sites of cottages, so that every inch of available space is
> likely to be speedily occupied.

Indeed, such was the hunger for housing that the decade witnessed the colonisation of the very tips which limited a more natural form of development. In March 1850, the *Morning Chronicle* told of how these tips had reached 'prestigious heights', with the greatest being around 300 feet high: 'Upon one of these heaps [the Penydarren tip], on the north side of the town, a long row of workmen's cottages has been erected, and the locality has been not inaptly named "Newfoundland"'.

Merthyr's physical environment also governed many of the materials used in building houses. Though the coming of the railways allowed for importing such goods, transport costs deterred their use and so an essentially local building indus-try relied on locally available materials. Perhaps the most striking outcome of this was the minimal use of timber, as local supplies were soon exhausted by the demands of industry. Consequently, builders were 'forced' to do without it and this 'contributed, in large measure, to the defective nature of the physical sur-roundings'. This cost factor governed all house construction other than that of the masters: economy was the name of the game for builders and this expressed itself too in their choice of stone. Though pennant grit characterised the geology of Dowlais and other parts of the town, 'Many of the houses were built of porous sandstone, which was damp and sponge like...'. As the *Morning Chronicle* explained in April 1850:

The houses are built of a peculiar grey sandstone, raised in abundance by the 'patchers' who quarry for the nodules of iron ore which are found near the surface of the ground. This stone costs little more than the cost of carting; consequently labour, wood, and iron-work form the most expensive items in the construction of these houses.

As we shall see, most of Merthyr's houses were built by speculators whose sole concern was to maximise profits. This led to the 'erection of dwellings which were deficient of most of the basic necessities, and houses were built which contained the bare minimum necessary to command a rental'. Continued immigration increased the pressure and so dwellings were thrown up in a 'monotony of disorder', exacerbating the nucleated congestion adjacent to the Cyfarthfa, Penydarren and Dowlais works.

According to the *Merthyr Guardian* in July 1850, 'cottage property in this locality is one of the most profitable forms in which money can be invested'. The *Morning Chronicle* argued that, given the accommodation provided, the profits accrued were far too high: 'A house which cost in the building £45, lets for at least 10/- a month... or £6-10-0d a year, thus returning upon the outlay about 14%' and it went on to suggest that with the best class of workers' housing commanding rents of 13s a month returns of 19% could be realised. However, by far the greatest profits were made from the lower end of the market. 'Second-class' houses, the majority of which had only two or three rooms and so were cheaper to build, were frequently rented out at between 6s and 8s a month, and in one instance cited by the *Morning Chronicle* one such house in Penydarren shared by two families and a lodger cost 11s a month. 'Third-class' accommodation, generally consisting of one-roomed hovels or cellars, proved particularly lucrative, especially when landlords adopted some form of insurance on their investment:

> Passing down a lane, we saw an instance of the truth that the poor pay more dearly for accommodation than the rich. In a small hovel, about 9 feet by 6, with a low tile-roof, unplastered and unceiled... the poor man told me he had to pay 2/6 a week. I have since heard that, in proportion to the likelihood there is that the tenant will be unable to pay regularly, the price is raised to provide against such contingency...

Landlords were also quick to respond to any upswing in the demand for iron. Hence, in May 1845 the *Merthyr Guardian* reported 'several of the proprietors of houses, taking advantage of the late advance in workmen's wages, have increased the rent of their cottages'. When trade slumped, however, they proved reluctant to lower rents accordingly.

Not all houses were built by speculators; many were owned by the iron companies themselves and some were built by working men either to let or for personal use.

Regarding the latter, in 1840 Tremenheere maintained that throughout Merthyr the most common reason given by workers for what savings did occur was the desire to build a house but 'The number so built, or in building, is far from being consider-able', and on the basis of his study of the 1841 census G.S. Kenrick argued that only ninety-one workmen owned their own houses. Yet evidence given to a Parliamentary Committee in 1854 painted a different picture:

> Is it not a fact that a great number of workmen both at Dowlais and Merthyr have laid out considerable sums in building cottages? A great deal...The general way of doing it is that when a man has £50 or £60 he starts upon three houses directly, he builds as far as his money goes, and he will borrow £80 upon a small mortgage for two or three years; that is done to a very large extent.

Only the labour aristocracy could afford to save such sums and as their aspirations would have been viewed sympathetically by their employers it was often the iron companies which lent the money needed. Evidence from Dowlais suggests that workers owned around 11% of the houses there, so the working-class stake in housing was small though not insignificant.

When they had first opened their works the masters had been forced to build houses, and statistics from the 1840s and 1850s suggest that about a third of all work-ing-class housing was still owned by the iron companies which rented them out to their skilled and semi-skilled workers. This stake was of major significance, not least in purely financial terms, since the rents charged for these houses, varying from 4s to 10s a month, were considerably lower than those demanded for similar houses by other landlords.

The remaining 60% of the market was controlled by Merthyr's small middle class. By common consent their houses were the worst available and their stake in the poorest areas was high if not total. Thus, though small in numerical terms, the influence they wielded was very considerable and it was this exaggerated influence which, in a great many respects, explained the lamentable condition of working-class accommodation in the town. Although Victorians spoke in terms of first-, second- and third-class houses for working people, perhaps a more accu-rate assessment comes from dividing the market into those houses occupied by the skilled, the semi-skilled and the unskilled sections of the workforce. Though by no means rigid, such divisions provide an illuminating insight into the differing status levels within Merthyr, as well as illustrating the gulf between the labour aristocracy and their unskilled neighbours.

First-class houses were occupied by those skilled artisans who alone could afford to pay rents of 10s to 13s a month on a regular basis or who had built their own homes.

According to the *Morning Chronicle*, these houses:

> ...are of two stories, have four small sash windows (which, by the way, are never opened),
> two above, and one on each side of the door. On the ground floor there is a roomy
> kitchen with a stone floor; adjoining is a small room, just large enough to contain a four-
> post bed, a chest of drawers, a small corner-cupboard, two chairs and a window table,
> which usually form its contents. The ceiling is not plastered, and the rafters are used for
> hanging up the crockery and household utensils. Above stairs are two bed-rooms, one
> large and the other small; the ceiling here is of lath and plaster. This is all, except, perhaps,
> a narrow cupboard, cut off from the lower bedroom, and dignified with the name of
> 'pantry'. There is no strip of garden, no backdoor or outlet, no place of accommodation,
> no drain to carry away house refuse, nor any pump or pipe for the supply of water.

Not all such houses were completely devoid of amenities, however, and the Plymouth
Company won praise from the *Merthyr Guardian* in April 1846 'for granting such large
pieces of land to the men for gardens and potato ground. The allotment system may
there be seen in miniature'. Similarly, the *Morning Chronicle* told of how:

> Mr. Hill has built 300 cottages, which, with the exception of Mr. Crawshay's new houses
> at Cyfarthfa Row, are the loftiest, roomiest, and best arranged of the workmen's dwell-
> ings that I examined in this neighbourhood. They have pumps which supply water, ovens
> for baking, and covered privies...

Such houses were exceptional, though, and the picture presented of four-roomed
houses lacking toilets, sewers, water and gardens is the one which should be regarded
as the norm throughout the period.

As to the interiors of first-class dwellings:

> These houses are, for the most part, the very type of cleanliness and order. They are stuffed
> with furniture, even to superfluity, a fine mahogany eight-day clock, a showy mahogany
> chest of drawers, a set of mahogany chairs with solid seats, a glass-fronted cupboard for the
> display of china, glass and silver spoons, forming indispensible requisites for the principal
> room. The other apartments are equally well furnished.

The 1851 census revealed that the High Street contained an abundance of shops
designed to satisfy this demand for furniture and household trappings from Merthyr's
highest-paid workers, whose 'desire for emulation and... joy of possession could be
most readily satisfied'. However, there was another reason behind this love of artefacts,
for, as Tremenheere discovered, 'small savings seemed to be often laid out in expensive

articles of furniture... which afford a fund under circumstances of pressure'. In 1840 there were only one or two pawn shops but by the end of the decade there were several, and for many, even those with a recognised skill, the fluctuating state of the iron trade meant the pawn shop became an all-too-familiar landmark.

Second-class houses differed only in terms of their size, most having only two or three rooms measuring eight feet by ten or twelve, and in their less elaborate household possessions. The Rhydycar cottages which have been re-erected at the Museum of Welsh Life at St Fagans provide us with a good example of these houses, which were occupied by miners and their families and which existed side by side with the larger dwellings of the skilled men and the hovels of the unskilled. Regarding the latter, generalisations are of little value because of the variety of accommodation utilised. Cellars, one-roomed shacks, back-to-back and over-and-under houses and even converted stables all provided accommodation. Newly arrived immigrants seeking employment, casual labourers, the Irish, vagrants, criminals, the sick, maimed, old, orphaned and widowed all found a niche at the bottom of the market and contemporaries have left us with an abundance of evidence from their periodic forays into the slums of Merthyr. According to one survey undertaken in 1854:

> The most striking features of vicious construction... are in the instances of houses being built *back to back*, or *under and over* – and of single or several habitations erected with high ground in their rear, frequently *abutting against the walls, or rising to a level with the roofs*. Others again, to the extent of whole rows, *without backlets*, or communication of any kind externally.

Back-to-back housing, often comprising just one room at ground level and a loft reached by a ladder, economised on land and building costs and thus increased the returns of those who invested in them. Similar in concept were the over-and-under houses or dual rows, which were well suited to the sloping sites so common in Merthyr and elsewhere in industrial south Wales.

Though overcrowding existed across the board, it was in the ghettoes and slums of Merthyr that it was at its worst. China, for example, was described by Rammell in the following terms:

> Some of the worst description of dwellings are those called 'the cellars', near Pont-y-Storehouse. These are small two-roomed houses, situated in a dip or hollow between a line of road and a vast cinder heap. In these miserable tenements, which are closely packed together, and with nothing in front or between them but stagnant pools of liquid and house refuse, it is said that nearly 1,500 living beings are congregated. The rents of these pest-holes are high, considering 'the accommodation', ranging from 3/- to 5/- a

month. Many of the tenants take lodgers, mostly, of course, vagrants and trampers who swarm daily into the town.

These cellars, 'mere huts of stone' as the *Morning Chronicle* described them, were considerably below the level of the road in many cases, and were reached by descending ladders. In 1845 De La Beche found one 'house' had just one room, measuring 7ft by 4ft 6in by 5ft 3in high, 'with a bed in it, and a stinking gutter partly under the floor'. For Merthyr's poor, the pressure on the housing market coupled with their lack of resources made even the worst of dwellings habitable, as the following reports from the early 1850s indicate:

> ...at half past nine last evening I saw Margaret Davies (living in a cellar, under a house in Ivy Bush Lane, Merthyr), and found her in the collapsed stage of cholera...The cellar... was until lately used as a cow house...
>
> Some huts in Pwllybaw in which cholera was very fatal in 1849, are in a filthy state. In one occupied by Patrick Brien in addition to the inmates and filthy bones and rags was a donkey...

A factor which exacerbated overcrowding was the taking in of lodgers, which was very widespread. The low-paid did it to supplement their wages, while for many people, especially female heads of households, lodgers provided their only source of income. Those deprived of a breadwinner by illness or injury or bereavement relied on the payments of their lodgers, and even those considered relatively well off – the skilled and semi-skilled – appear to have regarded the taking in of lodgers as a perfectly acceptable means of boosting the family income.

If lodgers led to overcrowding, conditions in individual homes were far better than those in the scores of lodging houses which were found in the poorest parts of the town. Owned by people whose sole concern was profit, comfort, privacy and hygiene were abandoned by all who stayed there:

> Michael Harrington's is a lodging house. On visiting today I found 45 inmates, but many more come in to sleep at nights... there are no bed-steads, but all the lodgers lie on the ground or floor. The children were sleeping in old orange boxes, and on shavings: that is, the younger ones, or they would be liable to be crushed in the night by persons rolling over them. Each party had with them all their stock, consisting of heaps of rags, bones, salt-fish, rotten potatoes, and other things... the stench was sickening... It is the common practice for these rooms to be occupied by relays of sleepers, some of them being engaged on work during the night, and some during the day.

The squalor and poverty found in these places was harrowing, but such was the demand that whereas in 1844 Merthyr was said to have some fifteen lodging houses, less than a decade later there were no fewer than 130, owned by just twenty-one individuals and one by the Dowlais Iron Company. Of the individuals, Josiah Atkins, the town's collector of rates and a man whose reputation as a slum landlord was without equal, owned no fewer than thirty-five, while the seven biggest owners between them controlled 76% of the market.

What then was the attitude of the people to their housing? Though contemporaries placed most blame upon the speculators and landlords, some degree of responsibility lay with the workers themselves. For the unskilled, the quality of accommodation was subordinate to cheapness and we should remember that the great majority of them were either first- or second-generation immigrants from rural Wales, where the typical cottage:

> ...had mud walls about five feet high, covered by a low thatched roof out of which there barely emerged a wattle and daub chimney... Such buildings inevitably became rat infested. The windows generally had no glass, and the floors no paving. Inside there was but one room, but this was usually partitioned into two by a box bed or a chest of drawers... [on the farms] the men and the lads slept in the out-buildings, in dark, badly ventilated lofts, over stables or cowsheds, or even in carthouses. Their bedding consisted only of clothes spread on the straw.

Having said as much, the blame attached to the middle-class speculators and the masters was well deserved. In most other spheres of working-class life, these people were responsible for a sustained and deliberate policy of overt action in order to bring about positive change. When it came to housing the workforce, however, they did little, and the contrast between the 140ft by 30ft of Crawshay's ballroom and the 7ft by 4ft 6in by 5ft 3in China hovel stands as a stark reminder of the fact.

When, in 1849, Inspector Rammell introduced that part of his report concerned with drainage, cleansing, sanitation and water supply, he stated that, while the town had long been notoriously deficient of such facilities, 'I was certainly not prepared for so bad a case as my own senses and the testimony of numberless witnesses proved to be actually existing here'. The same disregard for planning which characterised the housing market also manifested itself in the formation of the streets; the same indifference to comfort led to the lack of any proper sanitation or water supply, while the profit motive which drove those who controlled the town ensured that little concern was shown for drainage and cleansing. As the *Morning Chronicle* put it in March 1850:

The courts, and often the middle of the streets are obstructed with heaps of ashes, ordure, the refuse of vegetables and the clotted hay of which the Irish and some of the Welsh make their beds. Upon this is thrown all the slops from the houses... The roadways of the streets, especially in... Dowlais and Penydarren, are in rainy weather absolutely impassable; they are a mass of festering black mud, into which the wheels of the carts which carry coal to the houses sink deeply. Crossings are here and there made – not by the parish, for the roads have never been surrendered to their custody in proper repair, consequently the parish is not compelled to keep them up – not by the iron masters, whose houses form the streets, but by the inhabitants themselves, who, for their own convenience in crossing these stinking and poisonous sloughs, have here and there, in an irregular manner, placed stones in the mud.

The key to any understanding of this absence of authority lies in the evidence given by J.E. Price, a draper, to Rammell. He told of how the dust in the summer months adversely affected his trade and that 'The Board of Highways once partially watered the streets, but have discontinued it for ten years past, on account of economy'. This was the golden age of ratepayer mentality: the more savings and economies local government made, the lower the rates and the happier the ratepayers were – an attitude which explains the civic reluctance to address the roads and streets of the town. Such feelings played a crucial role in Merthyr's public health experience. For the great majority of the town's 1,300 or so ratepayers, the Parish existed to curb and not foster expenditure, and this stance permeated the minutes of the Vestry meetings throughout the period. To take the example of watching and lighting, at the beginning of 1839 at a meeting to decide on what action was to be taken, and which had already been adjourned once, 'the business was very quickly dispatched; it being resolved to postpone the further consideration of the subject for twelve months'.

Cleansing provides another example. In Dowlais, Rammell found that the Guests imposed a penny a week charge on each of their houses to finance the collection and disposal of household refuse, but collections were at best erratic and frequently non-existent because all such waste was universally thrown into the streets for collection by the company carts, and this rendered many of the streets, especially in winter, impassable. Elsewhere in the locality the streets were simply too narrow to admit carts at any time of the year. When collections did occur, the refuse was simply dumped onto tips and left to rot. 'In the upper part of Dowlais the refuse is taken to a "tip" on the north side of the town. At the lower part... there is a small tip... [which] consists entirely of the house-ashes and refuse... and it is immediately surrounded by a very dense population'. However imperfect cleansing was in Dowlais, Merthyr itself had no facilities at all. Rubbish of every description was scattered throughout the town:

the heaps of putrefying and fermenting refuse are as astonishing as they are pernicious... There is not a wall, a heap of scoria from the works, or a vacant spot of ground, that is not covered with abominations. The banks of the Taff form one vast and continuous mass of rubbish.

Closely associated with the problems of cleansing were those of drainage. Though naturally well drained, the growth of an unplanned and irregular maze of works, tips, tramways, roads and housing served to destroy the natural system without substituting any man-made one. Streams which had once fed the Taff and the Morlais turned into open and stagnant sewers or drained instead into cesspools which, as the breeding grounds for disease, came to haunt their immediate neighbourhoods. A good example of the lack of planning was provided by the somewhat inaptly named Bethesda Gardens where, in 1853, a surveyor reported, 'The place is still in a filthy state and will never be otherwise until it is properly drained. This will involve some expense as it lies in a hole formed by the Penydarren cinder tip'. The practice of building houses in parallel rows up the sides of the surrounding hills also created problems, as was explained by Robert Frederick, a Dowlais grocer:

> In consequence of the conformation of the ground, which is here extremely steep, the liquid refuse of one row of houses often drains down the back of another row of houses below it, and it frequently overflows the floor of the lower houses, and creates an ill-feeling between neighbours...

The wretched state of Merthyr was exacerbated still further by the almost total lack of sanitary provision:

> The inhabitants... make use of chamber utensils, which they empty into the streets before the doors, sometimes into the river, or, in the case of males, relieving themselves upon any of the numerous cinder-heaps... or by the sides of walls, or backs of houses, all without the commonest regard to decency. Children are placed out in open chairs in the street to perform their necessary operation.

Such was the lack of regard for building 'privy accommodation' that when schools were opened in Dowlais the pupils had to be taught how to use the toilets. As far as their owners were concerned, a dwelling could just as easily be rented without a toilet as with one, and so sound business sense dictated that privies were unnecessary. Indeed, building them increased the costs, which led in turn to higher rents and reduced demand. Though undoubtedly the major factor, proprietors produced a variety of reasons for their failure to erect toilets. For example, the Josiah Atkins of lodging house notoriety told Rammell quite blandly that he did not think the people *wanted* toilets. Another reason, perhaps, was that the lack of sewers meant that those toilets which did exist invariably became 'overfull'. The Rev. Jenkins, Vicar of Dowlais, viewed them with total disgust and argued that they were '*worse* than nothing'.

Throughout the period Merthyr's authorities viewed the problems of drainage and sanitation with complacent indifference, and even after the horrors of the 1849 cholera epidemic nothing was done. In August 1852, when J.S. Benect presented for approval a comprehensive plan for systematically draining and disposing of sewage in the town, it was rejected out of hand because of its 'excessive' costs of £33,056 19s, a cost which would have represented much less than £1 per person.

What horrified visitors to Merthyr was that the filth was not confined to the poorest parts of the town: it was everywhere. As Dr Holland of the General Board of Health wrote in 1853:

> The first circumstance that most strikes every visitor at Merthyr is the extreme and universal dirtiness and wetness of the town. I have visited many dirty places, and have generally been taken to see the worst parts of most of the worst towns in England; with the worst parts of London and Manchester I am familiar, that extremely dirty city of Bristol I have recently examined but never did I see anything which could compare with Merthyr...

For Rammell, the 'crowning evil' was not the overcrowding or the lack of drains, sewers or toilets but the total absence of any proper water supply. The ironmasters sank their own wells and the middle class paid between 6d and 2s a quarter for access to private ones, but the workers were forced to rely on artificial springs, known locally as *pishtyllion,* which were merely permeations from nearby bodies of water such as the Taff or the canal. In upper Merthyr between six and eight of these existed in the winter, but during the summer the number fell to three and queueing daily for water became a fact of life. 'At these water-spouts I have seen 50, 80, and as many as 100 people waiting for their turn... They have been known to wait up the whole of the night'. In lower Merthyr women and girls waded the Taff to secure water, or if it was in flood walked a mile to cross the iron bridge. Such journeys proved a daily necessity:

> because the occupation of the colliers and miners is of so filthy a nature that they are compelled to wash themselves all over at their return from their day's work, for which purpose a large quantity of water is... daily required.

Indeed, such was the demand that the river and canal were resorted to despite the all too obvious pollution. H.A. Bruce told Rammell of how he frequently travelled along a road which forded the Taff and 'I scarcely ever pass without seeing people close to me... easing themselves, whilst only a few yards off women and girls are filling their pitchers with water'. In Dowlais, according to Henry Murton, even when people relied on the spouts, what they received was little more than 'a very inadequate supply of diluted mud, absolutely in motion with living organisms', while Dr Holland from the General Board of Health wrote:

> I can hardly expect credence for such facts as the following, yet it is perfectly free from exaggeration. I saw a young woman filling her pitcher from a little stream of water gushing from a cinder heap the surface of which was so thickly studded with alvine deposits that it was difficult to pass without treading on them, in some of which I saw intestinal worms, and the rain then falling was washing the feculant matter into the water which the girl was filling into her pitcher, no doubt for domestic use.

All this must be seen in relation to the fact that Merthyr received a high rainfall and the surrounding countryside had abundant supplies of water. As the *Morning Chronicle* observed in March 1850:

> the traveller who, on his way to the town, passes fine reservoirs kept up apparently regardless of expense, and with extreme care, might suppose that at least the streets, if not the houses, would be well supplied. But the water in these reservoirs, and the copious streams of the rivers Taff and Morlais, are absorbed entirely in the works. The iron masters have a long-vested and absolute right in them, and the only question affecting them in this particular instance is whether, knowing the condition of the town, they ought not to have assisted the inhabitants in procuring a supply from a quarter which would not affect their interests.

Even in the 1850s water was the major source of power at the Cyfarthfa and Plymouth works, while its regular supply was also crucial at Dowlais and Penydarren. As far as the masters were concerned, its importance to industry far outweighed the problems its shortage caused their workers, and for many years Crawshay and Hill fought any attempt to remove their monopoly on its supply. They 'resisted to the bitter end any scheme to construct a reservoir higher up the valley. They even demanded compensation of £10,000 each should they be overruled'. Despite such entrenched opposition, however, a reservoir was finally built in the 1860s, although compensation was indeed paid and the masters benefited to the tune of an unlimited supply of water during wet weather and ten times the supply they had been accustomed to in dry weather.

Having examined cleansing, drainage and the supply of water, Rammell turned to the problems encountered by the people in burying their dead, and once again the crucial factors of ratepayer mentality and the profit motive were clearly demonstrated.

Despite the six-fold increase in population between 1801 and the late 1840s, and the fact that the town's mortality rates consistently exceeded the national average, 'No adequate general provision appears at any time to have been made for the probable requirements of an increasing population'. In 1849, as a direct result of this lack of planning, Merthyr had twenty-one burial grounds scattered throughout the town, the great majority of which were said to be 'in an overcrowded state'. Many graveyards were held on lease only, and when these expired landlords were quick to put the land to more lucrative use, as was the case at the Bethel graveyard in Dowlais:

> It has been for many years quite neglected. I have seen coffins, bones, and flesh exposed in the yard... the present leaseholder – Henry Protheroe... had the intention of clearing a portion of it away, in order to erect some cottages upon it... A portion of the ground was carted to the 'tips', and to the Morlais brook, and thus disposed of. Before this occurred, I have seen pigs nuzzling amongst the graves. I have also seen dogs endeavouring to make their way into the coffins.

Turning away from the physical realities of Merthyr in the middle of the nineteenth century, some attempt needs to be made to analyse how its people regarded the state of the town. Many of those who wrote about Merthyr commented on the cleanliness of the people in the face of the filth which surrounded them. The *Morning Chronicle*, for example, argued that:

> The habits of the women, in respect of their houses, are those of cleanliness, decency, and order. They are always scrubbing the rooms, polishing and regulating the furniture, or with long brushes laying white or yellow washes upon the front of their houses. In short, the people themselves do their duty.

Similarly, although the absence of toilets produced scenes which so horrified observers, Dr Carte informed Rammell 'I do not blame the people; they have no other place to go. I think they are naturally the cleanest people I ever saw'. As Ieuan Gwynedd Jones has noted:

> The contrast between these ideals of comfort and of possessive pride with the physical appearance of the town was indeed a shattering comment upon the failure of the government of the town to provide any of the decencies of community life for a people which struggled so hard to provide for itself.

As for the landlords, the filth was for the most part either ignored or taken for granted. Josiah Atkins maintained: 'The streets in Merthyr are generally well cleaned, in my opinion, and there is an abundant supply of water for those who make application for it'. When Henry Wrenn was appointed as Inspector of Nuisances in October 1848, in a belated attempt to clean up the town prior to the inevitable appearance of the cholera which had just reappeared in Britain, there followed a series of court appearances as proprietors defended their interests against 'orders of removal' and Wrenn's enthusiasm for the task. Such cases did very little to disturb the prevailing complacency, however, and when a Mr Overton was summoned after failing to clear away some 'obnoxious nuisances' as ordered, he informed the magistrates that the whole public health movement and its trappings was nothing more than 'a piece of vexatious officiousness'. Despite such open hostility he was only fined 5s a day for ten days which, under a law which provided for a fine of 10s a day until such time as the court was obeyed, was hardly a punishment calculated to provoke much activity.

What then of the town's authorities? Rammell remarked 'for all intents and purposes of civic government, Merthyr Tydfil is as destitute as the smallest rural village in the Empire'. Under the terms of the 1848 Public Health Act, legislation could be introduced if the annual mortality rate of a community exceeded twenty-three per 1,000, or if the General Board of Health was petitioned by at least one-tenth of the ratepayers. At the end of October that year, at a meeting held at the Vestry Room 'to consider the desirability of introducing the Public Health Act to Merthyr', those in favour of such action were defeated by opposition led by Anthony Hill. He argued that it was the small proprietors and the speculators who caused the problems, and as this was the case then why should the gentlemen of the town be forced to pay in order to clean it up? Hill favoured the introduction of local legislation, attacking the National Act for its huge bureaucracy, which would serve as a 'massive drain' on the ratepayers. Not all of Merthyr's ratepayers shared this hostility, however, and a petition signed by 185 of them, around 13% of the total, was duly forwarded to Westminster in November 1848, and it was because of this that Rammell came to the town in May 1849. The opposition did not give in, though, and in the intervening months a hurried attempt was made to clear some of the most obvious nuisances away in order that Merthyr could be presented as a model of the health, wealth and happiness which could be accrued from unfettered industry and enterprise. Such efforts coincided with Wrenn's campaign to improve the town before the onset of cholera, and so it was that when Rammell did arrive and expressed his astonishment at the state of the town he was told by Walter Thompson, a banker who was in the vanguard of the public health movement, that 'The town is now particularly clean, and I have seldom seen it in so good a state as at present'. Echoing such sentiments, Dr Carte said of Dowlais 'It is now the West End of London, compared with what it was. This is since the Commission has been spoken of'.

Given the dominance of the ironmasters and the divisions within the middle class, the state of affairs which so appalled visitors was not easily rectified. Commenting on the general condition of industrial south Wales in 1850, Tremenheere concluded: 'Attention to the means of cleanliness, decency, and comfort about the houses in these large "cottage-towns" is the subject that has made on the whole the least progress within the last ten years'. In October 1850 a Local Board of Health was finally established, although events were to prove that the Merthyr of the 1850s was as bad as, if not worse than, the previous decade, for as the Medical Officer to the Privy Council put it in 1866:

> This place used to be abominable. It had almost the unwholesomeness, with but a fraction of the apology, of Liverpool. In our statistics for 1851–1861 it showed every possible evidence of sanitary neglect; in fever, in diarrhoea, in cholera, in smallpox, in phthisis [tuberculosis] and other lung diseases, in mortality of children, test it how one would, it always was conspicuously bad; and when medical inspections were made there, every report told the same lamentable story of sanitary non-feasance to the utmost.

It was not until 1861 that piped water reached the town, and it was to take another seven years to establish a sewer system. For most of the mid-nineteenth century, therefore, Merthyr remained, in the words of Thomas Carlyle, 'the squalidest, ugliest place on earth'.

4

DISEASE, DEBILITY AND DEATH

COFFINS – It is not, perhaps, generally known that the iron masters supply their
workmen with wood to make their coffins...
Merthyr Guardian, 22 July 1843

There can be no doubt at all that mid-nineteenth-century Merthyr was a disease-
ridden town. Tuberculosis, typhus, typhoid, smallpox, influenza, scarlet fever, whooping cough, measles, rickets, diptheria, dysentery and cholera all combined in the
decimation of its inhabitants and gave the town the unenviable distinction of being
surpassed only by Liverpool and Manchester, the two worst towns in the kingdom
and each many times Merthyr's size, in terms of percentage mortality. In the ten
years between 1846 and 1855, the annual death rate averaged thirty-three per 1,000
at a time when twenty was considered to be the norm, and in 1849, as a result of the
cholera epidemic, it reached a staggering sixty-seven per 1,000.

At the heart of these figures lay the horrifically high rates of infant mortality:

> In the *seven* years, from 1841 to 1847 – 11,454 children were born, and 4,276 children,
> *under 5 years of age*, died – 37.3%; or more than 7 in 20. And, in the *six* following years
> from 1848 to 1853 – 11,399 children were born, and 4,555 children, *under 5 years of age*,
> died – 39.9% – 8 in 20 – 2 in 5! The naked figures tell their own appalling tale.[7]

Over the thirteen years from 1841 to 1853, a quarter of all deaths in Merthyr
involved infants under one year old, while over half were of children younger than
five. Little wonder, therefore, that the *Morning Chronicle* should inform its readers
in March 1850: 'whatever it may be, there is something prejudicial to infant life in
Merthyr...'.

What then were the causes of this massacre of innocents? In the first instance, children, and especially young children, had yet to build up sufficient resistance to infection, and if their parents were infected they were almost bound to suffer. Those born in the overcrowded hovels of Merthyr's poorest districts were highly susceptible to respiratory infections and other conditions communicated by airborne droplets. The lack of adequate washing facilities increased the risk of gastro-intestinal infection and their poverty effectively denied them proper nutrition or medical care.

The newly born were most at risk, and in national terms there were three main reasons for this: the employment of mothers, improper feeding and the administering of drugs. We have already seen that women were employed about the works and mines in Merthyr and there can be little doubt that when the mother was working twelve-hour shifts, six and sometimes seven days a week, her children could not possibly receive the same care and attention as those whose mothers did not work. As far as feeding was concerned, as soon as they had been weaned infants ate the same food as adults, albeit mashed to a pulp and possibly sweetened. If the parents ate balanced diets there was little to worry about, but if, out of poverty, they existed on bread and cheese alone or, as was the case with many of the Irish, ate only potatoes, the deficiencies are obvious – and the same factors, of course, would also have affected the quality of their mothers' milk. We will return to malnutrition; suffice to state here that its effects on infant health were considerable.

Regarding the drugging of babies and infants, this has historically been associated with the industrial towns of the north of England and Scotland. A Manchester chemist gave the following account of its incidence:

> The mother goes out to her work in the morning leaving her child in the charge of either a woman who cannot be troubled with it, or with another child of perhaps 10 years old. A dose of 'quietness' is given to the child to prevent it being troublesome. The child thus drugged sleeps and may waken at dinner time; so, when the mother goes out again, the child receives another dose. Well, the mother and father come home at night quite fatigued, and as they must rise early to begin work for the day, they must have sleep undisturbed by the child, so it is again drugged, and in this manner young children are often drugged three times in each day.

This particular chemist sold five gallons of 'quietness' a week, which contained 100 drops of laudanum per ounce and was sold for 2d an ounce. He also sold half a gallon of 'Godfrey's Cordial', which contained similar quantities of opium. But what was the position in Wales? No Welsh historian has ever mentioned it, but in May 1844 the *Merthyr Guardian* reported on the inquest on the death of a newly born infant in Dowlais. The mother said in her statement to the coroner that she had sent to the druggist 'for a pennyworth of Syrup of Poppies' in order to make the child sleep, as she had often done for her other child. The chemist, a Mr Harrison, said in evidence that:

> He had no recollection of the last witness having been to fetch Syrup of Poppies – in fact it was an article so frequently called for by so many people... that it was impossible he could recognize her; he considered half a teaspoonful a sufficient dose for a strong child'.

It would appear, therefore, that drugs too had an adverse bearing on infant health in Merthyr.

Such was the scale of child mortality that, in an attempt to replace the children who had been taken by disease, Merthyr produced high birth rates, approximately forty-two per 1,000 in 1841 and forty-four per 1,000 ten years later. Such were the conditions in the town that these efforts were very largely fruitless, however; as Dr Kay wrote laconically, 'this increase is an unproductive increase; an increase of children for the most part born to die'.

Before moving on, some mention of the darker side of life needs to be made:

> In the new industrial world, children were apt to be a nuisance, a drag on their parents, until they came to be old enough to earn a wage, and legislation increasingly discouraged child labour. The 'burden of dependency' in these days meant dependent children, not dependent old people. Some parents succumbed to the great expectations of the Burial Societies. Infanticide and near infanticide were not uncommon.

In Merthyr, according to evidence presented to Royal Commissioners in 1844, so many children were born illegitimate that desertion and infanticide were considered inevitable, and evidence contained in the *Merthyr Guardian* would seem to corroborate this. In March 1841, for example, Harriet Lewis, aged twenty-two and single, was discharged from custody after the case of her killing her own child by 'throwing it in a certain privy' was dismissed for lack of evidence. In May 1850, children playing in a wood near Twynyrodyn found the remains of a child in a blacking box which had been buried beneath some turf, while a year later some dogs were seen dragging an infant's corpse from the Penydarren cinder-tip where it had been secreted.

Because of infant mortality, the average life expectancy in the town was abysmally low. In 1852 it was calculated that the average age at death was only 17.6, though in Penydarren and Dowlais it was less than 16. Turning to what actually caused such death rates, the only comprehensive breakdown for mortality is that which Dr Kay, the town's temporary Medical Officer, produced for 1852. This revealed that almost 30% of all deaths resulted from epidemic, endemic and contagious diseases and in all probability a further 30% were occasioned by tuberculosis and other pulmonary complaints. Over 20% came under the rather nebulous 'other diseases' and 'unknown', with 'convulsions' at 16% and 'accidents' at 4% rounding off the total.

Why, then, was Merthyr so unhealthy? Enough has already been said about the appalling lack of public health provision in the town, but this alone does not account for all illnesses and deaths. Poverty was also a factor, in as much as it both caused disease and was a result in many cases of its ravages. The poor were forced to congregate in the very worst areas of the town and the slums of China, Quarry Row, Caepantywyll, Ynysgau, Pedwranfach and Caedraw were never free of disease. Without the means to eat nourishing food or buy decent clothing or live in anything other than squalor, the poor proved easy targets for infections of all kinds, particularly the very young and the old, who were most susceptible. Another link between poverty and disease concerned vagrancy. Without a workhouse until 1853, Merthyr proved particularly attractive to the thousands of itinerants who wandered about south Wales in search of relief, and throughout the period vagrants were seen as carriers of infection, a reputation probably well deserved. Those supported by the parish were not the only ones to experience poverty, however, and many of Merthyr's workers knew only too well the consequences of a poor diet. When the *Morning Chronicle*'s reporter asked an old Irish woman who worked around the calcinating kilns at Dowlais to produce her dinner, she brought out a piece of bread and said she couldn't afford any cheese to go with it. Those employed in filling the furnaces had bread and butter for their dinner as well as tea, but none could afford cheese or meat. One Irish labourer, supporting a wife and five children on 10s a week, 2s of which went on rent, said 'During the two years that I have been here I have not used a pound of butter or cheese altogether'.

Without further elaboration, thousands of Merthyr's workers suffered from poor diets and many of the afflictions which characterised the town stemmed in part from malnutrition. As one eminent doctor put it:

> Although death directly produced by hunger is rare there can be no doubt that a very large proportion of the mortality amongst the labouring classes is attributable to deficiency of food as a main cause, aided by too long continued toil and exertion without adequate repose, insufficient clothing, exposure to cold and other privations to which the poor are subjected.[8]

Immigration too had a bearing on mortality rates. Between 1831 and 1851 Merthyr's population more than doubled, but the town was as unprepared to receive these immigrants as they themselves were unprepared to live in an urban environment. The habits so condemned by observers – throwing slops and emptying chamber pots into the streets, keeping pigs inside houses and urinating or defecating wherever the urge occurred – were habits brought from the Welsh countryside, where they caused relatively little concern to low-density settlements. In Merthyr, however, such customs made disease inevitable.

If any one group of migrants was particularly associated with disease, it was the Irish. Driven by poverty and starvation from their homes, they were arriving in south Wales in ever increasing numbers, 'bringing pestilence on their backs [and] famine in their stomachs'. In Cardiff, the Police Superintendent reported:

> …many have the itch. I have seen a party of 20 young Irish men almost all scratching themselves at once, before settling into their rest in the straw. Lice exist in great numbers upon them… The most mischievous disease is a low kind of typhus fever, which particularly attaches itself to the Irish… it has generally proved fatal amongst the Irish only, and those in immediate contact with them, attending them as nurses or washing their clothes.

As for the provision of medical facilities, the town did have its private practitioners, but access to their services involved expenditure beyond the reach of most working people. This did not mean they never saw a doctor, as each of the iron companies employed surgeons paid for by weekly stoppages out of their workers' wages. The masters had gone to considerable lengths to recruit and train labour, and disease and accidents tended to negate their investment. It needs to be pointed out, however, that Merthyr had to wait until 1888 before a purpose-built hospital was opened, and the contemporary medical profession was severely limited by its ignorance of infection and disease. Consider, for example, the following advice issued in July 1849 at the height of that year's cholera epidemic and following the deaths of several washerwomen:

> CHOLERA – NOTICE – IT IS THE OPINION OF MEDICAL MEN, that there is LESS DANGER IN WASHING IN COLD WATER THAN IN HOT, the clothes, bed-linen etc., which have been used by persons while they were ill, and who have died of cholera. The Cholera Committee, therefore, begs to urge on all parties the great desirability of washing all such things in COLD WATER…

Cholera was the most feared of all diseases and there were four major epidemics in 1832, 1849, 1854 and 1866. In 1849 alone it was responsible for 1,467 deaths in Merthyr, and given that the single most important cause was drinking polluted water the only wonder is that it did not claim more victims. As Dr Kay put it, '*cholera is the direct result of sanitary neglect* – the direct infliction and penalty entailed by dirt, filth and impurity. It is an *invited*, a special, not an obtruding or indiscriminate visitant'.

Though cholera was the most spectacular killer, other diseases were endemic and typhus and typhoid, dysentery, tuberculosis, diptheria, scarlet fever, smallpox and a raft of others all served to keep the grave-diggers busy.

The most persistent and devitalising fever of the first half of the nineteenth century – socially as well as physically – was typhus, which, for most of the period, smouldered in the wynds and courts of the cities, breaking out with renewed virulence whenever a new crop of susceptibles came within its reach. Typhus sapped the strength and morale of the people. The disease was not highly fatal, but its victims were chiefly young adults and it had far-reaching economic effects: it was one of the most powerful causes of pauperism.

In Merthyr typhus caused one in every nine deaths, a higher proportion than anywhere else in south Wales. A disease greatly encouraged by hunger, dirt and overcrowding, it is carried in the faeces of lice which dry to a light dust, thus enabling a person to become infected by breathing in the dust or by a scratch on the hand. It not only caused poverty but bred on it. As for typhoid, like cholera, it was a water-borne disease and again it is hardly surprising that Merthyr in 1860 had the unenviable distinction of being among the worst ten towns in Britain in terms of mortality from the disease.

Tuberculosis, an airborne illness, caused at least one in five deaths in Merthyr and probably far more. An endemic disease, it selected its victims from among those whose resistance was diminished, and it thrived in deprived bodies whose lungs it eventually drowned. While no single factor may be said to cause it, poverty – which led to undernourishment and overcrowding – and TB were linked in an ugly alliance. Almost exclusively an urban disease, the lack of any previous exposure was particularly important, and when we remember the scale of the immigration from rural Wales it is not difficult to understand why it was so prevalent. One medical historian has argued that the experience of these migrants was comparable to that of Africans, Amerindians and Maoris when they first came into contact with tuberculosis. In as much as the disease is the product of the environment, TB morbidity also provides a sensitive index of living conditions, and thus its incidence provides a stark reminder of just how poor living standards were in Merthyr.

Those children who did survive infancy were subject to a variety of communicable diseases, especially scarlet fever, diptheria and smallpox. Scarlet fever declined after the turn of the nineteenth century, only to rise again in the 1830s, culminating in a forty-year period of severe and frequent epidemics between 1840 and 1880, when it was the leading child-killer. As far as diptheria is concerned, unfortunately little is known about its incidence, as until 1855 it was confused with scarlet fever. Smallpox, however, received far more attention. Posing a continual threat throughout the eighteenth and nineteenth centuries, it 'smouldered endemically in city and town, flaring up recurrently into epidemic outbreaks' such as those experienced in Merthyr in 1837–38, 1841, 1844, 1848 and 1851. Although Jenner discovered vaccination in 1798, the first Vaccination Act only came into operation in 1840, at a time when the disease was the fifth most fatal in Britain. Despite legislation, smallpox continued unchecked largely because of the repugnance vaccination held for the working classes, and in Merthyr this was certainly the case as the number of children vaccinated was nowhere near half the registered births, prompting the town's doctors to conclude that only compulsory schemes could hope to succeed.

Another affliction to hit great numbers of children was rickets. A vitamin-deficiency disease produced by a variety of dietary and environmental conditions, although it was not entirely restricted to the poor, 'rickets in Victorian Britain can be described as a disease of city slums, of ignorance, poor hygiene, and a paucity of sunlight'. There can be no doubt that it was endemic in Merthyr and reports like the following from the *Merthyr Guardian* in May 1847 were by no means isolated: 'scurvy and other diseases springing from bodily weakness are making their appearance in the poorer districts...'.

Before concluding this survey of disease and mortality, we need to look at the effects of employment and the incidence of industrial accidents. Contemporaries were certainly aware of the relationship between certain diseases and particular occupations, especially in regard to underground workers. Dr Greenhow noted in 1861 that men 'who are usually of a ruddy and healthful aspect when presenting themselves for employment at the mines, soon... lose their florid complexion and become pallid and etiolated after working for some time...'. At the end of March 1850 the *Morning Chronicle* maintained that:

> There exists no material difference, in the statistical value of life, between colliers and miners. Both die, for the most part, of pulmonary diseases, of which the most frequent is phthisis [tuberculosis]. Their occupation sufficiently accounts for this. From a third to one half of their time is passed in the depths of the earth, amidst an atmosphere contaminated with gases inimical to human life, and loaded with highly contaminated particles of coal dust, which irritate the delicate textures of the lungs... But even if the above were insufficient to account for this proneness to pulmonary complaints, another cause is to be found in the vicissitudes of temperature to which these classes... are subject.

In every contemporary statement, the 'impure atmosphere' was given as the major cause of disease for underground workers, and this arose 'from want of proper ventilation and economy of mining operations'. Throughout the south Wales coalfield methods of pit ventilation were crude, and even at the end of the 1850s the Dowlais Company's Fochriw Pit, which was 390 yards deep, was still being worked with just one shaft.

While tuberculosis was by no means restricted to those who worked underground, what made miners and colliers particularly susceptible was the continual inhalation of dust, together with the dampness and great fluctuations of temperature in the pits. Furthermore – though again a factor by no means restricted to underground workers – tuberculosis was 'the characteristic disease of overwork' and the long hours and heavy loads of miners and colliers in Merthyr have already been noted. Deaths from pneumoconiosis and silicosis alone must have been considerable, and though not yet recognised as diseases – indeed, it was to take until the 1920s for the incidence of pneumoconiosis to be officially accepted – nevertheless contemporary surgeons were well aware of dust pollution; as the *Morning Chronicle* related, 'Mr. Edward Davies... informed me that, in making *post mortem* examinations of the bodies of colliers and miners, he often found small black patches in the tissue of the lungs, which he believed were portions of carbon from the coal'.

Perhaps those who suffered most were the children. In 1842 Mr Kirkhouse, manager of the Cyfarthfa mines and collieries, stated that 'The infantine ages at which children are employed cranks their growth and injures their constitution', while the most damning observation came from Mr Probert, surgeon for the Plymouth Company:

> The employment of children in mines at a very early age tends to *produce disease*, by exposing a constitution not matured to foul air; but other causes contribute to this effect. Such children are very much exposed to wet and cold, especially during winter and the rainy season. They are, moreover, deprived of *solar light*, which is as necessary to the proper development of animals as vegetables.

Because of the unhealthy nature of their occupation, the early age at which they started work and the constant threat of accidents, the *Morning Chronicle* argued that the average life expectancy for underground workers in Merthyr was only forty-two years at a time when nationwide it was forty-nine, and even this was ten years below the national average for all men who had survived their nineteenth year.

Turning to the works themselves, once again a combination of factors served to diminish workers' resistance to disease. The *Morning Chronicle* deplored the fact that only the Cyfarthfa works were roofed and elsewhere those who worked at the furnace heads and hearths were compelled to do so exposed to the elements. As the reporter noted at the time of his visit to the Dowlais works: 'the snow lay two inches thick upon the ground... There is no other excuse for this neglect of the well-being and protection of the labourer than that of expense'. The largely female labour force of pollers, coke-girls, limestone-breakers, tippers and pilers was, more often than not, constantly exposed to the vagaries of the weather, so it was little wonder that 'great numbers find an early grave'.

So intense was the heat emitted by the furnaces that in the summer months firemen often fainted, and puddlers went blind after working at their furnaces for many years. Those who worked about the furnaces became recognisable as a distinct group by their very appearance. Indeed, founders, refiners, puddlers, ballers and rollers:

> …in fact all who come under the denomination of 'fire-men'… have a peculiarly sallow appearance… The face of the fireman is often ghastly white, with a peculiar shining waxy texture; his eyes are sunken, and so tremendous and so unremitting is the heat he has to endure that he never shows the slightest particle of fat – his limbs are gaunt and thin, and his muscles desiccated and hard like wire… [They] generally die from a breaking up of the constitution; frequently from pulmonary diseases, superinduced by the trying vicissitudes of heat and cold to which they are exposed… They get, it is true, the best wages of all classes employed in the works, but they barter their life for this increased pay.

Given such hazards to health, Robert Thompson Crawshay's statement 'I do not think that the men, from the nature of their occupation, are long lived' would seem particularly apt, and yet care needs to be taken to distinguish between those diseases actually caused by employment, such as pneumoconiosis, and those afflictions for which resistance was diminished and susceptibility increased by the nature of the job.

Before concluding on the subject of disease, it needs to be remembered that 'recorded mortality was only the tip of a vast iceberg of ill health', as all who were attacked or afflicted did not necessarily die, though those who succumbed to the more infectious diseases rarely escaped unscathed. As one Medical Officer of Health put it in 1856: 'Those attacked do not simply recover or die. I shall not be exaggerating when I say that all recovering… are permanently injured'.

Turning finally to accidents, just how dangerous employment was in the town is largely a matter for conjecture, as the masters kept no records. Having said this, their very absence provides a grim pointer to the historian, for, as one of the 1842 Commissioners put it, 'It is much to be regretted that an apparent unwillingness to communicate exists among those who alone are capable of affording the requisite information'. Though scanty and often vague, the evidence which does exist does much to explain this reticence. In Dr Kay's breakdown of mortality for 1852, the number of deaths from accidents was fifty-four, a mere 3.7% of the total. Though very small in percentage terms, it may well be that in other years there were greater fatalities, besides which even fifty-four deaths cannot be regarded as insignificant – and this figure does not give the slightest indication of the number of non-fatal accidents. After examining fatalities for the latter part of 1849, the *Morning Chronicle* reminded its readers 'this of course does not show anything like the number of accidents that occurred… the cases of fractured limbs, or burns, and other injuries – some disabling for life – have been… numerous, but the particulars have not been obtainable'.

Throughout the period, the *Merthyr Guardian* regularly included brief reports of fatal accidents, and between 1839 and 1851 it reported on 225 deaths. Given Kay's figure for 1852 alone, we can presume that this was but a fraction of the whole; nevertheless, the information provided does give some clues as to the extent and character of such accidents. Regarding the occupations of the victims, data exists for over 90% of the cases, with underground workers accounting for over 85% of the total. That such workers bore the brunt is also borne out in information concerning the causes of death. In all, 92% of these are known, and of these roof falls, gas and powder explosions and falls in shafts account for over 75%. If deaths by trams are included – and most of these occurred in the pits – then the figure rises to 85%.

Why then were the mines so dangerous? The *Merthyr Guardian* survey revealed that of those cases where the cause of death was recorded, nearly 48% were killed by roof falls. These 'were almost a weekly occurrence, causing over a period of any length more destruction of life than the occasional calamitous explosion'. The post and stall method of mining relied on leaving untouched pillars of coal or iron ore to support the roof, and the temptation to rob these was great. Skilled and careful propping was the main safeguard, but colliers and miners alike were paid for the minerals they dug rather than the timber they erected; hence the death toll.

Regarding explosions, while it was not until February 1862 that Merthyr claimed her own disaster (when forty-seven men and boys perished at the Gethin Pit), the 1839–1851 survey revealed that they were responsible for almost 16% of deaths, with the majority of victims being colliers as opposed to miners. It was in the coal-levels that the threat of gas was at its greatest, particularly in lower Merthyr where the pits were at their deepest. During the *Morning Chronicle's* visit to the Glynderris Pit in March 1850, its reporter 'heard a uniform and monotonous singing noise, like the humming of a gnat, only much louder'. On inquiry, he was told by his collier guide that this was caused by firedamp pushing through into the workings:

> I asked him to show me the place where it so came in. Holding his candle to the floor of the coal, and sweeping away the rubbish with the other hand it immediately fired, and continued burning over the crevice till he trampled it out... I wished to see a slight explosion, if it might be attempted without danger, and I was gratified. Cautioning us to stoop, the collier raised his candle with a rapid movement towards the roof, and as suddenly removed it, but without effect. The second time it fired, flashing like gun powder and moving with great velocity, and a whizzing noise a few yards forward and backwards, and then it died out.

Quite apart from raising serious doubts about the sanity of the reporter, this statement provides a useful insight into working methods in the coal workings. Although

Davey first marketed his safety lamp as early as 1815, the Inspector of Mines appointed for south Wales in 1851 argued, 'In nine cases out of ten the safety lamp is not used to work by, but as a test for the presence of fire-damp' and research indicates that this was indeed the case, since just as underground workers were charged for the candles, tools and gunpowder they used, so too were they expected to buy their own safety lamps. Expense was not the only deterrent, however, as the light given off by these lamps was much less than that given by an open flame and thus:

> Even the introduction of safety lamps into gaseous mines encountered opposition, not as was sometimes asserted because the men had a reckless disregard for danger, but because its poorer light meant that they could cut less, and this, in the absence of an adequate adjustment of wage rates, reduced their earnings.

So candles continued to be used, and the crude and volatile nature of the powder used for blasting, the increasing depth of the mines and their primitive ventilation all ensured that gas continued to claim lives and limbs with frightening regularity.

Some 12% of fatalities resulted from workers falling to their deaths, the majority underground. When the *Morning Chronicle*'s reporter descended the 462ft-deep Glynderris Pit, he did so via a platform which 'had no cagework, nor indeed anything to take hold of' and which was suspended by a single chain; two weeks before Christmas 1850, three sinkers were killed when one of these chains broke at a Dowlais pit. However, the evidence suggests that most falls did not involve main shafts but arose from unprotected shafts within the pits themselves.

Turning to the ironworks, these could hardly be regarded as safe workplaces. Burns and scalds, explosions and falls of iron and machinery were all too frequent. Indeed, boiler explosions were so common that when Adrian Stephens invented the steam whistle at Dowlais in 1832 it was used as a safety device to warn of impending explosions. As in the mines, many of the victims were children such as twelve-year-old Thomas Lewis, who was crushed to death by the rollers at the Plymouth works in February 1844; that many more were injured or maimed by accidents is beyond question. Hence when the 1842 Commissioners visited the Dowlais schools, they found no fewer than twelve children attending lessons solely because of injuries sustained at work.

It would seem that Merthyr's workers viewed the prevalence of accidents with a pragmatic stoicism, except when negligence or indifference on the part of the masters was considered apparent. As far as the masters were concerned, they expressed the opinion that accidents were either the result of forces beyond all human control or the direct result of their workers' ignorance of, or disregard for, safety procedures. The civil authorities took an identical stance, and for every one of the deaths reported by the *Merthyr Guardian* verdicts of 'accidental death' or 'death by misadventure' were returned by the coroner, prompting one of the 1842 Commissioners to seriously question the role of coroners and their juries. In evidence he was told, 'When a man dies the viewer looks at the body and sends to the coroner. He does not come, but sends an order to the constable to bury, and frequently the coroner does not attend until there are five or six cases to clear off'. Not only does this suggest that the office of coroner was something of a sinecure, it also tells us something about the incidence of fatalities and the prevailing attitude that accidents were inevitable. Not everyone agreed with such a proposition, however, and Dr Kay argued that the number of fatal accidents would only fall 'if those precautionary arrangements and appliances, which science has supplied, and the adoption of which humanity dictates, were rigidly enforced, and greater care and general vigilance was scrupulously observed in all departments of work'.

In November 1851, H.F. Mackworth was appointed Government Inspector of Mines for the Western Region, which included south Wales. Two years later he reported that the great majority of accidents he had to investigate were 'attributable to the neglect or recklessness of the proprietors or managers of the mines, whilst they generally content themselves with attributing the same faults to the men'. He found that, whereas some owners accepted his advice, many others, like John Evans, the principal manager of the Dowlais works, ignored him and rejected his position on the grounds that it constituted an unnecessary bureaucratic intrusion. It was to be many years before influential public opinion and effective Parliamentary control succeeded in breaking the indifference and hostility of men like Evans. Writing in the *Mining Journal* in 1846, one correspondent accurately predicted that in the absence of more careful methods 'South Wales would undoubtably become a huge charnel-house, before which Northumberland and Durham will sink into insignificance', and as a result Dr Kay found that in the first three years of inspection, fatal accidents in the mines of Merthyr accounted for, on average, 'nearly double the number which happened proportionately to the men employed... in the whole of the collieries in Great Britain'.

Once again, we should remember that fatalities did not tell the whole story. A Dowlais surgeon maintained 'the number of accidents... resulting in amputation is very great. I believe there are in Merthyr more men with wooden legs than there are to be found in any town in the kingdom having four times its population', while the *Morning Chronicle* described the streets of the town as being 'thronged with the maimed and mutilated'.

Mid-nineteenth-century Merthyr paid a terrible price for its industrial prominence.

5

PAUPERISM AND POVERTY

I t may I think be safely said that the working population of the industrial districts of South Wales enjoy a standard of living equal, if not superior, to any group of workers in Great Britain. I know no other part of the Empire in which, year after year, wages are so high, food and fuel are so cheap, and workers houses are so large and comfortable. Nowhere can a working population be better fed, better paid, or more comfortably housed.

H.A. Bruce, Dowlais, 1852

No survey of life in mid-nineteenth-century Merthyr would be complete without some examination of the extent and nature of poverty in the town; despite its reputation as some kind of El Dorado, for many of its inhabitants the realities fell far short of expectations, and thousands were forced to 'go onto the Parish' in order to survive. This meant that all those who, for whatever reason, could not support themselves or be supported by others had, under the terms of the 1834 Poor Laws, to apply to the Board of Guardians for relief. If this was granted, they became official paupers whose details were required to be recorded in abstracts published twice yearly.

A statistical analysis of these abstracts for the 1850s reveals the following 'league table' for pauperism in the town:

Illness	32.4%	Orphaned	2.7%
Widowhood	23.8%	Single women	2.2%
Infirmity	18.6%	Funerals	1.3%
Trampers	10%	Insanity	1%
Deserted	5.2%	All others	1.6%

That illness was the major cause of pauperism should come as no surprise, given our exploration of housing, public health and disease. Merthyr's guardians were legally obliged both to care for sick paupers and to alleviate the causes of disease by regulating their accommodation, removing health hazards and promoting vaccination schemes, but their expenditure on medical relief during the years 1840–1848 averaged only 1.6% of their total spending, and the asylum which both doctors and guardians admitted was of immediate priority was never opened because of 'financial considerations'. Instead, sick paupers without friends or relatives to fall back upon were farmed out to lodging houses where they infected others and helped perpetuate the vicious circle of disease and poverty. It was only when the financial cost, not the human one, of the 1849 cholera epidemic became apparent that the guardians began to think again, though the primacy of illness as a cause of pauperism throughout the 1850s reveals that the movement towards better public health was painfully slow.

The next biggest category involved widows, who accounted for almost 24% of claimants, although 70% of those relieved under this heading were not widows at all but their dependent children. Again, the high mortality rates occasioned by disease and accidents, coupled with the arduous nature of employment, sufficiently accounts for this, for although women did work they only represented a small proportion of the workforce. For those with young children, any form of employment was frequently out of the question, and even for those who were able to work job opportunities were limited and wages low. Although sympathetic, the guardians did enforce the laws, and widows whose 'parish of settlement' was not Merthyr were forced to search for work, to rely on friends or relatives or to submit to 'removal', even though in many cases they had never even seen the distant parishes from which their husbands had originated.

The lot of those widows who lived in houses owned by the iron companies was particularly difficult, as shown by the following letter to the Manager of the Dowlais Company written in January 1844:

> Sir it is with the utmost truble i now send you these few lines to you. My husband have been sick 8 months through severe illness, but now is dead this near 2 months by which cause i am plunged in the deepest distress and no means whatever for support having parted with many things out of the house. Sir should my misfortune and poverty move you to let me remain in the house and if i could have to lodgers to me, i have no living body in the house night nor day but myself. I do have 3/6 from the parish a week and that is all i have to live on and i am helpless, i can't go out of the house for a drop of water nor any thing else. Please be so kind as to let Sir John now my poverty, if his honour please to give me little, i shan't be long in this owld world and i am in Dowlais this 40 years and have got my living by slaving hard... Sir, please to take me under your consideration and... please to let me now. God bles you and all your family

I am duly and humbly oblige to you

I am sir your humble servant

Mary Bowen widow and poor.

Without the support of a wage earner, for nearly ten months Widow Bowen had relied on the pawn shop to ward off destitution. Now her husband was dead there was no compulsion on the Company's part to allow his widow to remain there, especially when she was in no position to pay the rent. Hence her plea to remain in the house and to be allowed to take in a couple of lodgers, though the latter too would have eased the obvious loneliness, as she was old and housebound. While the pawn shop and the taking in of lodgers were two ways of avoiding destitution, other widows became street-sellers, labourers, grave-diggers, road-sweepers, baby-minders and washerwomen to make ends meet.

The third major cause of pauperism was 'infirmity', which in most cases meant old age, and in over 70% of cases those relieved were old women. In general terms, Merthyr's guardians accepted their responsibility of looking after the aged without much debate. They strongly resisted Westminster's attempts to ensure that at least one-third of any relief should be in kind and directed their relieving officers to visit old paupers in cases where the latter were too infirm to collect their relief. They also entered into agreements with other unions in which old paupers belonging to Merthyr had become chargeable, so as to prevent them being removed. Nevertheless, those chargeable to other parishes where the guardians refused to send relief were frequently forced into removals, even though many of them had spent most of their lives in Merthyr. Those who were chargeable to Merthyr had first to convince the guardians that they were unable to support themselves, and so many worked until they were well into their seventies and eighties before being deemed genuine applicants. In the abstract for September 1852, for instance, was a ninety-nine-year-old woman described as a 'filler'.

Those who were recognised as eligible but who had no family or friends to fall back on were farmed out to lodging houses. In April 1850, the *Morning Chronicle* cited one instance when, during an inspection of an overcrowded two-roomed lodging house in Penydarren, its reporter discovered an old woman 'bedridden and supported by the parish' living in a small cupboard off the main room:

…she lay on a mass of woollen rags, spread on the floor, and she completely filled the closet. If it were not for the open door, she must have died from suffocation. Her allowance was 2/- a week, out of which she paid 6d. for lodging…

Not every case of infirmity was due to old age, and some recipients were the victims of Merthyr's high accident rates. Once again, those without family or friends to fall back on had little choice other than to seek relief, and those not chargeable to Merthyr were sent back to their own parishes as soon as they could be moved. The town became notorious for its hideously deformed beggars and its crippled or blind musicians and singers. As the *Morning Chronicle* reported in March 1850:

> It is a frequent practice of men disabled… to learn to play the harp, by which means they earn a precarious and scanty subsistence, by playing at public houses and merry-makings wherever they can find employment. I have seen men recently mutilated practising the harp for this purpose.

Before continuing, it needs to be emphasised that these three categories of illness, widowhood and infirmity accounted for almost 75% of the paupers relieved in the 1850s.

Of the remainder, perhaps the saddest group were orphaned or abandoned children. In 1847 some forty children aged between three months and twelve years were maintained by the Parish, and in August 1849, at the height of the cholera, there were seventy-five orphans alone. Until the workhouse opened in 1853, no provision at all was made for their accommodation other than boarding them out with anyone willing to take them in. H. A. Bruce, Merthyr's stipendiary magistrate, maintained that such children were:

> …farmed out, at about 2/6 a head, to such people as are willing to receive and feed them at that price… [and] it cannot… be doubted that some of them are harshly treated, are stinted in food, poorly clothed, and made victims to the desire of their keepers to realise some profit out of their miserable pittance.

In April 1850, the *Morning Chronicle* described a visit to a two-roomed hovel of an Irish woman in the Cellars in the following terms:

> The first thing we saw on entering was the corpse of a child… [which] had been dead two days, it was unprovided with a coffin. The odour of the house was almost unsupportable. Before the fire were three or four children, amongst them was a boy named Martin B----- 11 years of age, who had been placed there by the Parish, the allowance being 2/- a week. This boy had no shirt: he was barefooted, in rags, his hair bristled up and he was literally black with filth. He sat with the others on a low bench near the fire, and seemed more to vegetate like a plant than to live like an animal. I made him stand up and questioned him, but could get no answer. He stared with an air of stupefaction at the fire, and… appeared to take not the slightest interest at the entrance of strangers, or in the questions I put to him. Yet the woman told me he was not idiotic… His father… had run away, and his mother was an 'unfortunate woman'… On looking into the adjoining room

I saw three beds; two of these were occupied by two married couples, and the third by the children I had seen round the fire.

Even the guardians themselves admitted that many of the people who took such children in were 'of bad or doubtful character', like the Mrs Davies who was one of the biggest brothel keepers in China. Little wonder then that a visitor in 1852 was prompted to describe the town's pauper children as 'the sad and deplorable residuum' of society, but, deprived as they were, at least they had a roof over their heads. Police Superintendant Wrenn argued that some 150 children were homeless in Merthyr, sleeping rough wherever some shelter was to be found.

Apart from the ill, the widowed, the infirm, and the orphaned and abandoned, several other classes of paupers were regularly relieved. Among the women and children, for example, there were usually one or two whose husbands or parents had been gaoled or transported. Single mothers, too, were supported by the Parish and in the majority of cases these were well-known prostitutes. Merthyr also had a small number of the mentally ill and, as elsewhere in south Wales, 'it was customary to board [them] out... with relatives, or anybody willing to take charge of them, at a cost of 2/- or less per week'. Although an asylum opened at Briton Ferry in 1843 and others were available in the West Country, by 1850 each pauper in an institution was costing the Parish 10s a week. Whenever possible, therefore, the guardians preferred to leave the insane with relatives or anyone else willing to take them. This ensured that the treatment received by pauper lunatics was left very much to chance. Those sent to institutions were often incarcerated for life, while of those boarded out some seem to have been well looked after, but others were expected to fend for themselves as best they could and some spent most of their lives in close confinement under the most appalling conditions. It is hard to discover a more neglected class of paupers.

One further group to receive regular parochial attention, and which at times posed by far the greatest problem for the guardians, was the dead. The incidence of illness, consistently high accident rates and old age ensured that pauper graves were always in demand, and for many of those relieved by the Merthyr Poor Law Union an unmarked parish grave was ultimately their only possession.

Certain types of poverty were closely aligned to the fortunes of the iron trade, and it is to these that we now turn. Undoubtedly the greatest failing of the 1834 Poor Law Amendment Act was its inability to recognise the problem of industrial unemployment, and nowhere was this shortcoming so apparent as in Merthyr. The iron trade was never the most stable of concerns, and just as periods of high demand led to rising wages and increased job opportunities so the years of low production brought wage reductions, short-time working, lay-offs and redundancies. Unemployment was by no means a new phenomenon. The bleak depression which set in following the defeat of Napoleonic France witnessed thousands being laid off. Similarly, the continental upheavals which followed the 1830 revolutions saw another collapse in demand, and in 1831 at one of the Crawshay pits where between sixty and seventy workmen had usually been employed, all bar three were dismissed. However, the years which immediately followed the establishment of Merthyr's Union coincided with the first great period of 'railway mania' and so the problem of able-bodied applicants hardly arose. By 1838, though, the signs were already ominous, with the able-bodied making up 25% of Merthyr's paupers, and by 1843 this had risen to nearer 35%.

From its inception, the Merthyr Union had attempted to provide for the able-bodied by finding jobs for them and setting up parochial work schemes. Given the dominance of iron, finding alternative work was always problematic, to say the least, and the role of the Union as an employer was far more important. The 1834 Act made provision for the able-bodied to be given task work in exchange for relief, and in Merthyr stone-breaking or road-mending was the usual test applied. As the economy worsened in the early 1840s, however, with the rapidly increasing numbers of unemployed coinciding with a financial crisis for the Union itself, such measures provided scant comfort for those forced to fall back on the Parish. During 1842, for example, in order to avoid complete bankruptcy, the Surveyor of the Parish Highways was instructed to cut the payments for stone-breaking by no less than 66%, from 1/9d to just 7d a yard, so that more paupers could be relieved without unacceptable cost increases.

Given the scale and extent of the crisis, removals became daily occurrences, as the guardians could hardly cope with their own paupers let alone those from elsewhere. Until the early 1840s the great majority of such cases involved unskilled labourers and their families, but in 1842 and 1843 even skilled men, the aristocrats of the workforce, were unceremoniously bundled into carts and despatched. Thus in just one week in January 1843, orders of removal were issued against a miner, a plasterer and a puddler, together with some eleven dependants. The situation remained chaotic throughout 1843 and it was only the long-awaited upswing in the demand for iron during 1844 which brought about improvement. This second burst of railway-building proved short-lived, however, and by 1850 the picture was even bleaker than it had been in 1843 as Merthyr experienced the worst slump in living memory.

Though wages were cut by 40% between 1847 and 1850, and redundancies became more and more common, the *Morning Chronicle*, in an analysis of poverty in Merthyr on 1 July 1849, found that there were no adult males relieved because of unemployment, while the survey of the abstracts for the 1850s revealed only one case of a man receiving relief because he was unemployed. That there was unemployment, and on a considerable scale, cannot be doubted, so why then should the official abstracts have no record of the unemployed? The answer seems to be provided by a combination of factors; in the first instance, the class of workers which bore the immediate brunt of any downturn were the unskilled labourers, many of whom were single migrant males, women, children and the old. When women and children were deprived of work, many could fall back on the wages of husbands or parents, while the old could apply for or be given relief under the 'infirm' category. Migrant single men, however, simply went to look for work elsewhere, returned to the farms of rural Wales or were immediately removed to their original parishes. Such was the extent of these depressions that skilled workers also found themselves redundant, and these too were removed or went in search of jobs elsewhere.

Many of those thrown out of work took to tramping around south Wales and further afield in search of jobs of any kind. Applying for relief wherever they happened to be, they were usually granted aid as long as they moved on soon after. In 1844, De La Beche reported that nearly 11,000 trampers passed through Merthyr every year, while the 1850s survey revealed that they formed the fourth largest class of paupers, averaging 10% of the total. Although not everyone relieved under this heading was genuinely searching for work, as a percentage were 'confirmed vagrants', at times when work was harder and harder to come by the transition from tramper to vagrant was an easy one, especially for those without a recognised skill or trade.

Periods of industrial contraction and stagnation also led to increases in other types of poverty, notably those brought about by desertion and bastardy, since when wages and jobs were cut more men were tempted to abandon their families and take to the road. The 1850s survey revealed that desertion was the fifth most important reason for the giving of relief. In the half-year ending in September 1852, for example, it was the third major cause, with 14% of those relieved being deserted wives and children, while two years later, as wages and job prospects rose, it had fallen to less than 3% of the total.

When discussing the relationship between economic depressions and poverty, undoubtedly the greatest effect was on the health of working-class people. When wages were cut so too were diets; lower standards of accommodation became acceptable and longer hours were worked in an attempt to redress falling living standards. It can come as no surprise that most of the major epidemics coincided with periods of prolonged economic hardship when many workers had lost what little resistance they had.

Of all the sections of Merthyr's workforce, there can be no doubt that poverty was most insidious among the Irish. The cheapest labour in western Europe, they were prepared to accept the lowest wages, the worst accommodation and the most laborious tasks. Exclusively employed as unskilled labourers, they were always among the first to suffer when depressions set in and, condemned as they were to the worst housing, disease was never far away, especially when many of them worked exposed to the elements twelve hours a day, seven days a week. If their situation was hazardous in 1840, by 1850 it was chaotic, as the depression came in the wake of the unprecedented influx of the famine years. Most of the Irish entering south Wales in the later 1840s seem to have originated from County Cork, where landlords proved eager to evict tenants and 'encourage' emigration so as to reduce their rates, and according to Poor Law Inspector W.D. Boase this geographical connection was not their only characteristic. Reporting in general terms about the Irish in Britain, he maintained 'the general proportion seems to be four-fifths male, and one-fifth female, except of those applying for relief in Wales and neighbourhood, where the proportion is very different'. 'Indeed', he wrote:

> ...the contrast between the Irish immigrants at Liverpool and in Wales is most striking; the former... come from distant parts of Ireland, walking from Mayo to Drogheda, and from Roscommon and Sligo to Dublin, to take ship, which none but able-bodied could do. And they really are... chiefly lusty young men, willing to work and unencumbered by women or children. But on the contrary, those landing in Wales are nearly all helpless and burdensome to the community. The incredible number of widows with three or four small children... young girls and boys looking for parents, brothers and uncles... and... a very numerous class of old women.

Without further elaboration, it would appear that the majority of the Irish landing in Wales at this time were in no position to work and, having proved burdensome in Ireland, they were now to do the same to the Welsh Unions which, by sheer force of numbers, they were threatening to swamp. According to Cardiff's Police Superintendent Stockdale, the great influx of Irish began around 1843–44: 'at first 13 or 14 in a vessel, then increasing to upwards of 200 in one vessel'. That the movement gained great momentum may be seen by examining the statistics for those people relieved at the Newport House of Refuge, the great majority of whom were Irish. In 1846 the average monthly figure was 329, but a year later it was 2,110 and in the first quarter of 1848 it had increased again to 2,384.

No one harboured any doubts as to how they arrived:

> ...great numbers... are landed on the Welsh coast; but the amount cannot be ascertained or even guessed at. They are brought over by coal vessels as a return cargo (*living ballast*) at very low fares (2/6 is the highest sum I heard of)...

They were then landed clandestinely along the coast, usually at night, as captains were loathe to admit to port officials their role in such a business; as Boase explained, 'there is great odium attached to the traffic'. Some never even saw Wales, being found dead on arrival, while others died soon afterwards. In June 1849, for example, the *Merthyr Guardian* carried the following report from Cardiff:

> A poor, wretched Irish-woman was, a few days ago, observed near this town... with a dead child in her arms, and two or three other children around her – all apparently in

the most helpless misery. The emaciated body of the child was interred. On Wednesday evening the same woman was seen sitting at the relieving officer's door...with another dead child in her arms; and a boy of about 10 years of age standing by her side. Hunger seemed to have gnawed into the wretched little fellow's bones; his looks were ghastly, heart-rending. There seemed to be but little doubt that the infants... died from starvation. And these are far from being solitary instances.

Once landed, some wandered about the countryside seeking relief, others willingly accepted the discipline of the workhouse, but the majority gravitated to the Irish ghettoes which had developed over the previous quarter-century at Swansea, Cardiff, Newport and Merthyr, where they merely added to the existing misery. The *Merthyr Guardian* soon resorted to publishing racist descriptions of the squalor to be found in their 'milesian colonies':

> ...any day of the week there may be seen a whole colony of Irish women, girls, and boys, squatting upon... heaps of ashes... where they are lazily engaged in picking up the rags and cinders which the workocracy have thrown away as refuse. Another of the occupations of the boy part of the grubocracy is to climb up the scavengers' carts for the same purpose...

Turning now to the scale of pauperism in Merthyr, the absence of any official abstracts for the 1830s and most of the 1840s makes it impossible to determine the exact size of the problem. De La Beche maintained that during the early 1840s the Merthyr Union was relieving some 6,000-7,000 people annually, suggesting that well over 10% of the population was being relieved. Though the upswing of 1844 and 1845 brought a considerable reduction, it was short-lived, and by 1850 approximately 13% of the population were officially paupers. Though this was largely associated with the aftermath of the cholera epidemic, such was the scale of the depression that a year later it still stood at 12.5% and it was to take the economic upswing associated with the Crimean War to bring it down to just 5.1% in 1854. Thereafter came a slow but consistent increase, reflecting the decline in the fortunes of the iron trade and the increasing insecurity of the workforce, and Charles Wilkins maintained that in the period 1861–65 around 8% of the populace were paupers.

Such statistics, however, greatly underestimate the true extent of the problem, in as much as by no means all those who were sick, infirm, old, widowed, orphaned, deserted or unemployed sought, or were given, relief. Indeed, evidence exists to suggest that at times the official picture formed no more than the tip of a huge iceberg of poverty. In the first place, it should be remembered that by no means all applications to the Union were successful, especially at the height of depressions when the guardians' finances were stretched to their limits and none but the utterly destitute could hope for relief. By far the most important factor, however, was working-class antipathy towards the workings of the Poor Laws. The 1834 Amendment Act had never been accepted by working people, and its workhouses, the dreaded 'New Bastilles', were regarded with horror by the respectable workers of Merthyr and elsewhere. The 'barbaric' and 'immoral' operations of the Act saw mass meetings of Chartists express their determination to smash the Poor Laws, and in later years opposition did not wane but simply became less vocal, as large sections of the workforce adopted a stance of passive resistance by refusing to have anything to do with the Union.

Although Merthyr had no workhouse until 1853, many of its inhabitants were migrants whose own parishes had been far quicker to build such institutions, and, as we have seen, removals were commonplace during times of depression. For those who did not live under the threat of incarceration, the indignity of first having to plead for assistance and then being forced to break stones or repair roads for it was more than many workers could bear, especially the skilled ones. Those who were forced to apply, having first exhausted savings and pawned possessions, became increasingly angry as hand-outs were steadily reduced; on successive weeks during 1843, for example, one of the guardians and a relieving officer were stoned by an angry crowd of paupers while acting as taskmasters.

Such was the strength and depth of working-class opposition that the building of a workhouse was delayed for nearly twenty years. One of the Commissioners inquiring into the unrest in south Wales in 1844 was told in no uncertain terms that such was the popular feeling against a workhouse that a military barracks would have to be built before work could begin on its construction, and in 1847 the same argument defeated yet another demand from Westminster to build such an institution. Whether this was really the cause, rather than pervasive ratepayer mentality, we will never know, but it was only when the financial threat posed by continuing outdoor relief became too great and the cholera and the unprecedented depression had sapped working-class strength that the guardians finally sanctioned its erection.

It was not just the bastilles or task work which incurred the wrath of the workers, for the harshness of the entire system and the heartless attitudes of its bureaucrats were continually cited as examples of the general oppression associated with the Poor Laws. That there was a fairly rigid means test has already been noted, as has the fact that not all applicants were given aid. Certain cases involving such decisions were given considerable publicity within Merthyr and served to buttress working-class opposition. Just before Christmas 1841, the *Merthyr Guardian* reminded its readers 'if you become short of the necessities of life, you need not fear starvation; if the laws of the land did not forbid this, the greater law of humanity, and the still greater law of Christianity, would prevent this taking place'. Shortly afterwards, however, an unemployed man was found in a miner's cabin in a condition close to starvation.

He was promptly ejected by an iron company agent and died some hours later in a nearby ditch, after the relieving officer would have nothing to do with him, despite the threats of the local vicar to charge him with manslaughter if he did not help the man, and he subsequently died. In the event, these threats came to nothing and at the ensuing inquest, to which miners were refused entry because of their expressed intention to expose the inhumanity of the case, the jury returned a verdict of 'died of want of necessities of life', and the relieving officer absolved himself and the Union of any responsibility as 'the deceased had not been chargeable to Merthyr'.

Not only were the guardians and their agents seen to be heartless, they were also regarded as corrupt. In 1842 a woman came before the guardians with a notice of distress for rent and applied for relief so that her unemployed husband could pay the arrears. The Clerk to the Union abhorred the irregularities of the guardians and was not well liked, so whenever they 'wished to keep any information from him, they spoke in Welsh'. On this occasion, 'when one of them asked who the landlord was, the answer was given in Welsh by the Chairman that it was himself. The result was that the Board resolved that the money should be paid'. Thus, accused the Clerk, when rent was owed to the guardians they were quite willing to grant relief, but when they were not directly concerned such applications were generally refused. An inquiry by Assistant Poor Law Commissioner Day found that the Clerk was indeed justified in reporting the matter and that the only discussions to be held in the above case concerned whether or not the full sum of 45s should be paid at once or in instalments.

Scandal was by no means confined to the guardians themselves, and in June 1849 William Rowlands, the Vestry Clerk at that time, was the subject of:

> …some very severe charges… He was accused of neglecting to have the graves [of cholera victims] dug to the proper depth. He received from the Parish 4 shillings for the digging of pauper graves seven feet deep; out of this he paid 1/6d. to the digger, who, in consequence of the smallness of the pay, only dug them four feet deep. Mr. Rowlands pocketed the remaining 2/6d. as profit…

However, if any one individual was to incur working-class hatred it was Roger Williams, one of the town's two Relieving Officers. He had refused to help the sick miner back in 1841, and in the spring of 1845 a coroner's inquest 'severely condemned' him for refusing relief to a Mary Aubrey and her sick infant child who had subsequently died. In 1851 he was taken to court on a charge of neglect by John Troop, a brewer who maintained that Williams had stopped a shilling a week from the relief of Daniel Dixon, who had had an accident at the Plymouth works several months previously resulting in his losing a leg. Williams argued blandly that he had reduced Dixon's payments from 3s 6d to 2s 6d 'as the young man was so far recovered as to be daily in the streets'. This was vigorously denied by Dixon, who informed the magistrates that he had been forced onto the streets in order to collect his parochial allowance as Williams refused to take the money to him.

No matter what lay behind working-class opposition, there is no doubt that a large proportion of Merthyr's workers regarded applying for relief as anathema, and though hundreds were forced to queue outside the Vestry each week there were thousands who struggled on in conditions of awful privation to avoid the disgrace. Poverty itself held no stigma among workers but the indignity of having to beg for the reluctant charity of a hostile class did, and even during the very worst depressions the fierce pride and independence of working people ensured that large numbers of the poor remained outside the control of the Union. Thus, in March 1843 'a woman died in a part of this town last week whose whole household furniture consisted only of an iron kettle and two small stools', while in November that year the *Merthyr Guardian* noted laconically: 'POVERTY to a considerable extent prevails in the iron manufacturing districts, and we are informed that deaths are increasing weekly'. Deaths from destitution did not just occur in the bad years, however, and in January 1860, at a time when the local economy was in a far better state than it had been in 1843, the same newspaper was forced to concede:

> STARVATION... it is to be feared that the wealthier classes of Merthyr... have but faint conceptions of the hardships endured by their humbler... neighbours... we feel assured that few of them are aware that at the present time many poor persons...are now suffering the extremities of want, and absolutely dying from an insufficiency of food to sustain life. Yet evidences of the fact have repeatedly appeared at the inquests held by the Coroner. A case of death from starvation occurred a few weeks since at Twynyrodyn; and another case came to light on Monday last... [when] after hearing the evidence, the jury found that death resulted from exhaustion, consequent on the want of food.

Without further elaboration, therefore, it should be stressed that the levels of recorded poverty in no way reflected the true extent of the problem, and in all probability, especially in the worst years, the official statistics grossly underestimated the real distress.

This reality was understood by those shopkeepers and tradesmen whose businesses relied on working-class patronage, and 'bailing', or extending credit, became the norm for many of those who realised that if they were to retain their clientele then they had to accept 'the slate' as a necessary evil. A fair number seem to have sympathised with their customers, but even so one could not survive on credit notes indefinitely and some who proved too sympathetic ended up without shops or capital. By no means all were willing to extend credit, however, and one only needs to look at the role played by the small debtors' court in the uprising of 1831 and the Chartist-inspired boycott of certain premises a decade later to appreciate that certain sections of the town's shopocracy had no time for customers unable to pay in cash, no matter what the economic circumstances. These were the wealthiest tradesmen, who were also the parish and special constables, as well as guardians, and whose championship of the profit maxim left little room for compassion.

As far as Merthyr's elite were concerned, they had never known poverty, could not understand its causes and proved very largely indifferent to the problem, though it would be wrong to suggest they displayed no philanthropic tendencies. As the traditional response of paternalism, some charity was forthcoming and, as befitted their station and status, it was the wives of the masters, agents and professional men who were entrusted with such good works. Thus, in 1835, under the patronage of Lady Guest, the Dowlais Benevolent Institution was established 'For the relief of sudden accidents and rare infirmities' and by 1839 it could boast of two collectors and fourteen visitors, all of whom were volunteers. Similarly, the aptly named 'Wives Society' was formed 'to provide linen and clothing for destitute married women, during the period of their confinement, and their infants; and also for aged and infirm females'. In Georgetown, Mrs Richard Crawshay, 'horrified' at the wastage in the Cyfarthfa Castle kitchens, ordered that all food surplus to requirements be made into soup for the poor of the neighbourhood. Between 1846 and 1879 this was distributed three times a week and 'on each occasion 30 tickets were issued to those who might come to the castle and receive the soup'.

Despite such petticoated benevolence, the dominant attitude was uncompromisingly hostile. We think of the 75% of paupers who were being relieved as a result of illness, widowhood, old age and accidents. We remember, too, the orphaned and abandoned children, the insane and the unemployed, and then we read the words of H.A. Bruce, stipendiary magistrate, trustee of the Dowlais works, MP for Merthyr and subsequently ennobled as Lord Aberdare:

> …it must not be forgotten that of those who receive relief, the enormous majority owe their degradation to moral causes – to the faults of themselves or their parents. They owe it either to their own improvidence, intemperance and recklessness, or to the evil example of those who have been paupers before them.

As the controlling interest on the Board of Guardians, it was the masters who ensured that such matters as asylums, hospitals and industrial schools had to wait many years for implementation. Though the Vicar of Dowlais argued that God had ordained the rich to be charitable towards the poor, in all honesty this cannot be said to have been the case in mid-nineteenth-century Merthyr.

PART 2
RESPONSES

6

PROTEST!

Given the conditions outlined in previous chapters, it should come as no surprise to learn that Merthyr witnessed periodic working-class protests, and in our period the focus for much of this was provided by Chartism, which arrived in October 1838 when a 'Working Men's Association' was established, with Morgan Williams, a twenty-five-year-old weaver-proprietor-journalist of Penheolgerrig, as its secretary. Though at first dominated by its parent branch at Carmarthen, within a few months Merthyr became prominent in its own right and after 1839 it was the main Welsh centre for the movement.

When analysing why the town had become such a Chartist stronghold, Royal Commissioners argued that class conflict was inevitable, given the absence of any sizeable middle-class presence to provide a cushioning link beween the masters and their men. This they blamed on the prevalence of the truck system in the town's formative years. Other authorities stressed the 'neglect of duty' by the ironmasters to provide decent living and working conditions. Whatever the case, working-class radicalism in Merthyr was by no means a new phenomenon. In 1800, workers had imposed price controls by force and attacked truck shops, and were only put down by an influx of dragoons. A year later there was renewed trouble, this time with a political dimension. The army again intervened and two ironworkers were hanged 'as an example'. In 1816 the post-war depression brought rising prices and falling wages. Merthyr's workers went on strike, and marching gangs using violence spread the stoppage across the Heads of the Valleys. At Dowlais, Guest opened fire at the 'mob' while Crawshay went into hiding, and once again troops had to suppress the trouble. Then came 1831 and the Rising, which was subdued only by a massive influx of military. Within a fortnight, the first trade union branches in Wales appeared in the town and, despite their legality, the ironmasters, led by Guest and Hill and urged on by the government, locked out all unionists and starved the men back to work. Though only momentary, Gwyn Alf Williams wrote about the creation of a '*working class identity*' and argued that 'In Merthyr Tydfil in 1831, the prehistory of the Welsh working class comes to an end. Its history begins'.

Two years later, union lodges of the 'Miners' Association of Great Britain and Ireland', which was affiliated to Robert Owen's 'Grand National Consolidated Trades Union', were established in the town. Once again, the masters broke them with lay-offs and threats to blow out the furnaces. Nevertheless, the seeds of working-class solidarity had been sown, and in 1834 Morgan Williams and John Thomas published Wales' first working-class newspaper in Merthyr, the bilingual *Y Gweithiwr/The Workman*, with its demand for the radical reform of Parliament by means of universal manhood suffrage.

Trade unionism, though subsequently overshadowed by Chartism, did not disappear completely. In 1838, for example, Penydarren puddlers went on strike for better wages, and in the months leading up to the 'General Strike' of 1842 there was little doubting the links between trade unionists and Chartists, especially among underground workers. In 1843 and 1844 support was forthcoming for the 'Miners' Association of Great Britain and Northern Ireland'. In May 1844 a mass meeting of some 500-600 workers at Heolgerrig was told that the object of the union was to better the conditions of underground workers by limiting work to eight hours a day, promoting greater unity and being 'more discrete' about working practices. In the late 1840s and early 1850s, as wages collapsed, there were other isolated strikes, most notably by the colliers of Aberdare in 1849 and of Dowlais in 1853. There was also, during the winter of 1856–57, another strike in Merthyr against a general wage cut of 15%, which became so bitter that troops were once again called in. However, it was to take many years before effective trade unionism was established in south Wales.

By and large the leaders of Chartism in Merthyr were drawn from the ranks of the town's labour aristocracy and the lower echelons of its small middle class. Such men were educated and proud of the fact. Morgan Williams' mathematical ability was such that he was known as 'the Young Mountain Solomon'. At their meetings they toasted 'The March of Intellect' and ridiculed the stupidity of their opponents: the aristocracy, the hierarchy of the established Church and especially the 'fools' at Westminster. These men were the products of a tradition of radical nonconformity which stretched back into the eighteenth century and beyond, and which provided precedents for the effectiveness of both constitutionalism and revolution; nor were they isolated from the mainstream of town life. Through their radical nonconformist connections, they counted trade unionists, dissenting ministers and many fellow tradesmen, artisans and shopkeepers among their friends. Although their identity is fairly easy to document, that of the mass of workers who followed them – especially in the years 1839, 1842 and 1848, the focal points of Chartism in Merthyr – is much more difficult to ascertain, but it is evident that the movement won support from most sections of the workforce, even though this proved transitory.

Officially launched in Birmingham in August 1838, the programme of the National Charter Association was clear. It demanded the radical reform of Parliament, to be brought about by the implementation of the six points of the 'People's Charter', namely: universal male suffrage, secret ballots, equal electoral districts, the payment of MPs, the abolition of property qualifications for MPs and annual parliaments. Though it remained the central platform, Chartism was by no means limited to the six points and the objects of the movement could and did vary from place to place and from person to person and, although there was confusion at the time, it is possible to identify a number of common themes. Despite the reassurances offered by the National leadership to the effect that their object was not revolution, 'only equal rights and fair representation in Parliament', there can be no doubting that what many sought was, given the realities of the day, revolutionary. As Bronterre O'Brien, the Chartists' leading philosopher, explained, what they stood for amounted to:

> An entire change in society – a change amounting to a complete subversion of the existing order of the world. The working classes aspire to be at the top instead of at the bottom of society – or rather that there should be no top or bottom at all.

Within this revolutionary framework there were decidedly republican sympathies. Cromwell and Benjamin Franklin were Chartist heroes and there were frequent references to both the American and French Revolutions. The costs of the royal family were cited on many occasions, as in 1843 when George Morgan illustrated a lecture on the 'Idle and Unproductive classes' by citing the amounts of bread, butter, cheese and meat consumed by the Royal household at a time when some in Merthyr were quite literally starving to death. Ivor Wilks has suggested that the degree of positive republicanism and anti-monarchism in Welsh Chartism stemmed from an antipathy towards English domination. The reports of meetings at the Three Horse Shoes certainly reveal several instances of pride in a separate Welsh identity and contempt for the 'stupid English rulers'.

Throughout the period a constant theme was 'liberty', with the 'oppressors' and 'tyrants' being the ironmasters, the police, the army, the Poor Law guardians, the Church of England and the press, as well as Parliament and the monarchy. Chartism was pledged to achieve 'Civil and religious liberty all over the world', 'the rights of man' and 'the sovereignty of the people', as well as economic freedom for all. It was the universal panacea for all the indignities and injustices and cruelties suffered by working people.

The violent debacle at Newport early in November 1839 brought the Chartists of south Wales into national prominence. While historians still argue over its purpose, the consensus favours the view that it was to act as a signal for a more general uprising, and it was the timing of this revolt which led to dramatic splits in the local movement. Despite the fact that one of the men shot dead outside the Westgate Hotel was a card-carrying Merthyr Chartist and two Dowlais men were subsequently imprisoned for their part in the proceedings, there were deep divisions between and within the Chartists of Monmouthshire and Glamorgan.

While Dowlais was certainly represented at Newport, the Chartists of Merthyr and Aberdare rejected the march, which has invited subsequent speculation that they were centres of 'moral force' Chartism, while Dowlais and Gwent belonged to the 'physical force' school. In the context of south Wales, however, far too much has been made of this alleged distinction. In July 1839, the *Merthyr Guardian* condemned the local Chartists' liking for pikes. Matthew John, a leading Merthyr Chartist, discounted the threat of troops billeted in Dowlais, saying that the Chartists would 'make short work of such striplings', and Morgan Williams, regarded as the premier local moral force leader, was not averse to the company of Doctor William Price of Nantgarw, a known distributor of arms in Pontypridd and Treforest. Indeed, the sale of firearms and pikes continued in Merthyr throughout the early 1840s, with Chartists being urged to withdraw their money from the Savings Bank for this purpose, while several local benefit societies dissolved themselves during the winter of 1841–42 to raise the necessary finances. Subsequently, in 1843, when the horse belonging to Merthyr's Police Superintendent was shot dead, local Chartists congratulated the culprit as being 'A good hearty fellow' and hinted that the Superintendent himself might soon suffer a similar fate. It would seem that Merthyr's Chartists, in common with most of their counterparts elsewhere, agreed with Ernest Jones, who would later become the acknowleged leader of the movement, 'that physical force must always remain as a legitimate last resort of self-defence'.

Merthyr's radical tradition provided a precedent for violence and, given a situation in which the vote was denied, petitioning scorned and legal redress beyond their financial means, for many violence may have seemed the only possible means to achieve 'justice'. To live and work in Merthyr involved coming to terms with violence and so it should come as no surprise that working people were prepared to resort to it when threatened. It was not philosophical conflicts which divided the Chartists of south Wales but deep disagreements over the organisation, feasibility and timing of the proposed uprising, and with hindsight it is clear that the misgivings of the Merthyr and Aberdare men were well founded.

In the aftermath of Newport, the Chartist cause in south Wales was thrown into acrimonious disorder and confusion, but despite the hopes of the ironmasters the movement was kept alive through the efforts of Morgan Williams and his fellow leaders, and the following years were to see the Chartists reorganise themselves and initiate a series of campaigns designed to propagate the Charter and restore and mobilise mass support.

In the first instance, Newport had highlighted the weaknesses of an organisation fragmented into regional and local interests, and gave an added impetus to the call for 'a permanent leadership to guide a united popular movement'. In July 1840 this came to fruition when Chartist delegates meeting in Manchester decided to create a national political party, the National Charter Association [NCA] led by a National Executive. From now on, new members were only admitted once they had signed a declaration in support of the objects, principles and constitution of the NCA and handed over 2d for a membership card. Where possible, members were to form classes of ten people, hold weekly meetings and to elect from each class a leader to collect the weekly penny contributions. Such leaders were to report to the monthly ward meetings where the NCA's business was transacted, funds collected and speeches made.

Merthyr was divided into ten wards, led by Georgetown, which alone had thirteen discussion classes. In turn, each ward appointed a collector who channelled funds to the Town Council, which met weekly. This framework was complemented by a County Council, again based at Georgetown, and the National Executive itself. Regarding the latter, Merthyr's national importance may be judged by the fact that when the six-member executive was elected in June 1841, Morgan Williams received the third highest vote, and the largest number of votes cast by a single branch came from Merthyr.

As far as meeting places were concerned, Matthew John's smithy was one location and the Georgetown schoolroom of David Evans another, but in general it was in the pubs of Merthyr that Chartists met, and such houses as the Angel, Carpenter's Arms, Coach and Horses, Cross Keys, George Inn, Plough, Rising Sun, Rolling Mill, the Star, Chandler's Arms and – most famously – The Three Horse Shoes entered into popular folklore.

Throughout the period, the attraction of large open-air public meetings in the Market Square or the more traditional mountainside site at Heolgerrig remained constant as Merthyr's Chartists sought the reassurance of mass support, to show their strength to their critics and to hear the speeches of prominent local and national figures. One such rally on Christmas Day 1840 attracted 1,200 people; during the troubled months leading up to the 'General Strike' of 1842 crowds of up to 6,000 attended, while in 1848 several meetings drew audiences in excess of 1,000. At these meetings, as well as advocating the principles of the Charter, missionaries from other areas spread the gospel of unity and solidarity and tried to rally support during periods of relative inactivity. Beginning with Carmarthen's Hugh Williams, the Welsh representative to the first National Convention, a long list of Chartist luminaries visited the town, though Merthyr's favourite was always Henry Vincent, who addressed large crowds as early as January 1839, was given a hero's welcome by a crowd of over 3,000 after his release from prison in June 1841 and was still going strong in the 1850s. Given the town's national prominence, it was not surprising that Merthyr should export as well as receive such orators. Morgan Williams was particularly active in this respect, while at the end of 1840 Merthyr's Isaac Rogers became the NCA's official south Wales missionary.

'When the Press is free, the people will know their rights' had been the call in the mid-1830s, and Merthyr's Chartists were quick to see the need for their own news-papers to spread their gospel and counter the propaganda of their opponents. In the spring of 1839, Vincent's *Western Vindicator* was reported to have a weekly circulation of some 300-400 copies in Merthyr alone, and early the next year *Udgorn Cymru* (*The Trumpet of Wales*) and *The Merthyr Advocate*, edited by Morgan Williams and David John, built up a combined circulation of between 12,000 and 15,000 copies a month. Containing poems by Coleridge, articles on temperance and health foods, and hints on gardening, as well as Parliamentary and local news and Chartist intelligence, these papers struck such a chord that the authorities determined to suppress them. Such was their intimidation of the shopkeepers and publicans who distributed these and other Chartist tracts and pamphlets that the *Advocate* ceased trading towards the end of 1840, though *Udgorn Cymru* managed to survive until 1842. Throughout these years, such local publications were supplemented by what was to become the bible for Merthyr's Chartists, Feargus O'Connor's *Northern Star*. Launched in the winter of 1837–38, this Yorkshire-based journal soon became a truly national campaigning organ, and right through to its demise in the early 1850s it set an enviable standard of radical journalism.

Petitioning Parliament or the monarch, the traditional recourse of an aggrieved people, was another tactic. In 1839 the first National Petition attracted 14,710 sig-natures from Merthyr and three years later nearly 22,000 people signed the Second Petition, making Merthyr's contribution the fifth largest in Britain. In between, two other petitions from the town were sent to Queen Victoria, asking for a full and free pardon for John Frost and his fellow convicted Chartists. The first was signed by close to 16,000 people and the second, signed by women alone, had nearly 11,000 names. There is ample evidence, therefore, that Chartism could command mass support in the town.

Chartist 'martyrs' like Frost and Vincent held an important place in the organisa-tion and propaganda of the movement. The leadership already knew the publicity value of political prisoners and quickly realised that concern for them could also be a useful source of unity and continuity. Thus the campaign to free Frost started within days of his arrest, and throughout the era meetings at Merthyr frequently ended with calls for 'the speedy return of Frost, Williams and Jones' or toasts to 'Exiled Patriots'.

Another tactic much advocated by O'Connor and O'Brien was for Chartists to stand in Parliamentary elections. In England it was used frequently and with some success, though in Merthyr it seems only to have been considered on two occasions. In 1841, Morgan Williams stood against Sir John Guest and won a show of hands at the hustings only to decline going to a poll, as he knew the majority of his supporters were disenfranchised. Two years later the town's Chartist Council discussed nominating another candidate for the forthcoming election who would be no 'milk and water half and half, but a regular out and out supporter of the Charter', but in the event, and for exactly the same reason, declined to put anyone up against Guest.

Though stymied at elections, they enjoyed greater success in the field of local politics, where a favourite tactic involved the disruption and subversion of middle-class meetings. In April 1840, for example, Merthyr's Chartists took over a Vestry meeting called to congratulate Queen Victoria on her marriage, and having taken the chair they successfully moved an amendment to the Address to include a plea for a free pardon for John Frost.

Much more disconcerting as far as the authorities were concerned was Chartist-inspired intimidation of a far more direct kind. Early in 1839, for example, Lord Bute was told that unless a man could produce his 'Chartist Ticket' there was little point in seeking employment in and around Blackwood and Nantyglo, and after Newport, Merthyr's miners refused to work with anyone who had given evidence against Chartists, and threatening letters were dispatched to prosecution witnesses.

Urged on by Vincent, Merthyr's Chartists boycotted shopkeepers who refused to support the Charter and talked about setting up an exclusively 'Chartist Shop' near the Castle Inn. They also realised the value of price-fixing, or *taxation populaire*. Thus in June 1841 the *Merthyr Guardian* reported:

> The Chartists at Merthyr entered into an arrangement that they would not give more money for veal than 3d. per pound, and 4½d. for mutton and lamb – the 12th of June being the first market day after this arrangement. There was very little meat of any description in the market, and very little sold, persons being afraid to purchase, in consequence of threats... And on Sunday the 13th of June large bodies of Chartists were going about the town... nearly all day... to ascertain who had purchased, and who had not... They also laid out threats to those that did not adhere to their principles by remembering them that the Scotch cattle were still alive.

The reorganisation after Newport, and such tactics as these, meant that at the beginning of 1842 Merthyr's Chartists were well placed to exploit the growing unrest brought about by the unprecedented depression in the iron trade. Guest was forced to admit that 'the discontented spirit which prevailed, particularly in the district of

Merthyr Tydfil, is not extinguished. I fear rather that it has become more established...'. Chief Constable Napier reported to Westminster that talk of an impending insurrection was again in the air, though his intelligence suggested that local Chartists would not move until they knew the House of Commons' verdict on the second National Petition, the collation of which seems to have absorbed most of Merthyr's Chartists' energies in the weeks leading up to the NCA's Convention in April.

The Commons' outright rejection of the petition, together with ever-worsening economic conditions, saw unrest spread, and the *Merthyr Guardian* at the end of May called for the immediate formation of a military force to protect property, and for the silencing of Chartist firebrands who were exploiting industrial distress for political ends. In July, Staffordshire colliers struck against further wage cuts and the movement which was to lead to the first attempt at a general strike in British history began. At Merthyr, on 17 August, a 2,000-strong mountainside meeting resolved that 'they would not starve while there was food to be had', and within days the town's colliers and miners had downed tools. The authorities responded by drafting in police reinforcements and banning 'unlawful' meetings, but what finished it within a fortnight was the rejection of the strike call by most of the Dowlais colliers, the refusal of the town's furnacemen to join in, and the news that the movement had collapsed in England.

Though some Chartists took pride in the fact that they had succeeded in politicising a significant section of the workforce and instigated a peaceful stoppage and an orderly return to work, the fact was that over 100 local men found themselves blacklisted by the masters, and the strike was unquestionably a failure at both the local and national level. Once again, the movement had been stymied by the disunity of the workforce, the absence of effective leadership, the economic and political weaknesses of the working class and the power of the authorities.

While the *Merthyr Guardian* smugly reported early in September that the strike's failure 'will prove a death blow to the Charter and the Chartist leaders in the neighbourhood', in fact the latter displayed some of the same resilience that they had shown after Newport – although Morgan Williams retired from politics soon afterwards and it was to be a further six years before large crowds again demanded the Charter. This time, faced by a hostile police force only too willing to seize those who openly advocated Chartism, the movement went underground, shed its moral force mantle and began to talk more and more in terms of open conflict. Well aware that they were being spied on, however, not to mention the impossible odds they faced, it appears such talk was largely intended to scare their opponents into concessions, which were never forthcoming. Even before the economic upswing associated with the second great period of railway mania arrived in mid-1844, the Chartist arms clubs had been disbanded.

What appears to have galvanised many of Merthyr's Chartists in the second half of the 1840s was their support for Feargus O'Connor's 'Land Plan', which was officially launched in May 1845. Rejecting the socialism of Robert Owen a decade earlier, O'Connor advocated settlement in peasant smallholdings. With the capital raised by Land Plan branches nationwide, each member paying 2d a week, six estates were bought and divided into land colonies. The first to open, at Herringsgate, near Watford, was named 'O'Connorville' and 'The successful allottees were settled on May 1st 1847. Each house was worth £100, roads were named after the home towns of the settlers and a cow was christened Rebecca in honour of the Welsh Riots...'.

Nowhere was regard for O'Connor higher than in south Wales, and the region provided ardent support for the land scheme. Once again Merthyr provided the lead, with no fewer than three branches. Merthyr men provided O'Connor with a description of an estate within five miles of the town which they deemed suitable for development. They organised lectures on farming, helped to establish branches at Cardiff and Newbridge, and held notable recruiting and fundraising drives in Merthyr itself. An indication of the size of the town's contribution to the scheme came in 1848 when, out of a total Welsh donation of £172 2s 10d, Merthyr accounted for 45%. This was all the more remarkable given the lack of direct participation, as few Welshmen were successful in their bid to become settlers.

The Land Plan aside, the early months of 1848 were to mark the Chartists' final attempts to force the authorities into making the Charter the law of the land. Responding to a call from O'Connor for a genuinely national petition which no Parliament could refuse, Merthyr was in the van of the revival and, despite the best efforts of the magistrates to prevent public meetings, once again crowds took to the streets and hillsides to listen to such figures as Mathew John demanding reform. In the event, MPs treated the final petition with the same contempt they had shown the previous two, and as another economic depression began to bite it appeared that the Chartist cause had finally met its nemesis. Certainly, there were to be no more mass meetings or petitions and, despite continued support for the Land Plan, O'Connor's financial ineptitude, coupled with the scheme's limited capital, unfavourable sites and the fact that the great majority of those who did manage to settle on them had no farming experience, meant that soon that bubble had burst as well, the end finally coming in August 1851 when the scheme was wound up by Parliament.

So once again reform had failed, and before we look at the 1850s and 1860s it makes sense to examine the factors which served to stymie working-class solidarity and facilitate the subjugation of Welsh people in the first century or so of industrialisation.

Among their oppressors, first and foremost stood the ironmasters. Their fortunes were massive and their authority awesome. Not only did they control the means of production and therefore the size of the workforce, its wages and job security, but housing too in many cases. From the very beginning, those who owned the ironworks displayed constant, committed and concerted opposition to any semblance of independent working-class organisation. Individual troublemakers were taken to court for 'breach of contract', with almost inevitable prison sentences, and when trouble was widespread or even general there was always the recourse of dismissal and blacklisting, the importation of blacklegs and, as a last resort, the lock-out. Merthyr's masters were never afraid of stopping their works and starving their workers into submission, should the threat be deemed sufficient. Indeed, Dowlais in particular could be said to have pioneered such tactics, while they were to be taken to extreme by Robert Thompson Crawshay when in 1874, because of his workers' refusal to consent to a wage cut of 20%, he closed the Cyfarthfa works and stubbornly kept them closed until his death in 1879.

Nor were the masters reluctant to call upon the full force of the law and demand that examples be set. They did it in 1801 and they did it again in 1831, ensuring that Dic Penderyn went to the gallows, despite the misgivings of the military, a great many respectable middle-class citizens and even the protestations of the presiding judge. The simple if brutal fact was there for all to see: the masters were the law.

However, this was only one side of the coin, and a major consideration was the fragmentation of the workforce. There was no such thing as a working class in south Wales or anywhere else in Britain in this era. Workers were divided by criteria such as status, craft, skill and remuneration, and the gulf between the labour aristocracy and the unskilled was almost as stark and as absolute as between the masters and their men.

Another factor was the sheer scale of immigration into the town, which deprived all but the most skilled of workers of any real bargaining power. There was always another man, woman or child available and willing to take the job. What is more, as we have seen, many came on a purely temporary basis and such seasonal migrants were countrymen at heart. Urban Wales was an aberration – a temporary, if necessary, purgatory. Such people had no roots in Merthyr and wished for none; its troubles were not theirs.

Furthermore, for all Merthyr's El Dorado reputation, the very real threat of poverty affected all workers and their families and led inevitably to a more acquiescent, deferential and obedient workforce.

Nor was it always a simple case of 'us and them'. The masters might well have controlled the works but they rarely hired and fired directly, preferring instead to employ an elaborate system of subcontractors. It was the gaffers who by and large recruited, organised, ran and paid the workforce, and individual and group dissatisfaction with working conditions was often directed against individuals other than the master. The

perceived enemy was often not an absentee Crawshay or Guest, with their fine mansions and liveried servants, who might as well have lived on a different planet, but the
gaffer who lived down the road.

This dissipation of anger was exacerbated by what Ieuan Gwynedd Jones has
termed the particularism of the works, whereby each of Merthyr's four ironworks
and their associated communities regarded themselves as self-contained, self-
interested units. Indeed, until the last quarter of the nineteenth century 'Merthyr'
was not a town as such; it was simply the collective noun used to describe the communities of Cyfarthfa, Dowlais, Penydarren and Plymouth. Each was urged to wish
for better luck than its competitors and each saw the others as rivals, with perhaps the
most visible demonstration of this being the periodic set-tos between the Dowlais
and Cyfarthfa men in the Market Square – spats which in time disfigured the Chartist
and trade unionist cause.

This fragmentation of working people was made worse by the geographical isolation
of the different works and communities of south Wales, at a time when the industries
of the area had different interests. Particularism was not restricted to Merthyr but was
a regional, indeed a national, phenomenon. Iron, copper, coal, tin: working people
were one or the other and to hell with the rest. Propagating any kind of solidarity in
such circumstances was simply untenable. It was not until much, much later that the
domination of coal could be said to produce any kind of south Walian identity, and
even then the old rivalries scarred the coalfield. At the same time, industrial south
Wales was geographically remote from the great industrial centres of England and
Scotland. The existence of a British working class was an extremely difficult concept
to envisage and the isolation of Merthyr and the other industrial towns of Wales
contributed in great measure to the problems confronting those who attempted to
establish national working-class organisations. Indeed, until a truly nationwide rail
network developed later in the century, such problems proved insurmountable.

We have also to consider the tribalism of the Welsh. Since prehistoric times, geographical divisions have fractured relationships between people from different parts
of Wales, and such jealousies and feuds were perpetuated in Merthyr by a settlement pattern which revolved around roots. The men of Cardiganshire lived and
worked and drank together (and fought each other), as did those of Carmarthenshire,
Pembrokeshire, Breconshire and Glamorganshire. And, of course, if there was anything worse than a 'Cardi' it was a 'Paddy' – in the middle of the nineteenth century
the growing influx of Irish added a racial dimension to these fault lines.

We should remember too that the people of Merthyr, overwhelmingly first- or
second-generation immigrants from rural Wales, had no tradition of solidarity when
they arrived. Among the very poorest and most oppressed workers in Britain, it would
be many years before the railways allowed the exodus necessary to establish any kind

of bargaining power, and we really cannot talk of rural trades unionism in Wales until well into the twentieth century.

What tradition of working-class solidarity they did find when they got to Merthyr and the other towns of south Wales was one of total, abject and bloody failure. The message must have been all too clear: working-class protests not only failed to work but always backfired, and there was a very great deal to recommend silence, however sullen.

The fact was that throughout the nineteenth century every outbreak of organised working-class protest in Wales coincided with an economic downturn in the iron or coal industries or similar crises in copper or tin or slate or wool. Those in the van of the labour movement were never able to fight from a position of strength.

Another reason why radicalising working people was so difficult was the general illiteracy of the workforce; hence the Chartist emphasis on the demonstration, the debate, the public meeting and reading and the weekly night class.

Cultural factors were also important. Working people had very limited leisure time and an even more restricted choice when it came to using it. The chapel or the pub were for many the only options, and both, when it came to protest, acted as anaesthetising agents. The role of the chapel will be looked at in a later chapter, but, as far as drink was concerned, the National Chartist Executive admitted in 1852: 'Our movement has, in the past, been robbed of its moral stamina by the all-devouring cup'. Though the masters and Merthyr's middle class publicly decried the widespread drunkenness, their stake in the alcohol trade was enormous. They owned the breweries and the pubs and controlled the off-licences. There was big money to be made in beer and the fact that it had the added benefit of tranquilising the populace was not lost on them.

If all this were not enough, we should never forget the fact that throughout this period Parliament and Whitehall studiously ignored party politics and presented a solid face of opposition against any attempt by working people to challenge the status quo. The establishment, still dominated by aristocratic and landed interests, if increasingly influenced by nouveau riche industrialists and merchants, was determined to use every weapon in its armoury to retain control, and so it was that the militia, the army, the new police forces, the intelligence service and the courts were all stacked against any expression of working-class solidarity.

So it was that, when the *Morning Chronicle*'s reporter visited Merthyr in the winter of 1849–50, he concluded: 'The influence of Chartism, which was once great over the population of these hills... has not only lessened, but nearly died away...'. In terms of mass support this analysis was correct, but he was wrong to deliver the funeral rites, because in the years which followed the influence of the movement was to prove significant in Merthyr and elsewhere. In the first instance Chartists continued to meet in the town, rallied by a series of visiting lecturers such as R.G. Gammage who, in July 1852, gave a series of talks on the rights of labour, the incompetence of the government, the people's right to possess the soil and the evils of drink. Though he admitted that Chartism had been 'asleep' in Merthyr, he pointed out that he had been received by a vast and attentive crowd.

Interestingly, now the *Merthyr Guardian* could no longer see any threat, it came to accept those whose blood it had once demanded so vociferously. Thus when Ernest Jones, the leader of the movement in the 1850s and 'Chartism personified', visited the town in August 1851 and lectured to large audiences at the White Lion, the paper gave a glowing account of his rhetoric. Similarly, in June 1855, on the occasion of one of Henry Vincent's many visits to the town, the paper launched into a long testimonial to this 'remarkably able, eloquent, temperate, and consistent advocate of social, moral, and political progress'. The emphasis placed on education and temperance by such Chartist speakers did much to foster this rehabilitation, but such messages were by no means new to Merthyr. Morgan Williams, for example, might well have retired from active politics for a while after the defeat of 1842, but he did not withdraw from public life. Believing that education was a prerequisite for democracy, he was a pioneer in the field of working-class education in the town. A founder member of the Subscription Library, which opened in 1846 and by 1851 had the fourth largest collection of books in south Wales, he was a committee member for many years and a keen lecturer who took particular delight in demonstrating the achievements of working men.

Nor was education the only sphere to attract Chartist attention. In 1854 John James, a Chartist surgeon from Thomastown, made an unsuccessful bid to be elected onto the Local Board of Health arguing 'that in matters of health one was not bound to look to wealth. He supported men who were independent of the iron interest. The iron masters would carry their own clique but he was interested in the wants of the people'. Two years later, when he chaired a public meeting called to discuss the introduction of a public water supply, Henry Thomas, another prominent local Chartist, denounced the town's lack of proper drainage. Local industrial issues also concerned radicals, and throughout the period William Gould displayed a passionate concern with the question of arbitration between masters and men, going as far as to suggest the setting up of a 'Court of Arbitration' for the readjustment of wages, while constantly urging workers to explore and exhaust all legal and political avenues in their struggle for justice.

All through the 1850s and 1860s, prominent Chartists continued to demand reform. In 1855 Morgan Williams lectured on the theme 'There is something rotten in the State of Denmark' and, together with the Revd Thomas Davies, William Gould, John James and Henry Thomas, formed an association to promote administrative reform.

Eleven years later, when National Reform League delegates visited Merthyr, a reform demonstration held in the Market Square was chaired by James, who 'proudly stated that he had held the same position and views 20 years ago when the six points of the charter were advocated'. Along with Gould, who was the Treasurer of Merthyr's Reform Association, James was an active speaker in the campaign leading up to the Reform Act of 1867, which increased the town's electorate more than ten-fold from less than 1,400 to over 14,500. Having helped to secure the breakthrough, these same men worked tirelessly to secure the election of someone who would fairly represent the new voters and the triumphant result was the election in 1868 of the Liberal non-conformist Henry Richard, with over 80% of the vote, and the resounding defeat of the sitting member, H.A. Bruce.

The 1867 Reform Act also marked the acceptance of working men into local government. William Gould, for example, was elected onto the town's Burial Board that year and at the time of the 1875 Miners' Strike he was a Poor Law guardian, while Morgan Williams held the office of Registrar of Marriages until his death in 1886, aged seventy-three, when, as Charles Wilkins later noted:

> In tribute to his memory it must be added, that when failing years compelled him to become a spectator instead of an actor on the social stage... nearly all the 'points' he had advocated by voice and pen had become part of the constituted laws of the country.

7

CRIME

For all the mass meetings, we should remember that Chartism and trade unionism affected only a small proportion of the population at any given time. The conditions outlined in previous chapters provoked a variety of responses, one of which was turning to crime, and therefore the incidence of certain forms of criminal behaviour may provide a more sensitive index of socio-economic tension and frustration.

At the outset, however, serious statistical difficulties emerge, as most of Merthyr's petty sessional records have disappeared and, though the Chief Constable's Reports do exist for most of the 1841–64 period, the 'Merthyr Police District' to which he referred was considerably larger than the town itself. Furthermore, the dark figure of unrecorded crime was undoubtedly high and the period witnessed significant changes in both the numbers and the attitudes of the police, which in turn had an impact on crime rates in the town.

For all the deficiencies, enough information has survived via Quarter Sessional and Assize returns to allow general assumptions to be made about the nature of Merthyr's crime and the character of her criminals. During the period 1846–66, for example, almost 90% of charges from the town involved larceny, with assaults and miscellaneous offences such as embezzlement and forgery making up the remainder. As for the offenders, almost 60% were male, with an average age of twenty-six, and although 'labourers' formed the biggest single group to appear before the magistrates, those classified as single women, wives, widows, youngsters and the elderly accounted for over a third of defendants.

For ease of analysis, the following has been divided into sections concerning crimes associated with poverty, employment, leisure and sex and the family. Merthyr's professional criminals are also examined, as are contemporary attitudes towards community law and policing.

When dealing with crimes associated with poverty, we are overwhelmingly concerned with theft. Nearly 70% of such cases concerned stealing clothes, food and coal and stealing from the person, and as the last two will be dealt with elsewhere we will concentrate here on the theft of clothes and food, which accounted for almost 40% of such offences. In both cases, the majority of offenders were male and almost all the articles they stole were either sold or pawned immediately. Poaching was always spoken of as being undertaken for sale, and in March 1838 the *Merthyr Guardian* argued ,'The destruction of game in this neighbourhood by these midnight marauders, is carried on to an incredible extent'. As regards pawning, at the midsummer sessions of 1847 the chairman stated in no uncertain terms '…if there were no pawnbrokers' shops there would not be half as many thieves in the county as there are'. Though women also indulged in illegal selling and pawning, they were far more likely to steal goods, and clothes in particular, for their personal use.

As far as juvenile thieves were concerned, the common denominator was the temptation offered by food, and especially bread, and there can be little doubt that many of Merthyr's young criminals were motivated by hunger. In other cases they were driven by desperation, as in November 1849 when:

> *John Groom* and *Jacob Morgan*, two miserable-looking vagrant boys, were charged with having wilfully broken a square of plate glass… at the Royal Exchange beer-house. It appeared that the prisoners wilfully threw stones through the glass, but did not attempt to escape. In their defence they said they had nothing to eat nor any place to go. In default of paying the value of the glass and costs, they were sentenced to 14 days hard labour each.

As regards motivation generally, the Chief Constable was convinced that a positive correlation existed between larceny, the state of the iron trade and the level of unemployment. In June 1842 he reported:

> There can be no doubt that the present universal distress conduces in a great measure to the committal of crime, many persons having declared to me their intention to work when they could get it, but when that became impossible to steal, but never starve.

However, the statistics reveal little evidence of any dramatic increase in stealing when times were bad, prompting the late D.J.V. Jones to conclude that 'because of sympathy, intimidation and other factors' they failed to reflect the true scale of crime in periods of depression. Most first offenders found guilty of stealing served gaol sentences of two months or less, but far harsher punishments were not unknown. In 1850, for example, a fourteen-year-old boy with previous convictions for theft was transported for ten years for stealing just one and a half loaves of bread.

As for crimes associated with the ironworks, above all else it was the theft of coal which resulted in the most prosecutions and publicity. Rising steadily in the late 1840s and early 1850s, coal stealing accounted for 34% of all the cases heard at the 1854 sessions before a change in the law removed most cases from the county court-rooms in 1855. There was certainly a correlation with the state of trade, as it appears that during times of depression the numbers of people involved and the scale of the thieving led the masters to demand that examples be made, and it was the Dowlais Company which was the most persistent in this, bringing almost 60% of such cases to court. Its works were the largest in Wales and parts of them, together with a four-mile stretch of railway, were unprotected, though they did employ some vigorous watch-men together with a private police force. According to E.J. Hutchings, the company's principal agent, coal was stolen by employees to supplement their wages and also by others who carried out a trade in stolen coal:

> Colliers' wives put stones on the rails of railroads, to cause the trams to shake in their pas-sage so that the coal falls down, and children are always ready with their baskets to pick it up. It was the commonest trick possible.

The whole question of theft from the works, and especially of coal, brought conflict to the courts. As far as rural magistrates were concerned, the iron and coal masters had created much wealth in the towns of south Wales, but in doing so they had brought distress, disorder and even the threat of revolution. They had robbed the agricultural estates of much-needed labour and created huge settlements of turbulent, degraded and immoral workers. The industrialists had ignored the traditional ties between masters and men which made for peaceful and prosperous co-existence, and as a result the men now regarded their employers as enemies. Thus magistrates from rural Glamorgan were inclined to dismiss cases brought about as far as they were con-cerned by a lack of security on the ironmasters' part, which amounted to culpable negligence. Hence at the Epiphany sessions of 1850 no less than eight out of ten such bills were ignored, and even when successful prosecutions did occur the resulting sentences were always much more lenient than for other forms of theft.

Other works-related offences involved industrial discipline, wages and contracts. Having recruited their labour forces, the greatest problem facing the masters was their employees' reluctance to accept what E.P. Thompson described as 'the tyranny of the clock'. 'Saint Monday' was a concern throughout industrial Britain, as employers found that their workers did not wish to earn more and more money but simply to live as they were accustomed to, and so earned as much as was necessary and no more.

In Merthyr, drunkenness accounted for a great deal of lost production, especially following paydays, and a typical spree was reported by the *Merlin* in November 1844:

> The last Dowlais pay was on Friday evening last, and yet on Saturday morning dozens of the men may be seen reeling, sprawling and lounging about the streets of Dowlais having immediately on the receipt of their money hied away to the taverns; spent the money on midnight brawls; left their families to provide for themselves as they best could, and incapacitated themselves from following their work… out of seven balling furnaces in one mill, four were idle… and it has been moderately estimated that the Company lost upwards of a hundred tons of coal, and a hundred tons of iron, to say nothing of attendant losses…

The Dowlais Company tackled absenteeism in three different ways. Incentives of one or two pence per ton were offered for regularity of work, and when these failed, fines were introduced; in the last resort workers were taken to court. Thus in 1839 Evan Thomas, a puddler, was sentenced to a month in gaol for leaving his furnace and being drunk during working hours.

Fines and court cases were also employed to maintain production standards, since another considerable source of conflict was 'the readiness of furnacemen and puddlers to increase the iron make – and hence their wage packet – by producing slightly inferior metal'. Such malpractices probably accounted for the fact that the old Dowlais stocks were placed a few yards from the old puddling forge and 'It was a standing joke at the time, that its proximity to the forge was intended as a conspicuous menace to transgressing puddlers'.

The customary method employed by the masters to retain their skilled labour was the use of quite rigid and precise contracts, and these too brought conflict. When times were good, men were tempted by higher wages or better conditions elsewhere to abandon their work and break such contracts, and if caught they were inevitably prosecuted and ended up in Cardiff gaol. Workers, too, were quite prepared to take their employers to court as, for example, in early 1845 when Joseph Dickenson, a Dowlais agent, was prosecuted by Benjamin Thomas for having dismissed him from his job without the month's notice agreed to by contract. Throughout the period, prosecutions were rife as workers took agents and gaffers to task for not paying the right wages. In 1843, for example, one Dowlais miner summoned another for the non-payment of £1 12s 8d, while David Roberts, a Dowlais agent, was successfully prosecuted by a furnace-filler for the non-payment of wages amounting to £2.

Finally, court cases arose out of the willingness of certain employees to sabotage plant in order to avoid work, as in October 1839 when:

…some considerable damage was done to parts of the machinery of the Penydarren Iron Company by several of the boys employed there, who were anxious to enjoy the pleasure of 'a spell' or holiday, without the small trouble of asking leave of absence. To accomplish this, they put various pieces of iron into the nuts and spindles of the rolling mills; by which damage was effected to the amount of upwards of £5 exclusive of the loss of time occasioned in the works. The evidence being conclusive against Evan Thomas, a boy of 11 years of age, he was committed to gaol for one month, in default of payment of £5.

Crimes associated with leisure were dominated by drunkenness, and as the whole issue of drink will be dealt with in a later chapter we will restrict ourselves here to the connection between drink and violence; as the Chief Constable put it in 1846:

> There are no persons taken into custody in the Merthyr District for drunkenness unless it is accompanied with riotous and disorderly conduct or with assaults… or that they are so drunk as to be quite incapable of taking care or giving any account of themselves.

Throughout the period, assault and drink cases accounted for over a fifth of all crimes in Merthyr, and the true figure was far higher but, as H.A. Bruce pointed out, in 1851 more than half of the cases involving fights between men were settled out of court. Drunken brawling was very largely a male preserve, although in the same year almost 20% of assault cases involved fights between women, many of whom lived in the slums of Riverside, and were Dowlais Irish or China prostitutes, like the infamous Julia Carroll, 'the heroine of a hundred brawls'.

Contemporaries drew a clear correlation between violence and the Irish. Reporting on the district known as Quarry Row in October 1857, the *Merthyr Guardian* noted:

> This locality is the Irish quarter of Merthyr, and bears a very bad reputation, being continually disgraced by scenes of a most riotous description; drunkenness and fighting are of perpetual recurrence; the police are frequently assaulted in the execution of their duty, and heavy brickbats and missiles fly about on the slightest provocation.

According to H.A. Bruce, Merthyr's stipendiary magistrate, the Irish accounted for half of all assaults against policemen. In July 1860, for example, when Sergeant Thomas attempted to stop a fight in Brecon Street, Dowlais, James McCarthy and his wife assaulted him before making their escape. Having summoned assistance, Sergeant Thomas found the McCarthys waiting for him at their house. James had a large stick and:

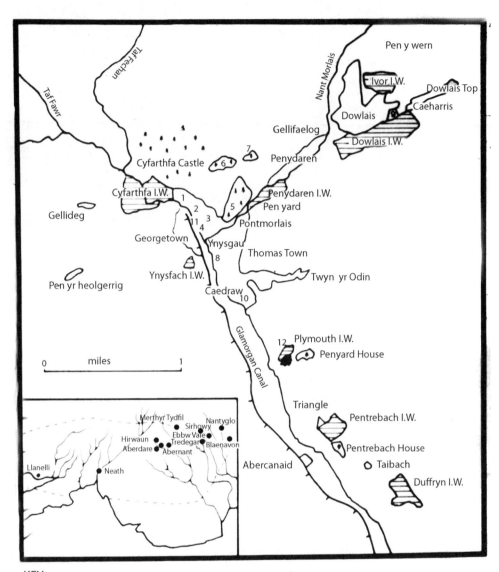

KEY:

1	Caepantywyll	5	Penydaren House	9	Dowlais House
2	Tydfil's Well	6	Gwaelodygarth House	10	Plymouth Street
3	Morgan Town	7	Gwaenfarren House	11	Pontstorehouse
4	China	8	Ironbridge	12	Plymouth Lodge

1 Merthyr Tydfil in 1851.

2 Cyfarthfa rolling
mill, *c.*1830.

3 Dowlais
ironworks, 1840.

4 Merthyr rolling mill at
night.

Above: 5 Puddlers, among the most skilled of furnacemen, removing the impurities in the pig iron so as to render it malleable enough for its first rolling.

Left: 6 A drammer dragging coal from the stalls to the main roadways, 1842.

7 A China hovel.

8 Iron ore patches, 1842.

9 Gas Row, Dowlais.

10 Cyfarthfa Ball,
1846.

11 Cyfarthfa Castle.

12 Following the death of an infant, the next child was often named after its late sibling.

13 Early, and much needed, mines rescue equipment in use.

14 A mass funeral, with benefit society officials escorting the cortège, following a colliery disaster in 1865.

15 Outside the pawn shop.

16 Outside the workhouse.

17 Saron Chapel.

18 Lady Guest at Dowlais
School, c. 1855.

19 Collier
stepping.

EMIGRATION !!

UNITED STATES & CANADA

CARDIFF
DIRECT TO
NEW YORK !
(Without calling at any intermediate port) by the

SOUTH WALES ATLANTIC STEAMSHIP COMPANY
LIMITED.

STEERAGE PASSAGE, £6 : 6 : 0
TO

New York, Baltimore, Boston, Portland & Philadelphia
FROM

All Parts of WALES and the South of England.

Including abundance of well-cooked Provisions served by the Company's Servants.

☞ STEWARDESSES CARRIED BY THESE STEAMERS.
AND MATTRESSES PROVIDED FREE.
A duly QUALIFIED SURGEON is attached to each Steamer.

Passengers BOOKED THROUGH to any Town in the United States, or Canada, at the Lowest Rates.
Parties securing Tickets in Europe or the United States for themselves or friends, are particularly requested to
guard themselves against disappointment by seeing that the Ticket is for the CARDIFF LINE OF STEAMERS.

For further Particulars apply to any of the Company's Agents; or, at the

Company's Offices, 1, Dock Chambers, Cardiff.

Above: 20 Workers at Merthyr's railway station departing for more prosperous towns, 1871.

Left: 21 Emigration poster.

…swore he would murder us or we should murder him before he would be taken to
the station; the female prisoner struck me several times with a hammer; the sister had a
poker – she struck us several times, but did not reach us…

One should not assume that only the Irish assaulted policemen or that such violence
was in any way peculiar to their ghettoes. In 1842, for example, a mob led by three
Welshmen stoned a police sergeant at Dowlais and then violently assaulted him 'by bit-
ing a part of his nose nearly off and otherwise ill using him…'. The navvies employed
to build the Taff Vale Railway had a legendary thirst for both drink and disorder. So too
did the bullies of China and the boatmen who worked the canal. Certain individuals also gained notoriety. In 1841, for example, the landlord of the Farmers' Arms in
Dowlais applied to the courts for warrants against one Thomas Thomas. Apparently
Thomas had an artificial limb and 'was continually involved in trouble of his own causing… as it was his custom, if refused beer where he went, or deemed himself affronted,
to smash the tables with his iron arm. He was the terror of Dowlais'.

Occasionally drunken violence led to deaths. In April 1843 John Hansell, a twenty-
three-year-old tinker, deserted his wife to live with a certain Mary Thomas at Caedraw.
After drinking all morning they quarrelled, and in the violent fight that ensued he
kicked her to death. In 1852 two labourers were gaoled for eighteen months for kick-
ing a third man to death outside the Black Bull: 'The prisoners said they were very
sorry for what had occurred, but they were too drunk to remember anything about
it'. Similar cases cropped up in 1858 and 1860.

Turning to crimes associated with sex and the family, then the very nature of
offences such as rape, indecent assault, incest, suicide, infanticide, desertion and bastardy ensured that many cases never came to court, as individuals preferred to forgo
the publicity of legal action or families decided to keep such unsavoury matters to
themselves. Thus, of the 10,887 people apprehended by the Merthyr police between
January 1842 and July 1852 only five were concerned with such offences and only
two were subsequently committed for trial. Then as now, judicial policy also explains
why so few cases of rape were brought, for the 'laws and their interpretation favoured
the offender rather than the victim' and in the majority of cases the defendant was
either found not guilty or the charge was reduced to that of common assault.

The attitude of the magistrates was illustrated well at the Epiphany sessions of 1852.
The chairman of the bench, Henry Thomas, referring to a case of assault with intent
to rape told the jury that:

…in order to put the prisoner on his trial there must be evidence that the girl did make
some resistance, that she afterwards complained to some female, relative, or friend, or that
from some satisfactory cause she did not make resistance or complaint.

Thomas advised the jury to ignore the bill and the prisoner was freed.

Even when the original charges were upheld, sentences, when compared to other offences, were comparatively light. In 1842, for example, when Walter Walters, a twenty-year-old Merthyr roller, was found guilty of rape and robbery he only received a twelve-month sentence, while a decade later a thirty-one-year-old Merthyr coal-weigher who had dragged a widow from the roadside, gagged and then raped her received exactly the same sentence as a Hirwaun woman convicted of uttering a counterfeit sixpence.

Only when the victims were very young did the courts treat offenders with any degree of severity. In 1846, for instance, a Dowlais man was sentenced to two years' hard labour for a 'felonious assault' on three young girls and in 1850 a twenty-year-old Merthyr ironworker was transported for ten years following a crime of 'grievous enormity' on a child of eight.

Turning to suicide, we are confronted by problems of interpretation. Although verdicts of such were returned by coroners, the many cases of 'accidental death' or of 'death by misadventure' may well have hidden more. When suicide verdicts were forthcoming, the majority of victims were either elderly or relatively young. It seems that the old resorted to it because of illness, the death of a partner or a fear of the workhouse, while the young, with few exceptions, killed themselves over matters of love and especially pregnancy.

The final offence connected with the family was bigamy, three cases of which were revealed by the Quarter Session and Assize survey of 1846–66. In 1856 a twenty-six-year-old Merthyr fireman received a nominal two-day sentence after the court had heard a testimonial on his behalf from Superintendent Wrenn and was told that the man's first wife had deserted him. Similarly, four years later an 'old man' from Merthyr whose wife had been transported was given a one-day sentence. A thirty-five-year-old mason from Aberdare, however, was given a nine-month sentence for the same offence, suggesting that when there were no mitigating circumstances bigamy was regarded as worse than rape in the eyes of the magistrates.

As far as the authorities were concerned, the overwhelming problem connected with sex was that of 'stealing from the person' by the town's prostitutes. Merthyr was very much a pioneer settlement – a wild-western town – and as such it had the usual complement of whores and gamblers, conmen and thieves. This criminal fraternity settled in the Cellars, a part of the district known as Pontystorehouse and later damned as 'China'.

In April 1850 the *Morning Chronicle* described the houses there as being:

> …mere huts of stone – low, confined, ill-lighted and unventilated; they are built with-
> out pretensions to regularity, and form a maze of courts and tortuous lanes… Like the
> unhappy and lawless people who inhabit it, the place has an alias, and is generally known

by the name of 'China'... Here it is that, in a congenial atmosphere, the crime, disease and penury of Merthyr are for the most part *located*. Thieves, prostitutes, vagrants, the idle, the reckless, and the dissolute, here live in a miserable companionship.

Now China was by no means unique and every large town in Britain had its equivalent, but by common consent it was just as bad as, if not worse than, the 'Little Sodoms' of Liverpool, Nottingham and Derby – all of which were far bigger towns. Just as the ironworks attracted those eager for work, so too did they draw those who preferred a more parasitic existence, and from the 1820s onwards they increasingly came to settle in that part of Merthyr in which the controls of authority were at their weakest. Early in the 1840s, Britain's Opium Wars with China introduced to a fascinated Victorian society a whole new bizarre culture and Merthyr's elite, faced by a deviant subculture of its very own, immediately rechristened the Cellars as 'China'. The *Merthyr Guardian* began to refer to the 'Celestial Empire', with its recognised 'Mandarins', 'Emperors' and 'Empresses'.

Just as puddler's sons became puddlers, and colliers' sons became colliers, so too there is evidence that this criminal class was self-generating and, given a favourable environment, it seized control of the district, succeeded in imposing its own authority within it and resisted all attempts by the authorities to clean it up.

So who were the Chinese? A newspaper report in 1850 concerning the theft of some potatoes described the accused, Samuel Tucker, as being 'one of the class of boys called "Rodnies" which infest the neighbourhood at Pontystorehouse', while a year earlier Evan Peters, William Richards and Thomas Thomas, 'three notorious thieves belonging to China', were charged with stealing a shop's till: 'The prisoners, who behaved in the most impudent and hardened manner, were all committed for trial'.

The police were well aware that several receivers operated out of China, and some at least certainly acted as Faginesque characters:

> John Sweeny and John Williams, two notorious thieves, living at 'China', were charged on suspicion of stealing a till containing about £3 from the shop of Mr. Jones... Superintendent Wrenn stated the prisoners were seen lurking about the premises at the time the till was stolen; they were notorious thieves; Williams had been in custody 20 times; they lived in 'China', at the house of Jenkin Rees, alias 'Shenkin Bach', who employed them and took them about the country to steal.

The Rodnies were also accomplished pickpockets, and China's proximity to the High Street and Market Square afforded easy pickings. Not that crime was restricted to boys. In February 1849, eight-year-old Mary Davies stole a bundle of clothes from one pawn shop and immediately pledged them at another. Described as 'a notorious thief', she was given a three-day prison sentence together with a warning that if she continued to thieve she would be transported. Nevertheless, at the March Quarter Sessions of 1851 she was again charged with theft, this time of 'a quantity of sugar, tobacco and bacon' and the Superintendent stated in evidence that 'She is the illegitimate child of an abandoned woman, and whom he feared took no care of her…'.

China also served as a refuge for those criminals who habitually travelled around the country in search of profit, and perhaps the most notorious of these were the 'smashers' or counterfeiters who periodically sent Merthyr's shopocracy into fits of aggrieved rage. While most, understandably, kept on the move, evidence suggests that some at least were tied to China. In November 1849, for example, the *Merthyr Guardian* reported on the capture of Mary Ann Jones, aged seventy-five, whose exploits had made her notorious in the district. Apparently she had been a smasher of coins for many years and had 'brought up her daughters (some of whom have been transported) in the same dishonest practices'. Given that Merthyr had been built on manufacturing iron, it should come as no surprise that some of her denizens turned such skills to criminal ends.

Then there were the 'Bullies', who were first and foremost protectors for their partners in crime, the prostitutes, in as much as they assisted the latter in robberies, attempted to prevent their capture and subsequent conviction and tried to ensure that no other members of the underworld deprived their particular girl of her earnings. In many cases the relationship between bully and prostitute was more than just a business one and both would live together in the Cellars. Bullies often assisted in robberies, either by actually being involved in the offence or by preventing the victim from repossessing his property. It was also the bully's job to ensure that the police did not apprehend his girl and, if they did, he was expected to secure her quick release. Consequently, reports such as the following were by no means rare:

> THOMAS TAYLOR, one of the 'bullies' belonging to China, was charged with having assaulted P.C. Joseph Hemmings on Sunday morning. It appeared that the officer had one of the women in charge for robbing a man… when the prisoner came up, swore she would not be taken and struck and kicked the officer…

If his attempts to prevent capture or effect an escape were unsuccessful, the bully tried his utmost to ensure that the case was dismissed by the magistrates and intimidation, bribery and perjury were the tools used to arrive at a not guilty verdict. The Chinese were experts at intimidation and most victims were easily persuaded not to prosecute, but if threats (and they could be on a large scale) were not enough, bullies would even return the stolen property in an attempt to have the case dropped.

Not only did the bully attempt to protect his girl from her victims and the police, he also had to protect her from other bullies and nymphs, as thieving between girls was a common factor underlying many of the cases of assault brought by the Chinese.

In the same way as the bully earned his everyday income from the proceeds of theft, so too, when the opportunity arose, did he supplement this by turning independently to robbery. Some bullies, like Rees Jenkins, *alias* 'Rees Trecastle', and Benjamin York, *alias* 'Ben the York', proved particularly adept at 'thimble-rigging', in which the punter was asked to bet on the whereabouts of a pea after it had been shuffled from one of three thimbles to another and, almost inevitably, had been transferrd via a thumbnail to the operator's pocket.

Unlike more normal theft, conducted as secretly as possible, thimble-riggers needed to draw attention to themselves in order to attract custom, and they also required a good supply of fresh, inexperienced and preferably idle victims. Hence racecourses, fairgrounds and major thoroughfares provided ideal locations. Furthermore, not only did the practice prove lucrative but it appears to have been remarkably free from prosecution as:

> ...they could only be brought to book on their victim's initiative; and the victim – left
> in an uncertain state of mind, and feeling that he had little prospect, whatever happened,
> of seeing his money again – was often reluctant to start proceedings that were bound to
> advertise his own gullibility.

In many cases thimble-rigging was used as a shield to disguise more straightforward theft. The game attracted punters who were then pickpocketed as they watched, or were later followed and robbed. Fairs were notorious for their drunkenness, and who better to rob the intoxicated than the bully whose paramour made a daily living from it?

Then there were the brothel-keepers. An Anglican missionary identified twenty brothels operating in 1860 and there would have been more in the 1840s. Brothel-keepers were notorious thieves and receivers, while their houses often doubled as lodging houses, cheap eating places and beershops.

At the heart of the Empire, however, were the prostitutes – although it was not prostitution as such which so alarmed Merthyr's magistrates and police but rather their wholesale use of it as a front for theft. Not averse to robbing the naive or unwary in the streets of the town, especially newly arriving immigrants, it was in the brothels of China that the girls enjoyed their greatest success. Merthyr's 'nymphs of the pave' were renowned for their ability to attract men into the bordellos, and numerous newspaper reports on robberies were preceded by such prurient comments as: 'Jane Lloyd, a young girl of rather captivating appearance...'.

Once enticed inside, the nymphs were experts at encouraging men to drink themselves into a stupor, thus ensuring the victim's powers of resistance and pursuit were suitably diminished. Once drunk, theft was easy and later identification frequently impossible; the frequency with which cases were dismissed due to victims being unable to verify identification drove successive magistrates into apoplexy. Some girls used drugs to dull their victims and, whether inebriated or doped, the rest was easy for such women as Margaret Llewellyn, *alias* 'Peggy Two Constables', Jane Thomas, 'Big Jane', Ann Phillips, 'Jonah', and Margaret Evans, 'The Buffalo'. Other girls would enlist the aid of bullies or work in pairs.

One survey of criminal records for the mid-1840s suggests that the average amount stolen was in the order of £2, still a considerable amount when one remembers that a collier's wage at the time was around £1 a week, but there were instances when far more was taken, as in October 1845 when £200 was stolen from an Aberdare man. Nor was theft restricted to cash and watches: handkerchiefs, snuff-boxes, boots, waistcoats, shirts and trousers – in fact, anything which could be quickly disposed of – were taken by the nymphs, continuously and by and large successfully for the best part of fifty years!

A recurring theme in the first half of the nineteenth century concerns the attempts to impose national laws and codes of behaviour stemming from an increasingly industrial and urban society on an essentially pre-industrial workforce. Those who tramped to Merthyr from the Welsh countryside brought traditional definitions of right and wrong with them. These, in common with most rural standards, were conservative in outlook and so tended to survive the transition bolstered by settlement patterns based on roots.

The evidence for the existence of 'community law' centres around newspaper reports on sexual and racial matters, and its most common manifestations occurred when a person or persons offended the moral standards of the community. In 1834, for example, three men and three women were fined for forcing Anne Harman onto a ladder outside her workplace and carrying her in a violent manner to Pwllyweiad, from where she was pelted with mud and stones to her mother's house: 'The justification was that she was an adulteress, and that such was their custom on such occasions'. This was a clear extension of the use of the *ceffyl pren* or 'wooden horse', the most typical of the punishments imposed on those who fell foul of the community in rural Wales. Its use, widely reported during the Rebecca Riots, normally went unpunished in country areas, but in Merthyr the local magistrates clearly regarded it as simply a common assault, to be dealt with as such.

The mob not only took matters into its own hands but also reacted when the police or magistrates were considered to be lax. Thus in 1846, when William Jones, a Dowlais shoemaker, was 'supposed to be keeping women of disreputable character in his house' he found a crowd of some 400-500 gathered, with the expressed intention of 'beating out the girls' and destroying his doors and windows. When the police intervened they were attacked and several were injured.

Of greatest concern to the authorities were racial manifestations of community law. Increasing antagonism between the Welsh and Irish led to an explosive outburst in Dowlais in July 1850. According to the *Merthyr Guardian*, what sparked the violence was a drunken brawl in the early hours of a Sunday morning in which the Welsh proved victorious:

> Maddened by their defeat the Irish perpetrated a most unwarrantable outrage, namely that of breaking the windows of the Welsh Independent meeting-house. This proceeding exasperated the Welsh, who assembled on Monday to nearly the extent of a thousand persons; and… commenced an attack on the houses occupied by Irish people – windows were broken – window sashes smashed; and in some instances, the inmates of the houses so assailed were hurt… [the] police… had very great difficulty in preventing further mischief as the irish were attacked in several places… On Tuesday night the disturbances were recommenced; but on this occasion a body of policemen… cleared the streets, hence no serious mischief occurred…

Nor was community law restricted to the Welsh. In February 1854, for example, following a report on a street brawl, the *Merthyr Guardian* noted:

> It appeared from the evidence, and also from a statement of the Superintendent, that an ill-feeling existed between the Irish men belonging to different counties, so that there were continual skirmishes between 'Tipperary and Cork boys', and others, in which pokers, tongs and similar instruments were pretty freely used…

Merthyr also drew agricultural labourers from the border counties of England and the West Country, and in 1833 one of these was responsible for a case that drew considerable publicity: 'Anne Vaughan, of Dowlais, was committed to take her trial… for marrying Thomas Wickley, her husband… being living. The ignorant delusion, that her husband could legally dispose of her by sale, appears to have actuated the prisoner'. This wife-selling has been shown by E.P. Thompson to have been a divorce action which was fairly commonplace in England in the eighteenth and early nineteenth century.

The influence of the mob declined significantly in the 1840s and 1850s and this:

> …may be seen as the result of the same process of industrialization which caused rural landowners to express disapproval of the erosion of a paternalistic ethic. Both were norms in an age-old rural society… which were now being destroyed with the concentration of the population in industrial areas…

As Charles Wilkins noted: 'as a rule, the social customs of the early years of the Iron Era underwent a change after the old people had disappeared'.

Turning finally to policing, traditionally Merthyr had been policed by a constable elected annually by the Parish and reinforced when necessary by 'respectable tradesmen' sworn in as special constables. In the days when it was little more than a hamlet this worked well enough, but industrialisation overwhelmed the old system. By 1831 the problems of enforcing law and order prompted the Parish to appoint an ex-metropolitan policeman at an annual salary of £80. Though efficient, he was dismissed a few months later on grounds of economy. Following the Rising the town and its neighbourhood were inundated with troops, so why bother to pay a policeman? As the military presence diminished, however, the fears of the ratepayers grew and from 1834 the *Merthyr Guardian* reported on two constables patrolling Merthyr, with another in Dowlais. These had to endure the inherent miserliness of the Parish and the disdain of working people, whose inter-district feuds no constable dared to interrupt.

As for punishment, the magistrates utilised two sets of stocks and a crude lock-up. The stocks in Merthyr had originally been placed in the churchyard, where offenders were not only exposed to public humiliation but could also 'hear themselves… alluded to by the minister, who aptly used them as illustrations of vice, and as warnings to the young'. For reasons which will become apparent, however, the location tended to disturb church services and so the stocks were moved to a plot opposite a pub, where they remained until around 1850. Although another set of stocks stood beside the tramroad at Dowlais, it appears that they were rarely used, as the local constable preferred to produce their keys and wave them threateningly to discourage 'unruly customers'. The Merthyr lock-up, known as the 'black hole', had been built behind the old church in 1809. A wooden shack about ten to fourteen feet square, it 'was a dark, unsavoury place, quite deserving of the name', and when the new police station was built it became a stable, for which purpose it seems to have been ideally suited.

The effectiveness of both stocks and the black hole was more than questionable; rather than spending their internment in miserable reflection on their wrongdoing, many offenders seem to have positively relished the experience. On the one occasion Henry Murton could remember the Dowlais stocks being used, 'on the expiration of his sentence the liberated man had to be assisted home quite glorious, from the profuse liberality of his friends during his confinement'. Similarly, the black hole had a large keyhole which:

> …was often used by the friends of tipplers to supply them with a little refreshment in the form of gin or brandy. A friendly call would speedily draw the prisoner to the door,

and then a tobacco-pipe placed through the hole, with the bowl outside, formed a mode of reviving them.

With the rise of Chartism at the end of the 1830s, the whole issue of law and order became far more pressing and the threat of revolution saw the middle class abandon its misgivings and move towards the establishment of a 'new-model' County Constabulary. Hence by October 1841 Glamorgan had its own professional police under the control of an ex-Rifle Brigade Officer, Captain Napier, and by 1844 Merthyr had a brand new, purpose-built police station, four-square and completely 'enclosed with a view to secure it from attack'.

Though Napier claimed from the outset that his force had brought about a great improvement, in fact the impact of the new police was limited by manpower shortages. Determined 'to retain none but the most efficient', each officer 'in addition to honesty, sobriety and a sound constitution... is required to possess a knowledge of the Welsh language, of keeping accounts, and of being able to read and write'. Because of such demands, 'it becomes no easy matter to obtain efficient men so qualified; and even when such men are obtained, they are frequently found to be totally ignorant of their duties as policemen, and must gain that knowledge by experience'.

Though several constables were dismissed in the 1840s 'for dereliction from duty', a far more serious problem was the attraction of higher wages at the ironworks. Despite the long hours and often dangerous patrols, sergeants received no more than 22s a week, constables 20s and second-class ones 18s. Though such rates were by no means insignificant, during times of prosperity they palled alongside those offered by the works. Thus in 1846 Napier noted that at a time when he needed all the men he could muster:

> ...in consequence... of the great demand for labour and the high rate of wages, a considerable number of the men have left the Force, and from the same cause, I experience a great difficulty in replacing the number with such men as I consider efficient, and likely to remain.

Because of such problems, the strength of Merthyr's police remained questionable throughout the 1840s. How could an average of just thirteen men hope to maintain law and order in a town of nearly 50,000 people? At times the odds must have seemed overwhelming, as in April 1845, for example, when at a time of considerable immigration only the Superintendent, one sergeant and a probationary constable remained to police both Merthyr and Dowlais. Little wonder, then, that certain localities like China remained to all intents and purposes 'no-go' areas throughout the period, while even in the main streets of the town 'The peace... is better preserved on moonlit nights than at other times'.

Napier was also confronted by continued ratepayer mentality, as was illustrated nicely in June 1842, when a meeting of Merthyr's ratepayers passed two not unrelated resolutions. The first, in response to Napier's request for additional constables, informed him that it was:

> …their unanimous and decided opinion that an increase of the number of constables is uncalled for and unnecessary. That owing to the great depression of Trade and consequent distress… it is with the greatest difficulty that the majority of ratepayers are enabled to meet the present calls upon them and any addition to the rate would be most severely and grievously felt.

On the other hand Napier was urged to:

> …memorialize the government on the present alarming state of the neighbourhood… [as] this meeting is convinced of the total inadequacy of the present military force to maintain the peace and security of the peace and that the government be earnestly solicited to immediately increase that force, as the present civil power or any… increase of it would be wholly inefficient to meet the threatened danger.

Merthyr's ratepayers wanted the protection of soldiers, paid for by Westminster, rather than policemen funded from their rates.

Despite such formidable problems, the determination of individuals like Chief Constable Napier and Merthyr's Police Superintendent Wrenn ensured that in time the new police would make a considerable impression, when such movements as temperance combined with economic factors to bring more stability to life. The Glamorgan constabulary was the most dramatic but by no means the only innovation to affect law and order.

8

RELIGION

When embarking upon any analysis of religion in Merthyr during the middle years of the nineteenth century, the obvious starting point is the unique religious census which was conducted there on the last Sunday of March 1851. This revealed that the town had sixty-two places of worship and a congregational strength of some 22,251, divided into the following denominations:

Denomination	Congregational Strength	%
Independent	7,244	32.6
Baptist	6,787	30.5
Calvinistic Methodist	1,970	8.9
Anglican	1,693	7.6
Calvinistic Baptist	1,478	6.6
Wesleyan Methodist	1,276	5.7
Roman Catholic	600	2.7
Mormon	580	2.6
Primitive Methodist	276	1.2
Unitarian	233	1
Wesleyan Reformed Methodist	80	0.4
Jews	34	0.2

Most striking of all the findings was the dominance of those sects categorised as evangelical nonconformist, with approximately 86% of congregational strength, and the very poor showing of the Anglican Church, with less than 8%. The fact was that Merthyr 'was Dissenter from birth'.

At the beginning of the nineteenth century, the Llandaff bishopric was 'The poorest diocese in Great Britain – in financial resources, buildings and manpower'. Of the five bishops to have governed between 1782 and 1849, one was a noted pluralist and the others all held far more lucrative appointments elsewhere. At Merthyr, prior to the arrival of the Revd Campbell in 1844, the vicar had been the Revd Maber, who as a young man had been tutor to the Marquis of Bute, under whose patronage the Merthyr parish existed, and 'When the Merthyr living became vacant he was presented to it by his old pupil'. Just how well he served his parishioners was summed up by the *Morning Chronicle*:

> The late incumbent, Mr. Maber for the last 32 years of his life was non-resident in his parish [preferring to live in the Mumbles in Swansea]. During that time he derived an income from it of about £1,000 a year; but he never paid a visit to the parish only once excepted, when he came in a post-chaise (almost as great a curiosity at that time to the townspeople as the sight of their Rector) *to vote for a Church-rate*. The consequence was, that the charge of the parish being confined to curates who were continually changing and had no permanent interest in the place, the congregation fell away... and dissent gained what the Church lost.

Within the space of thirty to forty years, the Llandaff diocese had been 'overwhelmed by a population explosion greater than that experienced by any other... in the Kingdom', and yet it was not until the 1840s that the Church began to acknowledge the fact. Even when these failings were confronted by men like the Revd Campbell, certain aspects of the Anglican faith ensured that its popularity would always be limited among the urban workforce. In the first place, it remained uncompromisingly hierarchical in structure and practice and had no time for lay participation other than of a passive nature. Furthermore, its legacy was one which displayed 'little concern for popular religiosity', and at a time when nonconformists were successfully appealing to a great many workers not only had the Church remained 'less sensitive to popular tastes and popular religious demands' but from the 1790s to the 1840s enthusiastic Anglican ministers tended to be discouraged, as 'the religious Establishment exhibited increasingly negative attitudes towards popular religious tendencies within its own ranks'.

This alienation was exacerbated by the fact that the language of the Church was English. As the Revd Jenkins of Dowlais expressed it in 1850:

> The Church in these mountains, so long as the people have two separate languages, will never prosper unless there are distinct places of worship for each nation. The Welsh are fond of their own language. There is but one spot, Merthyr Old Church, where the Welsh can be said to have a church of their own; but see the result – it is crowded to an overflow.

Of crucial importance in a town whose workforce had a clear record of radicalism, the 'Report on Religious Worship' which followed the 1851 census drew attention to the fact that 'the chief dislike which labouring populations entertain for [Anglican] religious services is thought to be the maintenance of those distinctions by which they are separated as a class from the class above them'. The Established Church was just that – the Church of the establishment – and practices such as the ironmasters possessing their own pews at the front, with the middle class renting the remainder and working-class worshippers having to stand at the back, 'only served to emphasize class differences'.

Given this catalogue of failings, the following statement from an article on Wales in *Blackwood's Magazine* in 1849 would seem to be more than appropriate:

> The wonder is, not that dissent should have attained its present height, but that the Church should have continued to exist at all, amidst so many abuses, so much ignorance, so much neglect, and such extraordinary apathy – until of late days – on the past of her rulers.

When analysing the rise of evangelical nonconformity, three major factors can be identified: the alienation of the Established Church, the popular receptiveness to nonconformity, and the fact that the latter did far more to satisfy both the religious and cultic needs of the workforce. Characterised by its unsophisticated approach, the willingness of lay preachers to take religion to the people wherever they lived, and its emphasis on Sunday school education, evangelical nonconformity was ideally suited to prosper in the newly emerging industrial towns. Furthermore, this emphasis on lay workers and, of necessity, on lay initiative, 'made for religious-cultural informality and spontaneity... It was a popular religious movement, sensitive to the understanding, taste, and outlook of its rank-and-file members'. In Wales this was given further impetus by the very language of itinerancy. The lay preacher, the Sunday school teacher and the visiting evangelist all used Welsh, and thus their message was even more direct and popular.

For all this, evangelical nonconformity, like any other brand of religion, offered both spiritual and cultic functions. The great majority of people accepted the concept of God and rejected secularism, and 'Such people could easily be mobilized by the evangelical doctrine of salvation, especially at times of crisis'. In Merthyr, the classic examples of this were the religious revivals which accompanied the cholera epidemics. In August 1849, for example, the *Merthyr Guardian* reported:

> Religious meetings are of frequent occurrence; great numbers of persons become members of societies who were previously indifferent to the subject; and in many chapels,

special meetings are being held in order to receive the number of aspirants for religious consolation, who flock to the altar. The outward visible sign of this is most apparent with the Baptists, who baptise in the Taff every Sunday afternoon, in the presence of thousands of spectators.

According to the *Morning Chronicle* the epidemic increased 'threefold the number of communicants in the churches and chapels', prompting one influential Independent minister to state, 'Who will venture to deny that the Lord had mercifully ordained this awful scourge as the means of accomplishing his gracious purpose of saving thousands?'

It should never be forgotten, however, that:

> …the spectre of terror beyond the grave, and the 'evangelical allurements' of justification and eternal life, were particularly potent weapons in the religious arsenal in an age when even normal times brought constant reminders of the poverty, powerlessness, and contingency of human existence for the great mass of the population.

As regards the cultic functions of religion, political, social and economic factors had a role to play. In the first instance, the element of protest was significant, for while evangelical nonconformity was not politically radical, its doctrine of natural equality and essential moral inadequacy of all men before God meant that the chapels cut across the hierarchical structures of contemporary society and gave their members an important sense of independence. In Merthyr, class and status differentiations were stark and absolute and yet in the chapels such differences were consciously ignored. So politically nonconformity provided an attractive alternative to Anglicanism, and as historian A.D. Gilbert has written: 'the element of social protest in commitment to a "chapel" rather than a "church" was vitally important'.

There can be no question either that the social function of nonconformity played a very important part in recruitment. Chapel membership helped to fill the vacuum created by the collapse of traditional social ties and expectations and:

> …involved the capacity for satisfying the profound associational and communal needs of people experiencing anomie and social insecurity in a period of rapid social change and dislocation in which increasing numbers of people found themselves… in unfamiliar, unstructured and largely normless environments.[9]

Many English observers commented on the gregarious nature of the Welsh and noted that it was to the chapel that many looked for their recreational and cultural needs. According to the journal *Y Drysorfa*, 'The Chapel… is the social centre around which its adherents gather; it is school, lyceum, club, church all in one…'. We should also remember that there were few alternatives to the pub, and while it would be uncharitable to say that thousands went to chapel in those days because there was nowhere else to go, such a statement is not devoid of all truth. Nor should one suppose that it was just the communal or recreational outlets which attracted people, for in a town where the threat of poverty was ever present:

> Membership of a chapel community often provided the best means of access to such basic necessities as housing, clothing, food, credit or employment in times of crisis. In a society bereft of adequate systems of social security, integration in a cohesive community was one of the best forms of insurance.

In Merthyr, the town's attraction to immigrants ensured that this economic function of collective insurance played an important role in the growth of its chapel congregations, as workers who flocked from rural Wales 'brought their religion with them in the form of a letter of recommendation – *llythyr canmoliaeth* – which handed the person over to the care and supervision of another chapel'.

Perhaps as a result of their own denominational loyalties, or in furtherance of the traditional outrage at the alleged treachery of the 'Blue Books', generations of Welsh historians have placed a seal of infallibility on the claim that 'the two things which were inescapable in Merthyr were smoke and chapels, industry and prayer, labour and religion' – and yet this was not the impression given by the 1851 census or many contemporaries, especially nonconformists. Thus when Calvinistic Methodist Dafydd Rolant was preaching on Samaria, he concluded 'Samaria was their ashtip. An ashtip where they threw all their stecks and rubbish. A hotbed of paganism and heresy and everything. Yes, my friends, Samaria was the Merthyr Tydfil of the land of Canaan'.

The fact is that, according to the census of 1851, 52% did not attend any place of religious worship – and by common consent this probably exaggerated religious affiliation. Enumeration techniques were questionable, 'adherents' as well as fully-fledged chapel members were counted, and the revival associated with the cholera had yet to wane. One thing is indisputable: a very considerable proportion of Merthyr's inhabitants did not go to either church or chapel. Rather than attempt to define who these people were, it is easier first to identify just who did attend, and we see that it was among the labour aristocracy that nonconformity won most support. This comes as no surprise, for if the fear of death was universal, the elements of protest, improvement and community held particular appeal for the skilled. Their pride lent itself to the independence of the chapel, their aspirations were recognised and encouraged by nonconformity, and as they represented that element of the workforce with the most commitment to the town, community and associational ties meant far more to them than they did to the more transient unskilled sections of the workforce who largely lay outside the scope of religion. Among the Catholic Irish, for example, the least rewarded and secure of Merthyr's workers, fewer than 20% of those born in Ireland attended mass at Dowlais on census Sunday.

But one should not suppose that it was only the unskilled who had no time for religion, for the period saw important changes in the character of nonconformity and its constituency, changes which were to lead others to reject religion. In the early years of the iron industry, the initial traumas of industrialisation and urbanisation produced 'a period of disturbed transition' in which evangelism prospered, but by the middle of the nineteenth century this transitionary period was coming to an end, and nonconformity responded by changing its emphasis from that of recruitment to consolidation. This trend was exemplified most obviously in chapel-building, and 'the primary functions of the chapel had to do with the social requirements of an existing Nonconformist community. A chapel was a symbol of status… It was "the public equivalent of the parlour mantel-Piece"'. There were only eleven chapels in Merthyr in 1815 and yet by 1851 there were forty-nine, over 60% of which had been built since 1830.

Itinerancy and the open-air or hired-room meeting cost very little, but the erection and upkeep of a chapel involved considerable expense and so this consolidation was accompanied by an increasingly upward trend in the constituency status of chapel membership. Quite simply, it was only the better-off section of the workforce who could afford to regularly donate money in sufficient quantities, and thus nonconformity began to appeal more and more to the labour aristocracy and shopocracy, at the cost of ignoring the less well-off sections of the workforce. It was for these reasons that the evangelical movement began to fragment, and Merthyr witnessed the growth of such bodies as the Primitive and Reformed Methodists, who 'captured the element of protest against organisational consolidation and institutionalisation'.

It was not just the goals of nonconformity which changed, however; so too did people's attitudes. Despite the connection between chapel membership and material satisfaction, during economic depressions recruitment fell, as people were either forced to go elsewhere in search of work or became disillusioned with the chapels. Regarding the latter, the crux of the problem was that while the community could cope with the problems of individual members during normal times, when the pressures of recession were general the chapel proved unable to help, and as we have seen the 1840s and 1850s were for the most part years of depression.

Evidence also suggests that the appeal of salvation was no longer universal. In 1860, for example, when Anglican missionaries visited Samuel Thomas and found him on his deathbed he proved 'an obstinate sceptic'. When they told him who they were he was very civil, but in answer to the question 'Would he mind if one of them prayed with him?' he replied:

That it would be an empty form if we would and that he did not wish to put us to such unnecessary trouble – that he made up his mind upon matters of religion a long time ago, at least 20 years, and came to the conclusion if there was such a Being as God that he was a good being and that he would not be so unjust as to punish him for doing a thing that was not conditionally laid before him when he received his being.

So by the middle of the century secular beliefs were emerging, and although the outright rejection of religion was far more a characteristic of the final decades of the century the fact that such trends can be identified in the town during the 1840s and 1850s is significant. Why then was this the case? Perhaps it was the drift towards a more skilled and comfortable constituency, or it may have resulted from disillusionment with the constituency itself. For example, the same missionaries reported on the case of Daniel Davies, who owned a four-girl brothel at China and yet argued 'that he had been belonging to religion almost all his life time... was received as a member at Zoar when he was only seventeen'. They also discovered another brothel owned by none other than an Independent minister!

That such hypocrisy should lead to disaffection is not surprising, but for far more working people it was religious indifference to major social problems which fostered alienation. As one historian has noted: 'Life for the working man was not to be lived in separate compartments; his religion and his social strivings had to be harmonized', but for the majority of ministers religion was above temporal matters. So it was that as early as 1833, when trade unionism first took root in south Wales, it was vigorously condemned by both Wesleyan and Calvinistic Methodists, and in 1839 when the Chartists were organising their first national petition and not a single Dowlais Methodist was said to have signed it, such was his appreciation that Sir John Guest donated £50 towards the building of their new chapel.

As it was the Chartist movement which represented the most sophisticated and prolonged form of working-class political agitation during this period, naturally enough it was the Charter which drew the most antagonism. The most vitriolic attack to emerge from Merthyr's religious community came in the form of a pamphlet, *Chartism Unmask'd*, written by the Vicar of Dowlais, the Revd E. Jenkins, in 1840. This diatribe began by pointing out that Satan 'may be called the *first Chartist Leader*... [as he] wished to be equal to the Son of God', before embarking on a systematic attack on each of the Charter's six points. Some sixteen pages of abuse later he concluded that Chartism provoked: 'Unholy desires, wicked counsels... unjust works... battle, murder... sudden death... war, hatred... discord... error and deception... scepticism, infidelity, and... anarchy... [leading] to poverty, misery, and transporation; the gallows, death and hell'.

That such a denunciation should have been penned by a vicar is not surprising, though the degree of support he enjoyed from nonconformist ministers is at first not so easily explained. One should not forget the history of dissent, however. Long regarded with suspicion and even hostility by a Parliament dominated by Anglicans, evangelical nonconformity took great pains to emphasise its respectability and acceptance of the status quo. Jabez Bunting, who dominated orthodox Methodism for most of the early nineteenth century, declared vehemently, 'Methodism hates democracy as much as it hates sin', while the Calvinistic sects took it a step further by quoting Luther: 'Even if those in authority are evil or without faith, nevertheless the authority and its power is good and from God'.

Though the secrecy, oath-taking and threats associated with early trade unionism (as well as the overt class-consciousness of Chartism and its rejection of the Anti-Corn Law League) provoked antipathy, what really lay behind this antagonism was the theology of evangelism. Its emphasis on the afterlife 'resulted in an attitude which took obedience to the will of God as implying complete satisfaction with, and acceptance of things as they were'. After all: 'If it was original sin that caused abuses to exist, what steps could man, the sinner, take to remove them?' Consequently: 'Religion became an apologist for social inequalities instead of a critic with a new standard of values to impose upon the life of men'.

One should not assume, however, that social reform was entirely beyond the realms of nonconformist ideology; hence the religious involvement in the Anti-Corn Law League, in education and in temperance. Similarly, not all ministers regarded unionism or Chartism with animosity. Back in 1833 when the Annual General Assembly of Calvinistic Methodists at Tredegar condemned trade unionism, its final resolution called upon all Methodist preachers and elders 'to sever their connection absolutely with the [workers'] Union', suggesting that some at least had embraced the idea of workers' control. Similarly, four nonconformist ministers were prominent Chartist leaders in Merthyr, with the Revd Thomas Davies, Baptist minister of High Street Chapel, attending the subversive Three Horse Shoe meetings, while the Independent minister, the Revd David John, 'was with his sons… at the centre of Merthyr's Chartist activity'. Indeed, the issue divided the Independents, as a number of Chartist chapels were established by congregations disenchanted with ministers opposed to the Charter. For such people Chartism in no way clashed with their theological beliefs, for as Ernest Jones expressed it, no doubt to the horror of the Vicar of Dowlais, 'Christ was the first Chartist and democracy was the gospel carried into practice'.

Generally, however, Chartists were not particularly religious and many were positively atheistic. Henry Hetherington declared that 'Truth, Justice and Liberty will never be permanently established on earth till every vestige of priestcraft and superstition be utterly destroyed'. *Udgorn Cymru* 'noticed as early as 1840 the apathy with which ministers of religion viewed the People's Charter, claiming that this neutrality was nothing less than active opposition – "He that is not with me is against me"', and David Ellis, a leading Merthyr Chartist, expressed his sorrow over the fact that so many Chartists continued to listen to 'those black-coated devils who are preaching hell to their souls all day'.

The impact of nonconformity was certainly complex. In as much as it fostered the goals of respectability and the work ethic and chose largely to ignore social reform, 'it reinforced the puritan values of the middle classes'. However, its popular roots ensured that it was bound to contribute to working-class movements. J.F.C. Harrison noted that 'As schools of practical democracy and self government the Chapels rendered valuable service to popular movements' and Eric Hobsbawm reminds us, 'The Labour Party owes more to Methodism than Marx'.

Before continuing, some analysis of the temperance movement which emerged in the 1830s and 1840s is warranted, as the chapels were certainly prime movers in its support. Having originated in England in 1828 as a middle-class anti-spirits lobby, the passing of the Beerhouse Act of 1830 saw the movement adopt a wider perspective, though unity was prevented by differences of opinion among its ranks. For example, the British and Foreign Temperance Society, formed in 1831, was in favour of moderation, while the British Temperance Association, founded in 1835, advocated complete teetotalism. In Merthyr, a branch of the 'British and Foreign' was formed in 1834, and the evidence suggests that the spread of teetotalism was not as spectacular as that in north Wales. In August 1837, for example, when the North Wales Temperance Association sent two nonconformist ministers to south Wales to lecture on total abstinence: 'Sceptics suggested they would remain alive until they reached Merthyr'. Nevertheless, in April 1841 the *Merthyr Guardian* reported that Easter Monday had witnessed the Fourth Annual Festival of the 'Total Abstinence Societies of Gwent and Morgannwg Districts' being held in Merthyr, suggesting that the town's first teetotal society probably dated from the north Walians' visit. By 1841 Merthyr also had an English Temperance Association for non-Welsh speakers, as well as its first teetotal benefit society, the Rechabites, and within two years the 'Tydfil' tent had been augmented by two others, as well as the Cefn-Coed-y-Cymmer Temperance Benefit Society.

Merthyr's reputation ensured that a steady stream of national figures visited in an attempt to win over new members and boost the morale of the converted. In May 1841, for example, some 350 new pledges were signed following a series of open-air and chapel lectures by a 'Mr. Scott, an agent of the British Temperance Society'. Twelve months later: 'The celebrated James Teare has been lecturing here', while in December 1843 1,000 teetotallers were reported to have marched in procession to hear a 'Father Watkins'.

Marches, representing the public affirmation of loyalty to the ideals of temperance and abstinence, were quite common in Merthyr, and apart from those which accompanied specific lectures or anti-drink campaigns, every Easter Monday saw a teetotal march. This was not the only form of demonstration, however; the public sports held at Cefn Coed in April 1841 and the public tea meeting at Merthyr in January 1843 bear witness to the reformers' attempts to show the inhabitants that alternatives to the pub and beerhouse did exist. By 1844 the town had a Teetotal Choir and four years later the Merthyr Tydfil Teetotal Cymmrodorion Society held its first eisteddfod, but by far the greatest display of this alternative leisure movement came in 1852, when the Merthyr Temperance Hall, capable of holding over 1,200 people, was opened.

Theology certainly played a major role in Merthyr. In 1842, for example, at Cefn-Coed-y-Cymmer: 'none are admitted members of the Welsh Calvinistic Methodists there unless teetotallers'. For evangelical nonconformists, drink was more than just a social problem – it was a personal sin and the 'rescueing of the working classes from the demon of drink was a mission of salvation'.

The movement, however, was not restricted to the religious constituency and some Chartists supported it on political grounds. Henry Vincent advocated temperance. 'David Ellis spoke in its favour [though at the Three Horse Shoes!] and David John, junior, advocated abstinence at the 1840 convention'. The government made millions out of the taxes on drink and thus abstinence would deprive the corrupt regime of much of its revenue. Some argued that temperance would lead to a material improvement in the working people's lot; it encouraged men to stay at home and look after their wives and children. If drink was avoided then the land previously given over to grow barley could be used for pasture, thus allowing more cattle to be reared, ensuring cheaper meat for the workforce. It would also lead to an improvement in Chartist finances and to more sober and constructive argument, and any increase in working-class sobriety would make the latter more receptive to Chartist propaganda. Despite such arguments, however, the important role of the pub as a working-class meeting place and community centre was recognised by many and 'Dependence of public house circulation caused most Chartist newspapers to fight shy of teetotal Chartism'.

Despite the strength of nonconformity in the town and the growth of temperance and teetotal societies, by no stretch of the imagination could Merthyr be described as a bastion of temperance. However, the 1830s and 1840s saw the foundations being laid for later successes in the 1850s and 1860s. Temperance was adopted by an influential section of the labour aristocracy, and the significance of the fact that by the early 1850s one of the biggest buildings in Merthyr was the Temperance Hall or that workers could be living in Temperance Street should not be ignored. By the 1860s the movement was a considerable force in Merthyr, and that this had much to do with the town's nonconformist communities cannot be denied, for 'The network of Bands of Hope, tract societies and Young Men's Improvement Associations built around the chapels soon became formidable auxiliaries in the battle to stamp out drink'.

In the same way that religious affiliation has been traditionally overemphasised, so too has the total picture been distorted through over-simplification, and the social and economic significance of Merthyr's Catholics, Mormons and Jews warrants some analysis.

Although Brecon and its neighbourhood had retained a core of Catholic families since the Reformation, the revival of the religion in Merthyr and elsewhere in south Wales was directly related to the influx of Irish in the nineteenth century. According to one priest, there were at least 300 Irish in and around the town in 1827, while the census of 1851 revealed 3,051 Irish-born inhabitants. As far as their religious wants were concerned, the first mass was said in 1824 by a Welsh Franciscan from Abergavenny, but no regular services were held until Father Portal was transferred from Poole in 1827 to serve the 'Merthyr District', which included Rhymney and Tredegar. He was not impressed by a mission he found 'one of the most severe and disagreeable I have ever heard of', as there was '…nothing here but hardships out and solitude at home…', and following the Rising of 1831 he decamped to Newport. For the next two years Merthyr had no incumbent priest until Father MacDermott, 'a man of means', arrived in 1833, to be replaced two years later by another Irishman, Father James Carroll, whose subsequent struggle can only be described as heroic.

Occupying a simple terraced house, he lived in the back room and turned the front room into a shop, where he sold vegetables grown in his garden to help support himself. Unable to afford to build a church, he rented, at £12 a year, a room above the public slaughterhouse at Pondside, described as 'a dark, low loft, without ceiling and gaping between the tiles in its roof… [access] being gained by a ladder flung across a brook'. Every Sunday he said mass there and did some teaching, before walking the six miles to Rhymney to hold similar services, this time in a hired wash-house. In Merthyr he also established 'a school for about 50 poor children of both sexes, in a one-horse stable, about 8 foot wide and 16 foot long'. Such was his poverty in 1840 that his house was 'without a single article of decent furniture', while he was 'often, it is feared without a sufficiency of food. He has declined a more comfortable mission offered him by the Bishop on account of the difficulty of finding a successor able to undergo such a continuous martyrdom…'.

If his position was difficult when times were relatively good, by 1844 it was desperate; the 'unparalleled stagnation of the iron trade' had seen many of his parishioners 'driven elsewhere in search of employment', while those who were left:

> …were unable to afford even their scanty contributions of former years for the support of their pastor. For weeks together the collections, and every other source of income, did not exceed…EIGHT or TEN shillings – frequently they were much less.

Sometime during the middle of the decade he moved to Dowlais, where, thanks to the charity of an unknown benefactor, a church opened in 1846. Then in June 1847 he succumbed to typhus. Such was his commitment that:

> ...a few days before, he was noticed, by a Protestant gentleman, making his way on foot
> over a bleak mountain to a sick call at a distance of several miles, in pelting rain, wearing
> a tattered coat, and his feet appearing through shoes and stockings. Being unable to get
> through a second mass, on Sunday, two days before his decease, he threw himself upon
> a mattress in his clothes, on the ground floor, that he might be better able to administer
> the Sacraments to any who should be brought for the purpose.

A Father Dawson took over the mission which, despite the bleak years of the ensuing depression, continued to grow until by 1859 somewhere in the region of 4,000 Irish-born residents were living in the town. A second church was opened at Georgetown on St Patrick's Day.

Financial difficulties were not the only ones, and these years witnessed a growing resentment on the part of the Welsh towards the Irish. This had not always been the case, and a source in 1828 told of how a visiting catechist called Lewis 'explains some tenets of our religion in the Welsh language to the Welsh' and subsequently 'from twenty to forty Welsh attend each Sunday quietly at Mass'. However, by the mid-1830s the growing numbers of Irish and the depression in the iron trade shattered any degree of sympathy between the two communities. The first serious clash occurred in May 1834, when the Irish were driven from the Varteg ironworks at Pontypool for accepting lower wages. Twelve years later the Catholic church and vestry in Cardiff, along with many Irish houses, were attacked by mobs and the authorities were accused of turning a blind eye. At Merthyr, such was the animosity that 'Someone [was] always on guard outside Pondside Chapel, [on] one or two occasions it was attacked'. Even Father Carroll felt unsafe:

> In 1837 the Irish navvies came into the district [Treforest] for the construction of the Taff
> Vale Railway. A Father Carroll used to come on weekdays and said mass very early in the
> morning... He used to dress in disguise, in moleskin like a navvy...

As we have seen, Dowlais was the scene of bitter clashes between Welsh and Irish in 1851 and for as long as the Irish continued to represent an economic threat, and it was many years before hostility dwindled to suspicion and semi-acceptance; even then the priests and their churches remained targets for antagonism.

In 1827, frontier drifter Joseph Smith proclaimed his vision whereby the angel 'Moroni' had revealed the presence of buried plates of gold with ancient characters inscribed on them, telling of Christ's American coming. Smith claimed to have located the plates and published his translation as *The Book of Mormon* in 1830. Despite Mark Twain's comment that it was 'chloroform in print', it attracted followers and soon afterwards the Mormons began their trek into the wilderness, settling in 1839 at Nauvoo, Illinois. It was here that Welshman Captain Dan Jones met Smith and his followers. Born in Flintshire in 1811, Jones had taken to the sea before settling in America some ten miles north of Nauvoo, where, with a partner, he built a steamboat to carry freight and passengers up the Mississippi – hence the title 'Captain'. Baptised in 1843, he remained with Smith until the latter's murder in 1844, when he returned to Britain as a missionary with Wales as his special concern.

Jones was not the first to arrive, and others based at Liverpool had already begun to preach in the north Wales coalfield. In south Wales the American Elder William Henshaw is reported to have baptised William Rees Davies, a miner, his wife and two sons at Penydarren in February 1843. That March, the 'Penydarren Branch' was organised by Davies, using his cottage as a meeting place, and 'To him, in all probability, belongs the distinction of being the first to preach Mormonism in the Welsh language'.

On his arrival in south Wales a confident Captain Jones chose Merthyr as his base: 'I have more places to preach in, round here, than I can possibly attend to… In fact the prospect is good everywhere for a plentiful crop of good souls ere long'. In July 1846 his monthly *Prophwyd y Jubili* (renamed *Ugdorn Seion* in late 1848) began to promote the saints' message. An eloquent and powerful preacher, he soon began attracting converts and by 1847, out of a total of 1,933 Welsh ones, no fewer than 804 were from Merthyr itself. Such was Jones' success that by March 1848 the 'Merthyr Tydfil Conference', which included Beaufort, Tredegar, Rhymney and Aberdare, was referred to by the *Millennial Star* as the 'Mother Branch' in Britain, giving credence to Jones' claim that:

> The great car of Mormonism is traversing over the Cambrian Hills with astonishing rapidity… as though it was destined to pick up thousands of the 'Ancient Briton' race in its golden carriages and land them on the everlasting hills of heaven.

According to the *Merthyr Guardian*, the half-yearly meeting held in January 1849 saw the hall packed with upwards of 1,500 people, with many more unable to get in. The next month saw the first exodus of Welsh Mormons to the Salt Lake, Utah, chosen in 1847 by Joseph Smith's successor, Brigham Young, as the new home for the faithful. Led by Captain Jones, some hundreds of Mormons left Swansea for Liverpool and passage to America.

On Jones' departure, William Phillips became President of the Merthyr Conference, and the deepening depression and the ravages of the cholera ensured that the millennial message continued to appeal to a considerable number of Merthyr's workers. Indeed, by 1851 there were five branches in the town. In February 1854 the *Merthyr Guardian* recorded, 'Mormonism still retains its hold on a considerable number of the working men of this Place'; in July 1856 Captain Jones took another 703 converts to Utah, and church records reveal that by 1857 a further branch had been opened at Troedyrhiw.

The impression given by the *Merthyr Guardian,* however, is that the fervour of the late 1840s and early 1850s was short-lived, and in February 1855 it announced 'we are happy to find… that the delusion in this district is dying away, and that Mormonism has lost its hold upon the minds of the people'. Just how accurate this was is questionable, for the newspaper was highly critical and took great delight in exposing Mormons as charlatans. In 1850, for example, it publicised the case of William Davies, a Mormon collier who was sentenced to a month's hard labour for attempting to emigrate, leaving his wife and child chargeable to the Parish. In 1851, David Williams, a labourer described in court as a Mormon preacher, and John Rees, another Mormon, were accused of stealing a blanket from a China brothel. In evidence Williams admitted that they had gone to China to sleep with two girls, one of whom had stolen 6s 6d from him and then run away, so he had taken the blanket by way of compensation. Similarly, in 1852 'President' William Phillips was summoned by Merthyr's magistrates to answer a much-publicised charge laid against him by his eighty-year-old widowed mother, to the effect that he had neglected her and forced her onto the Parish. Whether or not the newspaper was successful in its attempts to blacken Mormonism cannot be determined, but Captain Jones himself pointed out that such criticism often encouraged working-class interest in the sect, as 'The people tell such lies about us as to stir up the curiosity of many to hear us'.

Regarding who the converts were, an analysis of the first 350 baptised members suggests that the sect was probably exclusively working-class in character and had great appeal among underground workers, especially colliers. Just why this was the case is not known, but the very first entry in the church's *Record of Members 1843–1856* is that of William Phillips, miner, Elder and later President for Wales, while William Henshaw was a collier. It was probably the case that, working in the pits, they were most likely to convert fellow workmen. More cynically, the lure of gold in California was said by the *Merthyr Guardian* to have contributed much to the success of Mormon emigration during the period, and who better to dig for gold than miners and colliers? While such speculation does not shed any light on why far more colliers as opposed to miners became saints, perhaps the greater hazards of their occupation made the millennial gospel especially attractive.

The Jews constituted the last notable religious group, and, though very little information exists about them, it is likely that the few who had settled in the town were boosted by émigrés fleeing from the continental upheavals of 1848. The religious census noted that a synagogue dating from that year existed in Victoria Street, and, on the day when attendance was noted, some thirty-four people attended morning services. Numbers would seem to have risen shortly afterwards, however, for in February 1853 the *Merthyr Guardian* reported 'MERTHYR NEW SYNAGOGUE – We hear that the ceremony of inauguration of the New Synagogue will take place on Tuesday... when the Rev. A. L. Green, of the Great Synagogue, has, by special permission, kindly consented to officiate'.

Though most were skilled craftsmen or worked in the retail trade – and as such provided useful services rather than posing any threat – they were subject to the hostility of the Christian majority. As early as 1844, an observer could draw attention to the fact that the Jewish burial ground off the Brecon Road was completely separated from that of the Christians (which, in turn, was rigidly divided into Anglican, nonconformist and Catholic plots), while in April 1847 the Merthyr branch of the British Society for Promoting Christianity among the Jews was formed. Once again the *Merthyr Guardian* took some delight in denigrating individual Jews who could be shown to be of dubious character. Thus, in May 1847 considerable publicity was given to a court case in which Lazarus Harris, a Jewish clockmaker in Pontmorlais, accused Rachel Burke, a Chinese nymph, of stealing a silver watch. The newspaper informed its readers that Harris was in the habit of taking girls to his house 'at very unseasonable hours'. Burke argued in her defence that there had been several girls with Harris on the night in question, denied all knowledge of the theft, and a month later the case was ignored by the Grand Jury.

9

BENEFIT SOCIETIES

In a society bereft of any form of social security, workers were expected to rely on self-help, and one of the most fascinating manifestations of this – certainly one of the most traditional – was the benefit or friendly societies which originated in those areas which had experienced the earliest impact of the Industrial Revolution.

The earliest known date for a Merthyr society is May 1796, before which it is impossible to gain information, as prior to the Jacobin scares of the 1790s no attempt was made to register such clubs. Between 1796 and the 1830s, Merthyr mirrored the rest of industrial Britain, in as much as the main form of organisation was the local society characterised by its jealous regard for complete independence. 'Each Society had its own funds and was governed by its own rules as decided by its members.' However, due to the fact that many societies did not register while others proved purely transient, it is very difficult to gain an accurate picture of membership and organisation, and all that does survive is a scattering of statistics and an incomplete list of names. During 1803–04, for example, it has been estimated that fifteen societies existed, with a total membership of 1,874. In 1813 this figure had risen by something like 75% to 3,281, and in 1815, 4,115 members were registered.

Each society had its own officers, in most cases two to four stewards who were chosen by rotation for six-month or yearly office, and 'If a member refused to serve when his turn came round, the rules often provided for a considerable fine to be imposed'. Not all officers were chosen by rotation, however, and in cases where societies had presidents as well as stewards they were usually elected by the membership. Similarly, the landlord of the pub in which they invariably met was often the treasurer of the society and kept the box in which they kept their funds, a box which usually incorporated more than one lock so as to minimise the risk of theft. Another exception to the general rule of rotation was the office of clerk or secretary, as:

Obviously this officer had to be able to read and write sufficiently well to keep the club's accounts. Sometimes it was necessary to appoint an outsider as clerk. Even among registered societies the state of the annual returns – or their complete absence year after year – indicated that many clubs had no one competent to act as clerk.

As far as Merthyr is concerned, the set of rules for the Faithful Friends Society revealed that it fined members for refusal to take office and also for non-attendance at their meetings, which involved every member assembling 'between the hours of six and nine in the evening at the house of Mr. William Teague known by the sign of the Swan, on every fourth Saturday'. Its management was conducted by a general purposes committee, which appointed a secretary at an annual salary and two stewards to look after finances. Their president, elected at the annual general meeting, held office for a year and was to 'have insight and inspection of the society's affairs in general and the books and accounts in particular [and] he shall annually prepare a general statement of the funds and effects'.

Throughout the nineteenth century, the major reason for belonging to a friendly society was financial and concerned the provision of sickness or accident benefit and the payment of a funeral allowance. Provision was also made for payment when unemployed, and in certain cases for medicinal relief during periods of disease or debility, but in the main it was the sickness and accident benefit which was of paramount importance. 'Most societies incorporated into their rules some sort of provisions to save them from the most obvious financial hazards', and consequently those applying for membership were required to be in good health and age limits were imposed. For example, of four Merthyr societies for which details were noted in 1850 one imposed an age restriction of between nine and forty-five years of age, another restricted entry to those aged between twelve and thirty-five, the third allowed only those between fifteen and thirty-five and the fourth stated that new members had to be under thirty-five. Health and age qualifications were not the only barriers to membership, and the newly admitted were not eligible for benefit unless they had paid contributions for a minimum stipulated period, often of one or two years' duration, although in the one Merthyr case for which details exist an eighteen-month probation was in operation. Furthermore, contributions had to be paid regularly and lapsed members were denied benefit until they had once more served a probationary period.

In order to ensure that only genuine cases were awarded benefit, none was given to members who were unemployed or were unable to work because of their own laziness or folly, and many societies refused to grant funeral benefit following cases of suicide. Entry into the army or the navy meant automatic disqualification from benefit, and for much the same reasons 'it was quite usual for societies to exclude from membership men following occupations believed to have an unusually heavy incidence of sickness, such as coalmining'. Just what the position was in Merthyr is hard to ascertain, though it may well have been the case that miners and colliers were restricted to their own societies. Whatever the case, there can be no doubting that membership among underground workers was common. In March 1850, when the *Morning Chronicle* interviewed a miner of thirty years' experience, he informed the reporter that he belonged to a benefit society and 'the miners generally belong to such societies'.

Having overcome the barriers to membership, and the restrictions on relief once entitled to benefit:

> The general practice was to offer full sick pay for a limited period such as three months, followed by half pay for another three months. The actual size of the weekly payment would depend on the contributions the members could afford and varied considerably from one society to another.

Before examining contributions, it should be remembered that by the 1840s each of the iron companies had adopted a system whereby a fund was accumulated through weekly stoppages from each employee's pay in order to give sickness or accident relief when necessary. Thus, when the *Morning Chronicle* described the advantages of benefit society membership, it concluded 'By such means, in addition to his allowance from the "fund" at the works, he provides additional resources for the hour of sickness, or when he may be disabled by an accident'. Though a lack of information prevents comparative analysis, it seems likely given the size of the friendly society movement that the relief given by societies was at least equal to, if not greater than, that granted by the various works' funds.

As regards contributions, two factors governed the relationship between what was paid in and the amount decided on for benefit, local custom and competition. In 1852, according to H.A. Bruce, 'the monthly shilling... is the usual contribution', and yet given a situation where numerous societies already existed, as was the case in Merthyr, for a new society to attract members and establish itself it would have to appear more attractive. 'The inducement to join sometimes took the form of offering full sick pay for a longer period, in other instances it took the form of spending a larger part of the monthly contribution in liquor on lodge night'.

This last sentence points to the other form of benefit expected by those who joined friendly societies, that of companionship. Despite continually being castigated by the middle class for meeting in pubs and beerhouses, and for the amount of money they spent on alcohol, the fact was that those who managed such societies knew that although their members:

...expected insurance against sickness and death, they sought more than just this. They were also in quest of those convivial activities and the enrichment of their impoverished social lives which the friendly societies were expected to afford and which the very name seemed to imply.

As far as the social activities were concerned, these revolved around the monthly club night and an annual feast day. Club nights involved far more than simply collecting subscriptions, enrolling members and organising society business. While these were of prime consideration, so important were the convivial demands of full and would-be members that societies spent considerable amounts to ensure such evenings were pleasurable. Because pubs were working-class leisure centres, substantial amounts were inevitably spent on beer. According to Tremenheere, writing in 1840, benefit societies definitely encouraged excessive drinking:

> At the meetings of these clubs... a sum equal to two pence a head for each member, is allowed, out of the funds of the club, to be spent in beer. It seldom happens that more than a third of the members attend at anyone time. It is said that those present expend the sum allowed, and often much more; and that attempts to break through the custom rarely meet with even temporary success.

Tremenheere, an avowed anti-drink campaigner, not only appears to have relied on hearsay evidence but to have ignored the fact that pubs and beerhouses were the only places which could accommodate society meetings. Regarding feast days, the annual holiday was an expected provision and each society laid down elaborate rules governing arrangements and procedures. In time, the celebrations came to include processions and chapel services as well as the feasts themselves, and the evidence contained in the *Merthyr Guardian* suggests that a carnival atmosphere prevailed.

Given that the clubs were essentially social bodies, it is not surprising that, quite apart from the financial aid due to the family of a member upon his death, the society was also expected to ensure that its departed colleague had a fitting send-off. Some required its stewards and certain or even all of its members to attend the ceremony and fined those who neglected to observe such rules:

> Some societies laid down items of dress which the club mourners were to wear while others found it sufficient... that their members should merely appear clean and decent for the occasion. In some cases, societies purchased the symbols of mourning and appointed someone to take charge of them.

By far the greatest problem facing these societies was their lack of knowledge concerning how much money was needed in order to meet unknown future commitments. They charged flat rates regardless of age and therefore ignored the fact that as members grew older, so susceptibility to illness – and consequently the burden on society funds – would increase. As H.A. Bruce pointed out: 'The payments made by the members are barely sufficient to meet the disbursements of a club which has prolonged its existence beyond a few years'. Because of the increasing costs involved many clubs failed, as they were unable to attract young men into an ageing society. The competitive element, whereby societies attempted to boost membership by offering more attractive benefits, must surely have added to these problems by placing a proportionately greater burden on the funds of such clubs.

Another recurring problem was that societies relied on regular contributions, and yet during times of depression wages were cut drastically and hundreds were thrown out of work, placing an enormous strain on their finances. As the *Merthyr Guardian* noted in August 1842: 'There is scarcely a society of the scores existing in this town and neighbourhood but that the cash in hand has decreased to a considerable extent'. In 1850 one miner told the *Morning Chronicle* that 'the men are now too poor to continue their payments, and so must lose the advantage of them'. Furthermore, during depressions societies faced with empty coffers were frequently unable to pay the benefit due to members who had contributed regularly, and cases such as the following appeared with depressing regularity. In September 1842, a widow, Margaret Morgan, took two stewards of a benefit society held at the Miners Arms to court, for the alleged non-payment of £8 due to her upon her husband's death. 'The defence set up was, that there were not sufficient funds, which was proved by the production of the club books'.

It was due to such shortcomings that the mid-nineteenth century witnessed a very rapid increase in the number of clubs affiliated to national societies. 'While the small bodies are decaying or sinking into neglect, the affiliated bodies are growing rapidly in strength, and extending their branches into every part of the kingdom', reported a Select Committee in 1847, and Merthyr was certainly no exception. Of all the nationwide societies, it was the Manchester Unity of the Order of Oddfellows which seems to have had the most success in Merthyr. Founded around 1810, it was not until after a reorganisation of its central government in 1827 that the Manchester Unity spread beyond the north-west, but by 1850 Merthyr had at least twenty-five lodges. Though the 'Cambrian' lodge was the first to appear in Merthyr, the exact date of its foundation is unknown. According to an article from the *Oddfellows Magazine*, quoted by a speaker at an anniversary dinner in 1850, two Oddfellow lodges existed in south Wales in 1830, and it seems likely that at least one of these was based in Merthyr, for two years later the funeral of an Oddfellow in Merthyr was attended by 170 brethren from four lodges 'excellent and chaste in their deportment'. The movement contin-ued to progress and by April 1835 there were 759 Oddfellows in the town, two years later there were 1,388 and by 1839 membership had risen to 2,043.

If the growth of the Oddfellows was rapid, so too was that of the Carmarthen Union of True Ivorites. The first lodge opened in May 1839; by July 1840 there were at least eight others and in September 1840, when the *Ivor ap Alan* lodge opened, the *Merthyr Guardian* drew attention to the Ivorites' success by informing its readers, 'This is the 122nd lodge that has been opened in the short space of three years in the Carmarthen Unity, South Wales.' By the late 1840s the Oddfellows and Ivorites had been joined by at least thirteen lodges of the Ancient Order of Druids, at least one court of the Ancient Order of Foresters and three tents of the Independent Order of Rechabites, Salford Unity.

As regards organisation, the Oddfellows may be taken as fairly typical. They were controlled by a Grand Master and a central Board of Directors, 'elected by the Annual Moveable Committee, the latter being composed of delegates from all the districts... The district committees in their turn were composed of representatives from the lodges'. Though apparently democratic, by placing control outside each district the two biggest affiliated orders, the Oddfellows and the Royal Order of Foresters, suf-fered from a series of secessionist moves and schisms which gave rise to the Ancient Order of Foresters, as in Dowlais, and to the Druids and Ivorites of Merthyr generally. In each case, however, the advantages of belonging to an affiliated society remained the same.

The decade between 1835 and 1845 saw the most important period of growth for the affiliated societies in Merthyr, as in the rest of Britain, and by common consent the reason for this was the Poor Law Amendment Act. Writing about Merthyr in 1842, R.H. Franks stated, 'It is said that a very strong prejudice, conceived against the New Poor-Law Bill, has given an impulse to... [benefit society] establishment', and there can be no doubt that the workings of the Act increased the threat of poverty in working-class eyes and encouraged workers to group together for self-defence. Poverty was no stranger in Merthyr and neither was distress, as is borne out by the violence of 1801, 1816 and 1831. After 1834, however, the new and much-hated dimension of removal and workhouse came to haunt working people, and for many, membership of the affiliated orders appeared the best means of security.

When attempting to analyse why the nationwide societies were so much more attractive than the local ones, both financial and social factors emerge. In the first instance, the main advantage offered by affiliated orders was their pooling of funds, whereby a general funeral fund for that district was established into which each lodge paid its members' contributions and upon which each lodge could draw to meet its requirements. It was basically a case of there being, and being seen to be, financial safety in numbers. Furthermore, the existence of a relatively substantial amount of money enabled district officers to invest funds. In Merthyr this took the form of societies building houses and using the rents to relieve members. The size of funds, and therefore of society security, allowed stewards to act in a much less restricted way. In October 1841, for example, after an explosion which claimed several lives, the *Merthyr Guardian* carried the following:

> Odd Fellows – one of the poor men who was killed at the Penydarren works happened to have drawn his burial money, £10 in advance, and had repaid £2 by instalments: he was therefore £8 in debt. To the great credit of the order, the Brethren have ordered the full sum of £10 to be paid to the widow who has a large family – they have taken into consideration the melancholy circumstances of the case.

It was the better-paid urban workers who were first attracted to the affiliated orders and in particular to the Oddfellows. This was because not only were they able to pay regular cash contributions but the nationwide societies were able to offer some provision for mobility. Both the Oddfellows and the Foresters and, in all probability, the Druids and Ivorites developed a system by which a member who was moving could obtain a clearance certificate showing that he had met all liabilities to his existing lodge or court and present this to the lodge or court in his new district. Not only did such certificates help resettle workers displaced by unemployment, but, at a time when the vicissitudes of the trade cycle forced even the most skilled workers to tramp the south Wales coalfield and beyond, the travelling card issued by the Manchester Unity whereby a member could claim a travelling allowance from any lodge or the Foresters' issue of licenses and cheques for the same purpose (in both cases paid for out of central funds) must have been a more than welcome addition to the benefits acquired through membership of the affiliated orders.

For all their financial benefits, as was the case with the local clubs it was companionship which attracted workers to the national societies, and in this respect, by reason of their very size, they were able to offer considerably more. Apart from the monthly club nights and the annual feasts, the large orders organised social events, of which, in our period, by far the greatest was the Oddfellows excursion to Swansea in August 1855. On Monday 15 August at 6a.m., some 4,600 Oddfellows and their families marched in procession from Merthyr and Dowlais to the market square and on to the railway station, where two trains, numbering fifty-four carriages, took them to Swansea. After being greeted by the Swansea lodges, a huge procession was drawn up, which, 'having first favoured Greenhill with its presence, paraded the town. The streets... were gaily decorated with banners, flags, etc., many of them having appropriate devices... "Welcome to Swansea" etc.' Having marched around the town, they congregated on the sand dunes near the docks, where addresses of welcome were heard. When these were concluded the formal part of the day was at an end and:

> …all kinds of amusements that were to be had of a rational character were eagerly sought after by the visitants. There were omnibuses to the Mumbles, famous for its oysters… the doors of the Royal Institution were thrown open… and, above all, there was a 'grand concert' [featuring the Cyfarthfa and Dowlais bands] at the Town Hall at 3 o'clock, and several trips in the bay…

The festivities continued throughout the evening and though one train returned to Merthyr at 11p.m., the second, and largest, did not arrive back until after midnight.

The Affiliated Orders were able to offer more than enhanced social events. They inherited and cultivated distinctive mystiques which were developed through lectures, oaths, passwords, particular ways of shaking hands and so forth into elaborate forms of ritual. Initiation ceremonies involving blindfolds and sacred promises, the wearing of distinctive and ornate uniforms and the accumulation of banners and regalia were widespread in Merthyr. When in July 1840 the brethren of the True Ivorites met at their different lodge rooms at 8.30a.m. one Monday in order to initiate several new members, the occasion was deemed important enough to warrant 'Divine Service' at Bethesda Chapel and a grand parade of 846 Ivorites in nine different lodges through the streets of Merthyr and Dowlais. The whole affair was faithfully described by the *Merthyr Guardian* – 'Ivor Dowlais with their Pant Cad Ivor motto on their banner, their treasurer bearing his golden key; the officers with their supporters and swords' – and a few weeks later the *Guardian* could hardly disguise its disappointment when, on the second anniversary of the Dowlais Druids, the three lodges walked in procession to Bethania Chapel: 'But the Derwyddon did not wear the robes of their order in public'.

Upon analysing this delight in ritual, two underlying factors emerge. In the first instance, its use fostered a sense of fellowship among members, which was enhanced by the knowledge that those outside the brotherhood could not share in its mysteries. Secondly, the environment must not be forgotten and the societies helped to provide a touch of colour and ceremony, as well as providing an outlet for organisational ability. It was not just the physical environment which was bleak in working-class Merthyr: so too were the prospects of security and opportunities for recreation. In the harsh world of a working class deprived of most outlets for control and self-expression, the friendly societies served as an institutional focus for large sections of the workforce.

One should not assume that with the coming of the affiliated orders the financial problems which beset the local clubs disappeared, and the development of the Oddfellows, Druids, Ivorites and Foresters was by no means continuous in Merthyr. The greater sums of cash involved prompted at least one case of theft when, in 1842, the secretary and a member of one of the Oddfellows' lodges attempted to flee to America after absconding with £146 belonging to their lodge. However, by far the greatest problem continued to be depression in the iron trade. In 1842 those societies which had invested in property went through a traumatic period due to their lack of liquid capital, and the unprecedented slump of the late 1840s and early 1850s – coinciding as it did with the worst epidemic of cholera ever to hit the town and which alone broke many of the benefit societies – saw even the largest of the affiliated orders in serious financial difficulties.

Faced with a massive debt of £313 after the expenditure of no less than £440 in funeral benefits during the epidemic of 1849, Merthyr's Oddfellows held a public tea party to raise funds, preceded by a huge procession which was as much an expression of endurance, determination and pride as it was a demonstration on behalf of widows and orphans. Though successful in as much as the tea party raised £170 after expenses, there can be no doubt that the cholera, followed by the deep depression, continued to put a check on society development. As far as the Oddfellows were concerned, for example, whereas membership had spiralled from 759 in 1835 to over 2,000 in 1839, by 1850 their numbers had fallen to 1,851.

Just as the problems which caused so much distress to the independent societies remained to hinder the progress of the affiliated orders, so too it would be a mistake to assume that the emergence of the latter signalled the end for the purely local clubs. In July 1844 the *Merthyr Guardian* reported enthusiastically on the recently established 'funeral club' at Dowlais, which already had 114 members each contributing 1s to every funeral. Two months later a similar club opened in Merthyr, and by August 1845 it had more than 480 members and was turning away hopeful applicants, 'as the full number had already been enrolled'. Thus some societies at least insisted on restricted membership, although whether this was an attempt to limit the possible financial outlay or simply to promote their exclusive nature is impossible to determine.

By far the most successful societies outside those of the affiliated orders were those established in the name of temperance, and the greatest of these, the Rechabites, formed yet another national order. Established in 1835, the Independent Order of Rechabites was founded by teetotallers who realised that when belonging to other societies they were exposed to the temptation of drink every time they attended lodge meetings. In order to overcome such temptations, each 'tent', as their lodges were called, met in halls or rooms which had no association with alcohol and each member took the following pledge:

I hereby declare that I will abstain from all intoxicating liquors, except in religious ordi-
nances or when prescribed by a physician, nor engage in the traffic in them, but in all
possible ways will discountenance the use, manufacture and sale of them, and to the

utmost of my power I will endeavour to spread the principles of abstinence from all intoxicating liquors.

The first Merthyr tent, the 'Tydfil', which met at a room in Pontmorlais, was established in 1841 and had somewhere in the region of fifty members at the time of its first anniversary. By August 1842 this had been augmented by the 'Virtue' and 'Juvenile' tents and two years later the 'Tydfil' and 'Virtue' tents were reported to have a combined membership of around 150 people. Though unquestionably small when compared with the Oddfellows, the significance of the Rechabites and of such societies as the Coedycymmer Temperance Benefit Society, the Plymouth Temperance Society and the Merthyr Total Abstinence Society lies in their impact on the temperance movement generally in Merthyr, as they demonstrated that working men could still enjoy the financial benefits, the companionship and the ritual of friendly societies without having to resort to pubs or devote a proportion of their contributions to drink. An alternative was available.

As far as the size of individual clubs is concerned, the scarcity of evidence means one must rely on generalisations based on the limited data which has survived. For example, in July 1848 Dowlais societies marched in celebration of Guest's successful renegotiation of the Dowlais lease and though the number of Oddfellows was not reported, the names and the number of marchers of no fewer than seventeen other clubs were given. In overall terms, the average individual contingent was around the eighty-three mark, but there was considerable disparity between clubs. Of the seventeen, four were represented by between twenty-four and fifty members, seven had between sixty and eighty, five had between 100 and 150, and one, the Dowlais Firemen's Society, had 200.

As regards the membership of benefit societies, the growth of the affiliated orders, the existence of firemen's societies and the miner's comment 'miners generally belong to such societies' all point to the fact that the skilled and semi-skilled were well represented, but, given the weight of contemporary opinion, it would be a mistake to assume that membership was in any way restricted. In 1840 Tremenheere argued, 'The habit of belonging to benefit clubs prevails very extensively', and in 1842, even during depression, R.H. Franks reported membership as being very common 'amongst all classes of the working population'. In December 1848 the *Merthyr Guardian* stated 'There are in Merthyr District, comprising Merthyr, Dowlais, Aberdare, Hirwaun and part of Gellygaer, 144 benefit societies, containing not less than 13,342 members', the majority of whom would have lived in Merthyr and Dowlais, and the *Morning Chronicle* noted that in Merthyr 'the workman is always a member of one, sometimes of two Benefit Societies'.

Even the most insecure section of the workforce, the casually employed women, were represented. Even when they did work women were seldom the main breadwinners, and the married woman suffered from 'a legal incapacity to acquire and hold earnings independently of her husband. From the moment she acquired any earnings they became the property of her husband'. In England, due to these circumstances, 'the typical local friendly society did not admit women to membership', and, though some solely for women did emerge, they were very few in number. In Merthyr, however, the evidence points to a fairly sustained tradition of female club activity. Of the 116 societies to have registered between 1796 and 1848, twenty-one, or 18%, were female. As early as 1800 a Women's Friendly Society was meeting at the house of Thomas Miles, innkeeper, and information presented by the *Merthyr Guardian* shows that this tradition was still strong in the 1840s. In August 1843 it reported on the anniversary celebrations of several female clubs without, unfortunately, naming them. It also provided information on the Female Ivorites in October 1841, as well as the Loyal Alfreds Lady Lodge in September 1846. Interestingly, the Female Ivorites and Alfreds suggest the emergence of women's societies modelled on those of the affiliated orders with whom they certainly marched. In August 1847, during a report on an anniversary parade involving 'great numbers' of clubmen and women, the newspaper noted 'two or three clubs of females' and informed its readers that of all the participants it had been the ladies who:

> …found most favour in our sight. And it must be admitted that they formed quite a
> pleasing spectacle. Black shawls and white, blue shawls and grey, with dresses of various
> colours gave a charming variety to these long files of fine women and pretty girls.

This report, apart from indicating that uniforms were as common among female societies as they were for their male counterparts, gave some hint as to the numbers of women involved. Two weeks later this was reinforced when a report on the sixth-anniversary celebrations of the 'Temple of Love' female society mentioned that over 130 members sat for dinner at the Morlais Castle Inn. As to why women joined such societies:

> The main object of the early female societies was to provide benefit for the 'lying-
> in-month'… [but] In addition to following convivial practices associated with male
> societies, the societies for females also showed most of the other organizational and prac-
> tical characteristics of societies for men…

By the 1840s it appears that women who did not work also joined clubs, which, in a very real sense, were the only organisations other than religious ones to cater for the social needs of women.

Up until now, membership has been discussed in relation to status, occupation and sex, but two other factors may also need consideration: neighbourhood and birthplace. A workman residing in Georgetown would be unlikely to enroll in a Dowlais society, and vice versa, while as early as 1804 a Pembrokeshire Society was registered in Merthyr and in January 1850 the *Merthyr Guardian* reported on the existence of a Caledonian Lodge for those of Scottish origins. In many ways neighbourhood and birthplace were not unrelated; the clanship of the Welsh has already been noted and, just as chapel membership provided the newly arrived immigrant with a passport of sorts to society, so too did the benefit society.

Before concluding, an examination of the hostile stance of the middle class provides a fascinating insight into the character of those who controlled Merthyr. That their attack on insobriety ignored the lack of alternative recreational facilities has already been noted, while their stake in the town's alcohol trade was extensive. Essentially, however, what lay behind such criticism was the working-class rejection of enshrined middle-class norms and standards. As H.A. Bruce expressed it, 'the Club system has many and serious drawbacks. In the first place it does not assist the careful and temperate workman in making himself independent'. Whereas if that same man were to turn instead to a Savings Bank he would reap a great benefit, for:

> …we must not suppose that the man who sees his little capital steadily increasing in the course of years, would limit his savings to the monthly shilling…the pleasure of possessing something he can call his own adds to his desires of possessing more, leads to the foundation of those temperate, self-denying, habits which not only tend to gratify that desire, but lead to the formation of a manly, independent character.

He continued by emphasising his belief in the 'decisive superiority which Savings Banks possess over clubs', stating that it was due to the former's encouragement of 'the habit of providence… the *habit* of thrift is the important object. It gives a sense of dignity, a spirit of independence and self reliance…'.

Once again, however, such arguments were very largely invalid, as Merthyr did not possess any facilities for the small saver. A Savings Bank had been established in 1836 under the presidency of Guest and in October 1837 the *Merthyr Guardian* could report 'Deposits are rapidly on the increase and amount to a very considerable sum'. In 1839 Tremenheere stated that port 146, 'Colliers, miners, and others connected with the iron works', as well as six friendly societies were among those who deposited £3,391 into its care, and in March 1843, at the nadir of the depression, the paper could report on a healthy balance of £4,380 6s 9d. Despite such a promising start, however, the Bank collapsed dramatically soon afterwards when its manager absconded with £2,000.

Not only were benefit societies seen to hinder the progress of middle-class ideals but, as far as many of the latter were concerned, the lodges and courts provided a natural camouflage for working-class political and trade union organisations, suspicions which during the 1830s and 1840s would appear to have been well-founded. In national terms, 'where for some reason local societies were confined to men of one particular trade, at times they developed into trade unions' and, given Merthyr's one-industry labour force, the clear evidence of craft-based friendly societies and the well-documented evidence for trade union and Chartist activity during the period, it would seem that Merthyr provided a good example. It should be noted, however, that by no means all of Merthyr's benefit societies were sympathetic to Chartist or trade unionist aims. As early as 1831 the *Merlin* reported 'A genuine Oddfellow... will never trespass beyond the pale of the law in attempting to redress any private injury or public grievance'. In 1839 the *Merthyr Guardian* published a letter extolling the peaceful, anti-union, respectable nature of the Oddfellows, one of whose lodges was named 'The Lord John Russell'. Similarly, among the Druids, several lodges were named after ironmasters and their families, and the Cyfarthfa firemen chose Robert Crawshay as their patron. Having said as much, it should be remembered that during the period of the most intensive growth among the affiliated orders they were unable to register and thus were denied any of the benefits held out to Registered Societies. In view of this, the spectacular growth of the affiliated orders 'forms an interesting commentary on the attitude of contemporary working men to the State'.

It is also worth illustrating that Merthyr's workers were not unaware of the political implications of independent organisation. In 1850, the *Morning Chronicle*, when discussing the absence of a Savings Bank, was 'told that the men, from an apprehension that the masters might learn the amount of their savings and lessen their wages, never favoured establishments of this nature', while two years later H.A. Bruce was forced to admit:

> It is, I am sorry to say, a prevalent opinion that one principal reason why no Savings Bank, and Provident Funds in connection with it, have been established in Merthyr, is the jealousy and fear of the masters, lest the men, as a body, should become too rich, and so be enabled to support themselves during strikes, and force the masters to accept their terms.

That such ideas could find root in Merthyr says much about the level of paranoia in the town.

The middle class openly displayed a strange ambivalence, in as much as they too joined societies for social and occupational reasons. As early as 1804, a 'Tradesmen's' benefit society was registered in Merthyr, and in the 1840s organisations such as the Good Samaritans Tradesmen's benefit society existed in both Merthyr and Dowlais. By the 1840s a whole raft of organisations had emerged designed to further middle-class interests in cultural, charitable, temperance and religious affairs, as well as purely social ones such as the Saint Leger club and the Merthyr Cricket club. Without any doubt, however, the most influential one was the Loyal Cambrian Lodge of Free and Accepted Masons. Entirely restricted to Merthyr's professional and managerial elite, the masons held prestigious social events such as the ball in February 1841 to celebrate the christening of the 'Princess Royal of England', and displayed all the mystery and ritual so beloved by working-class societies. In December 1849, for example, they marched in procession from their headquarters, the Bush Inn, to the new Anglican Church, led by E.J. Hutchings, the principal agent for the Dowlais Iron Company, and the 'Provincial Grand Master for the South Wales, Eastern Division'.

So the middle class adopted a characteristically hypocritical stance towards the benefit societies. The criticism of the drinking ignored the reality of working men's recreational facilities; their cynicism concerning the financial stability of the clubs was proven unfounded by the resilience of the affiliated orders; and their own free-masons practiced rituals just as elaborate as any found in the lodge rooms or courts of working-class Merthyr. With this in mind, it is not unreasonable to suggest that the real reason for this antipathy lay in their distrust of anything which displayed even the slightest hint of workers' control. The very success and stability of the clubs, their nationwide connections and their organisational flair constituted a threat to the self-appointed supremacy of the middle class.

10

EDUCATION

There are few, if any towns, where the necessity of providing for the instruction of the very young children of the poor, is more glaring than at Merthyr Tydfil.
Merthyr Guardian, 14 March 1840

In all the various Parliamentary Reports on the state of south Wales which emerged during the mid-nineteenth century, one theme remained constant: the general ignorance of the working class. It was this, above all else, which led to the insurrection at Newport, the continuing support for Chartism, the widespread drunkenness, immorality and vice, the poor standards of housekeeping, the careless acceptance of debt, the reckless disregard for personal safety at work, the brazen flouting of the law and the general turbulence of the region.

When, in 1840, Tremenheere first examined the provision of education in south Wales, he took the number of children aged between three and twelve as being somewhere in the region of one-fifth of the total population. On that basis, he calculated that throughout the area over 70% of working-class children did not receive any day-school education at all, and as a result he informed his superiors:

> ...that of the adult working population a large proportion could neither read nor write; that very many had only acquired the art of knowing the letters and words; and that very few could read with ease to themselves, and with understanding.

According to Tremenheere, this ignorance was the direct result of working-class antipathy to education. As the vast majority of parents had never received any formal instruction, they failed to see why their children needed any. Furthermore, given the iron industry's reliance on child labour, parents knew that 'their children are sure of being able to gain an ample livelihood at an early age, without the aid of "learning"', while as far as girls were concerned parents 'think instruction of any kind very little necessary for the girls, whose assistance at home they are unwilling to dispense with'. As for adults:

> Their occupations are such, that in general the absence of any previous mental culture is no obstacle to their obtaining good employment... Even those individuals among them who are appointed to situations of responsibility, possess in general very slight attainments. It occurred recently in one of the largest works, that, out of eleven competitors for a situation of that nature, only one could write.

Turning to what educational opportunities did exist, there can be no doubt that Sunday schools provided the most important focus for working-class education. G.S. Kenrick's analysis of the 1841 census revealed a total of 4,931 Sunday scholars for Merthyr and Dowlais, and he argued that almost 80% of those who did receive some form of instruction did so in Sunday schools. The prime movers here were the non-conformist chapels. In 1840 Tremenheere found that of Merthyr's nineteen Sunday schools seventeen were organised by dissenters, while some idea of the scale of the movement was provided by the *Morning Chronicle* when it reported in April 1850:

> The English and Welsh Wesleyans educate 550 scholars. The Welsh Baptists have 1,554 Sunday Scholars, The English Baptists 180, The Welsh Independents have 2,067 (one school at 'Bethania Chapel' has 600 Sunday Scholars); the English Independents 100. The Welsh Calvinistic Methodists educate 810 scholars; one chapel alone, 'Hermon Chapel', accommodates not less than 500, and has 105 teachers. The Primitive Methodists have 40 scholars, and the Roman Catholics 60.

As far as the organisation and curriculum of these schools was concerned, the great majority of teachers were volunteers who aided their ministers and deacons in the teaching of both children and adults, for the latter were just as welcome. Tremenheere indicated that something like two and a half hours was the usual period allocated to meetings and continued by stating, 'Unquestionably these schools have done inestimable service in communicating widely among the rising generation the elements of religious knowledge. But the instruction conveyed in them appeared to be limited by the want of books, maps and other necessary apparatus'. Tremenheere found this to be especially regrettable, 'as so large a portion of whatever information the working classes here obtain from direct instruction comes through the medium of these schools'.

Instruction was not just limited by a lack of equipment and apparatus, however; the religious dogmas of the most influential sects also played a part in restricting what was taught, in as much as the ability to read was encouraged but the ability to write was strictly limited by the belief that writing was essentially a secular art, which held no place in spiritual teaching. This may well explain why Kenrick found that nearly twice as many people could read as could write. In spite of such shortcomings, the role of dissent in the initiation and provision of working-class education cannot be belittled, for without chapel involvement of a sustained and highly organised nature the vast majority of Merthyr's working people would have received no education at all.

As regards day schools, Tremenheere found a total of forty-seven private schools in 1840, in the majority of which conditions were such that he concluded:

> It is manifest that, under the most favourable circumstances, the instruction offered to the children of the labouring classes… could not be expected to have much permanent effect in disciplining the mind, raising the taste and habits, and correcting the disposition.

Of the teachers, five were dismissed as being 'under the care of females' and of the remaining forty-two:

> Sixteen had been unsuccessful in some retail trade. Eleven had been miners or labouring men, who had lost their health, or met with accidents in the works, and had subsequently 'got a little learning' to enable them to keep a school. Ten had received some instruction, with the view to adopt the profession of teaching. Four were ministers of dissenting places of worship [and] One was the clerk of a parish church.

Each pupil usually had to pay between 3d and 8d a week for the privilege of being taught in rooms which were:

> …for the most part, dirty and close… The books being provided by the parents, mere fragments consisting of a few soiled leaves, appeared to be generally deemed sufficient to answer the purpose for which the children were sent to school… In many, silence was only maintained for a few moments at a time, by loud exclamations and threats… In one, a deserted chapel, half the space was occupied with hay piled up to the roof… In eighteen only were the principles of English grammar taught: in four only was a map of any kind used.

Given such conditions, Tremenheere concluded: 'they seemed in general to be not so much places of instruction, as of periodical confinement for children whose parents were at work during the day'.

Seven years later commissioners found thirty-seven private schools providing for working-class children, of which twenty-one were dame schools. In these the school-room was generally a kitchen, 'and instruction was given upon no plan or system whatever. Of the entire number; not more than three can be pronounced even moderately good; twenty-six indifferent; and eight very bad'. Without further elaboration, private schools for working-class children cannot have made anything more than a very marginal impact.

Given the dearth of educational provision within the town, the importance of the Dowlais schools cannot be overstated. From the standpoint of establishing schools for the education of the working classes, the Guest family of Dowlais was probably the most important, and also the most progressive, in the industrial history not only of south Wales but of the whole of Britain during the nineteenth century. The Guest schools, the largest of their kind in the country, achieved as much fame as the Guest ironworks, and the educational scheme planned and implemented by Sir John and Lady Charlotte Guest was the most comprehensive and practical ever to be attempted during the nineteenth century.

As early as 1814 the Dowlais Company had opened a school for its workers' children, and by 1818 the idea of establishing a National School connected with the Company, run on Anglican lines, was firmly established, and applications for positions within the school were already being made. In 1828 the Dowlais boys' and girls' schools replaced the older one. Instruction was 'conducted on Dr. Bell's system' and 'At that period, the attendance of the boys was from 50 to 60; of girls, from 40 to 50. The payment was 1d. per week, evenly spent on books and rewards'. By the early 1840s, however, the Guests were admitting that 'The means of education for the labouring classes in the large village of Dowlais, with a population of about 12,000 were very meagre and unsatisfactory' and they were also concerned by the long waiting lists for admission. Consequently, they decided to build new and larger schools in which the standard of instruction was designed to be 'well-calculated to meet the wants of the labouring portion of the community, and to be of a quality – both from the religious and secular point of view – to leave a lasting impression of good on the minds of all who partake of it'.

The opening of the new boys' and girls' schools in 1844 and of an infants' school in 1846 saw the foundations of the Guests' scheme being laid. The infants' school, at Gwernllwyn, had one trained master who was aided by two female assistants and an average daily attendance of 200 children, the majority of whom, unless backward, left at six years of age. Though it came in for some criticism in 1847, when commissioners asserted that its classroom was 'a small room of a very inconvenient description', on the positive side it was 'well supplied with apparatus, and the master appeared an efficient one'. It also boasted an enclosed playground which had been newly laid with broken slag, offering a 'dry surface, though rather a rough one, for children to play upon'.

As regards the girls' school, the 1847 Report found it to be:

> ...well lighted and ventilated. It has the advantage of three adult teachers, two of whom have been trained... Each afternoon the girls sew from half past three to quarter past four. On Fridays they bring work from their own homes. There were maps of the World and Palestine on the walls. Arithmetic is taught both from the board and slates. The children were neat and clean, and the school quiet and orderly.

The commissioner was not entirely satisfied, however, as he 'expected a great deal more proficiency than I found in this school'.

Turning to the boys' school, this was divided into upper and lower sections, which at the time of the *Morning Chronicle's* visit provided instruction for forty and 130 pupils respectively. The 1847 report told of how the two sections:

> ...occupy two unequal parts of a big room well lighted and ventilated. The entrance is into the larger part, or lower school, which is fitted up with a gallery, running longitudinally and divided, like boxes of a theatre, into transverse sections, by curtains. Each class has a section. The curtains however can be drawn back and two or more classes united for simultaneous instruction. The teacher of each class occupies the floor in front of its section of the gallery... Opening out of this, and partitioned off from it, is the upper school room, which, in shape, is nearly square, and also fitted with a gallery. It contains a piano, drawings from solid figures, done by the boys, upon the walls; maps and every kind of needful apparatus. It is by far the best provided school-room which I have seen in Wales.

Throughout the boys' school all instruction was undertaken by trained teachers and its curriculum set it apart from any other school. In the lower school boys were taught reading, writing, arithmetic, English and Scriptural history and the Church catechism, while in the upper school, which boasted 'a very well furnished laboratory', arithmetic, algebra, etymology, mensuration, music mechanics, reading, writing, drawing, Scripture history, religious knowledge and English history were all studied. It specialised in the teaching of science and mathematics, and later trigonometry and logarithms were introduced. Throughout both sections 'discipline and good order prevailed. The boys were neat and tidy in appearance, and were much interested in their work. The Rector of Dowlais, The Rev. E. Jenkins, came to give religious instruction twice per week'.

Before continuing, it should be made clear that only a small minority of boys were taught in the upper school and that most received only elementary instruction. In the three years prior to the 1847 commission, for example, of the 110 boys who had left the Dowlais schools over 30% did so without even experiencing the first class of the lower school, and of the remainder over 70% failed to reach the upper school.

It was because of this early withdrawal that the Guests laid such an emphasis on the provision of infants' schools. Well staffed and properly organised, they would do a great deal 'to improve the character of the preparative instruction... towards carrying on the education of young children by ten years of age to a higher point than was obtained previously'. Consequently, by February 1849 some 467 children were being taught in four infants' schools established at Dowlais, Gwernllwyn, Gellifaelog and Banwen. Because of this emphasis on infant instruction, Matthew Hurst, headmaster of the Dowlais Schools, maintained that even when most children left school at nine or ten the majority could generally read and write fairly well 'and would also be able to do the simple rules of arithmetic'.

However, the Guests remained dissatisfied and, as a result, perhaps the most ambitious element of their scheme came into operation: provision for adult education. By 1849 both male and female evening classes had been established for the benefit of those who were employed by the Dowlais Company, although the female class did accept 'servant girls and girls who had left the day school'. Classes were held in the school buildings from October to April each year and were conducted by five teachers and a superintendent in the male classes and seven teachers and a superintendent in the female ones. As for the curriculum, the men and boys were taught 'to read and write, cipher, History, Geography, and Grammar' while the women and girls studied 'reading, writing, arithmetic, geography, history, needlework and cutting out'. As in all the day schools, religious instruction was also given great emphasis. Attendance for both men and women was said to be high. The *Morning Chronicle* maintained:

> The adult school for women has an average attendance of 100 [while] the average attendance of men was for some time 170; it has been now reduced to 110, this was accounted for... by a statement that there had been a want of efficient teachers, but I was told this would be obviated in future. It was cheering to learn that this falling off was not the fault of the workmen.

The Dowlais adult classes were widely acclaimed by both residents and visitors alike. The Revd Jenkins, for example, asserted that the evening schools had done much good: 'The Shopkeepers... have more than once in the course of conversation intimated that the effect of them has been greatly to improve the language and conduct of young men and women in the streets and everywhere', while in 1853 a schools' inspector reported that the evening classes were 'producing highly beneficial results. Everything pleased me... the earnestness of purpose shown by all engaged in them...

the good behaviour, and cheerfulness of pupils and teachers… and the progress made'.

When it came to finances, great store was placed on the fact that the Guests provided free instruction, equipment and materials, as well as the actual school buildings themselves. However, the overwhelming majority of those who attended both day and evening schools were either employed by or were the children of people who worked for the Dowlais Company, and as such had their wages automatically docked in order to finance both the sick fund and the schools. Furthermore, Commissioner Lingen, reporting in 1847, stated that 'Besides the stoppage upon wages, the children pay, in the infant, girls; and lower boys schools, 1d. and in the upper boys' school 2d. per week'. According to the Company's own records during the year 1848–49, the total expenditure on education was £521 7s 2d, of which £342 17s, or 66%, came from stoppages and the small government grant for which the schools were eligible.

It would be foolish, however, to attempt to measure the Guests' contribution in purely financial terms, for if it had not been for them then very few educational opportunities would have existed, and in this the driving force was Lady Charlotte Guest, whose efforts during the 1840s and 1850s ensured that the Company schools became an educational showpiece of such renown. Though it was her husband who initiated the schools, she 'developed them, secured new buildings, and extorted a more liberal curriculum. It was most certainly her inspiration and vision that called into being the extensive evening schools, which culminated in an elaborate and complete educational structure'. Throughout 1849, 'so enthusiastic was she that she took to visiting some of the schools every day. She even, from time to time, gave lectures or lessons herself', all of which seems to have been regarded by her husband as being too enthusiastic, for he is reported to have 'found the extent of her school activities excessive, and she undertook to limit her evening school visits to two a week'.

Matrimonial tension apart, the Guests' educational scheme was a resounding success. It provided Dowlais workers and their families with opportunities for instruction very largely denied elsewhere in the town. It recognised that child employment meant more emphasis being placed on infant schooling and supplemented this with adult education, and it endeavoured to provide equipment and materials of a high standard under the supervision of properly trained teachers working in purpose-built schoolrooms. Given the prevailing indifference and apathy, it was unique: 'It was without question, the largest and most successful experiment in the field of elementary (and to some extent higher) education, during a century which was more concerned with the minimum in educational attainment and school provision'.

Once the Dowlais schools were seen to be of value, others imitated them. When the Revd Campbell first came to Merthyr he found two National schools which, between them, had a capacity of 350 children, 'but they were neither of them well filled, and one (the boys school) was in a bad state of repair'. By 1850, however, he felt more confident: 'I am happy to state that, in more efficient hands, there has been a considerable improvement both in the attendance and in the progress of the children'. As soon as the new Church was completed he organised the fundraising and building of new schools for 150 boys and an equal number of girls, and at the time of the *Morning Chronicle*'s visit its reporter found the schools staffed by a small number of paid superintendents augmented by something in the region of 120 volunteer teachers, 'who gave their services for one or more nights in the week'. At the boys' school:

> I found that the average attendance was about 120 daily. The boys were mostly well clothed and clean; only one of them was barefoot. The master, who is from the training school at Westminster, observed that they were children who 'but for the school, would have been running the streets'. The course of instruction at present comprises reading, writing and arithmetic, geography, and the outlines of history. When the highest-class boys are sufficiently advanced, they will be taught grammar. I tried the second class, consisting of boys from seven to nine years old, in the Gospel of St. Luke, and they acquitted themselves very creditably, reading without hesitation, and correctly... As a body, the master informed me, the children show great acuteness and capacity.

In the girls' school the mistress was also Westminster-trained and the curriculum was more or less the same as for the boys, 'with the addition of the feminine arts of sewing and knitting... Most of them were sewing when I entered. They may bring work of their own, but they are mostly occupied on work for a town charity for supplying the poor with clothes'.

The Revd Campbell took pains to tell the *Morning Chronicle* that even before they were opened as day schools the buildings had been used for adult evening classes, and it was these which most impressed the reporter:

> I could scarcely credit my senses when the governess told me that the girls I saw were those whom I have formerly described as stacking coal for coking, loading trams, and cleaning ore on the slopes of the mountain, black, coarsely clad, and repulsive. Here they were clean, orderly, and well dressed. The average attendance at present is 60. They meet 5 nights in the week... from October to June. The Governess... said 'You would be surprised to see how rapidly they get on. Even married women have learnt to read the Testament and to write well, in one season'. They were mostly writing when I entered, using steel pens and copy books – a far preferable system to the slate and pencil...

On the negative side, he noted that 'There was no infant school here attached to the church… but a club-room had been taken for the purpose… which, I was told, would shortly be opened, and would accommodate about 170 infants'.

Elsewhere in Merthyr it was left to the ironmasters to establish schools and night classes, although the speed with which this was done varied from district to district. The Cyfarthfa school opened in 1848 and immediately began adult classes under the tutorage of volunteer teachers who:

> …were obtained by rotation, each set… taking on duties a week or a month at a time
> and were recruited from the clergy, the gentry and the tradespeople. The men and boys,
> girls and young women dressed themselves in their best clothes, came with clean hands
> and faces, as if to a feast, and when within the school walls worked with a steadiness and
> diligence that soon produced its own reward.

The Plymouth school was probably opened in 1850, while at Penydarren the school, catering for 200 children, did not open until 1852. In all three cases finance was provided by stoppages from workers' wages and the small government grant.

There can be little doubt that the practical lead provided by Dowlais received a massive ideological boost by the arrival in 1847 of the *Reports of the Commissioners of Inquiry into the State of Education in Wales*, which became damned as the 'Blue Books'. Though quite blatantly prejudiced against both nonconformity and the Welsh language, their other criticisms were largely well founded and the hostility which they engendered had the perverse effect of stimulating many of the educational developments which followed their publication, in as much as they shattered much of the apathy which had until then characterised education in Wales. Consequently, in a great many ways 1847 may be regarded as the watershed, the year in which those in authority began to wake up to the realities of working-class ignorance and started to discuss and implement schemes to overcome it. As regards their motives, education was seen by many as the panacea for a whole range of problems ranging from drunkenness to the threat of revolution. It has been seen that, having attracted a workforce, the main difficulty confronting employers involved the essentially pre-industrial mentality of their workers, which expressed itself in forms such as irregularity of attendance and general indiscipline, and 'An educational structure which provided for religious and moral instruction was a direct attempt to counter this influence'. A stable, methodical workforce was not the only goal, however, as a constant supply of skilled labour was essential and education was one of a variety of schemes employed in order to ensure this supply. At Dowlais, for example, 'Sir John Guest's particular interest was the Upper Boys' school, where he drew freely on the older boys who were given posts in the works which required a good deal of technical knowledge and skill', while a school inspector wrote, 'It is intended to train those acute engineers and miners, upon a proper supply of whom the prosperity of the great ironworks at Dowlais depend so much, and as no expense is spared, the object is readily obtained.'

As well as attempting to inculcate norms associated with the smooth running of their works, and trying to ensure a steady supply of superior workers, the masters were actively concerned with the propagation of a new morality more suited to their tastes. According to Tremenheere, 'Domestic discomfort aids the attractions of the public-house while the low standard of education among the adults deprives them of better means of enjoyment', and H.A. Bruce argued that education operated to disgust the workman with the lowest and most degrading forms of indulgence. When he addressed the Young Men's Mutual Improvement Society, in 1852, he told his audience:

> It is to institutions such as these that I look not only for supplying means to the more highly gifted among you of raising themselves to higher positions in society, but for the general and permanent elevation of the working classes to a higher moral and intellectual station… others will make the discovery which you have made, that when the day's work is over there are better, and purer, and nobler pleasures in store for them than to drown thought among the intoxicating fumes of beer and tobacco.

In the belief that it led directly to increased prudence and foresight:

> Education… was an attempt to incite moral restraint and to provide an influence which would curb the excesses of individuals. The grim physical surroundings, which were so often the deep seated cause of excess had to be provided with an emotional and moral counterweight.

Education was also seen as one of the best methods of diffusing working-class agitation and discontent. Bruce was certain that education provided the workman with 'clearer and juster views of right and wrong'. Not only could education eradicate Chartism and other heretical aberrations, it was also regarded as an ideal method of fostering a belief in the existence of a community of interests between masters and men which, once accepted, would banish practices which disrupted production, whether by individuals or groups of workers. As a letter written to the *Merthyr Guardian* in March 1840 expressed it:

> Can the proprietors of the iron works expect the minds of the population to be well disposed without cultivation? As well might they look for the land to produce wheat if suffered to lie waste. As certainly will the human mind, without education, produce evil as the land will produce weeds, thorns, and briars if left to itself.

As far as the masters were concerned, therefore: 'Activity in the educational sphere represented a mixture of philanthropy, enlightened self interest and paternal benevolence'.

The opening of schools and adult classes was not in itself enough, and the curriculum delivered in them had to accord with the desired results; hence the importance placed on religious studies. Similarly, the emphasis in all the Anglican and works' schools was on English culture, seen as encapsulating all that was modern, industrious and progressive, whereas Welsh culture was dismissed as primitive, stagnant and worthless. Not only did this occur in the history or geography lesson, it dominated all forms of instruction, in as much as English was the language of the schoolroom and evening class – and quite deliberately so, for as Tremenheere expressed it: 'Good schools will aid materially in spreading the English language; the ignorance of which is one of the great causes of the backward state of the Welsh part of the population'. Thus, although Welsh was the language of the overwhelming majority, only in the Sunday schools were people taught in their own tongue.

Despite the example of the Guests, the publication of the 'Blue Books' and the political and economic expediency seen in extending the provision of working-class schooling, in 1850 the great majority of Merthyr's population still remained outside the scope of formal education. Dowlais apart, Tremenheere argued that in proportion to its need it was the most inadequately provided town in the whole of south Wales. Twelve months later, in December 1851, the *Merthyr Guardian* complained bitterly about a situation in which out of:

> a population of 45,000 persons, there are probably NINE THOUSAND children of school age; but, according to the returns of 1847, the number in schools was only 2,301. If we allow an increase of 700 for the intervening four years, we shall still have to provide schools for a remainder of full SIX THOUSAND CHILDREN.

Furthermore, those children who did attend schools did not necessarily do so regularly. Tremenheere noted in 1840 that in almost all the various day schools:

> …the number actually present was much below that taken as the number frequenting the school at that time of year. The attendance is of course larger in summer than at the period when the inquiry was made, but it was confessed that even in summer it was very irregular… the complaint of irregularity… was universal… it was said that the general practice was to send the children for one, two, or three months continuously; they were then withdrawn for similar periods.

Ten years later, when the *Morning Chronicle* interviewed a schoolteacher at one of the new National schools, it reported:

'The only difficulty I have' said he 'is to get them to attend regularly; when they stay away for a few days, of course, they fall back. Mondays and Fridays are the worst days for attendance'. He could give me no reason why on these days the attendance was small.

Even in Dowlais, attendance was erratic. During October 1850, for example, daily attendances varied between 1,141 and 674. This irregular attendance and the school-teacher's evidence concerning Mondays and Fridays suggests that Merthyr's children followed their parents' example and made 'Saint Monday' and the elongated weekend as much a part of school life as in the adult world of the pit and foundry. Tremenheere's point about children attending for a period and then being withdrawn for a similar time may have its explanation in irregular job opportunities, or it may have been the case that parents economised by sending their children to school in shifts. Whatever the case, according to the *Morning Chronicle* irregularity of attendance was:

> …an evil that will in time abate. It must be more the fault of the parents than the children, for it is in their power to compel attendance. But in reality the people have not yet begun to feel the advantage of these schools… When they see the striking improvement in manners, language, and turn of thought which these schools eventually must bring about, they will then properly estimate the value of such instructions and will be anxious to profit by them as largely as they can.

Illness also affected instruction, which may well explain why Tremenheere found attendance lower during the winter months. This was especially evident in 1849 when, by common consent, the cholera epidemic dealt the cause of education a severe blow:

> Everywhere I found a great falling off in the attendance since the visitation of the neighbourhood with cholera, as compared with the numbers previously to the coming of that destroyer. This reduction was generally one fourth, and sometimes nearly a half of the former average attendance. The Rev. Mr. Jenkins observed of it, 'The cholera has unhinged and broken up everything'.

When looking at those who remained outside the sphere of education, it becomes clear that for the most part they were the unskilled and transitory who worked for the lowest wages in the least secure jobs and whose children began work at the earliest opportunity. Similarly, it was among these people that religious forces held least sway and thus Sunday school attendance would not have been common. Ignorance, like disease and insanitary housing, owed much to the culture of poverty in which many families were trapped.

It was not just the poorest sections of the workforce who remained uneducated, however, for the limited nature of the increase in educational opportunities points to the fact that even the children of the skilled often experienced little or no instruction. That this lack of progress had much to do with the attitudes of those who controlled Merthyr cannot be denied. As far as the shopocracy was concerned, the 'Blue Books' drew attention to the inertia caused by ratepayer mentality when they reported 'the tradesmen and shopkeepers of Merthyr naturally feel that they ought not to be called upon to contribute *pari passu* with the… great Iron Masters of the place to educate a population in the profits of whose labour the latter get the lion's share'. Not all ratepayers were indifferent, but even those who supported schooling were influenced by pecuniary matters. Thus the object of a public meeting held in March 1847 and chaired by E.J. Hutchings was 'to consider the best means of providing a good, cheap and unsectarian education for children of the working classes in the town and neighbourhood of Merthyr'.

Turning to the masters, with the notable exception of the Guests, they were hesitant and miserly in their approach. The 'Blue Books' found that as far as the children of those employed at Cyfarthfa, Plymouth and Penydarren were concerned, 'no provision has hitherto been made, further than some trifling subscriptions by the proprietors to the national schools'. However, the major criticism which can be levied at the masters, Guest included, is that their determination to employ children ensured that even when schools were opened education was limited. As H.A. Bruce argued, 'At the very moment… when instruction really begins to tell upon them, they are carried off to the rolling-mill or the colliery, where the little they have learned is speedily forgotten'. In spite of this, however, after Sir John Guest's death in 1851, when Bruce became a trustee of the Dowlais Ironworks, children continued to work in its mines and foundries. Every attempt to limit or curtail such employment by Parliament was vigorously opposed by the Dowlais management. It would appear that Bruce, in common with other employers, was prepared to promote schooling as long as it did not threaten profitability.

One should not suppose that the 1840s saw no improvements being made, for despite the limited nature of many of the innovations an extension of educational opportunities did occur both at the infant and the adult level. Similarly, though Tremenheere argued that Merthyr's parents saw nothing of value in education and the irregular attendance patterns suggest the same, other evidence points to the fact that by 1850 many of Merthyr's working class 'had begun to lose their suspicion of education'. At Dowlais, for example, the Guests repeatedly professed their concern over the long waiting lists for admission to their schools and the 'Blue Books' found both the upper and lower boys' schools 'always full to overflowing'. Even in China, parents clamoured for education. In 1850 when, accompanied by the Revd Campbell, the *Morning Chronicle* reporter visited the cellars, he recounted that while they were inspecting a house:

> ...some women of the neighbourhood gathered around the door, and beset the clergy-
> man with requests that their children might be admitted to the new schools; he sent
> away some smiling faces and gladdened hearts, with a promise that if they would send
> them at once, and pay attention to their childrens' habits, they should have the benefit
> which these excellent institutions afford.

The 1840s saw many working people experience education for the first time, and the decade witnessed a growing awareness of the value of instruction. This reflected a growth in the demand for literacy and numeracy, influenced by the burgeoning of the chapels, benefit societies and other working-class movements. When lecturing in 1852, H.A. Bruce pointed out that 'Twenty years ago the literary demands of the population were very easily supplied, a few religious periodicals formed their graver studies', while according to Kenrick's analysis only 445 workmen, 1.3% of the population, had books other than religious ones. By 1850, however, the *Morning Chronicle's* reporter could argue: 'I must again mention the booksellers, because I consider them in proportion more numerous than the other trades – that is – taking the usual ratio to population as shown in other places. Even the market house has two; if not more' and Bruce could state that 'A vast number of cheap periodicals relating exclusively to art, science and literature are now circulating' among the working classes.

Obviously, the demand for reading material had risen sharply in the 1840s, and perhaps the best index of this was the number of libraries which opened during the decade – libraries which, though initiated by the middle classes, owed their success to working-class support. The Dowlais Tradesmen and Workmen's Library, opened by the Guests in August 1845, had more than 200 volumes and a membership (which cost 1½d per week) of 120 within a month. Just over a year later, it was reported to have 700 volumes and took the *Times* and *Daily News* every day. Hours of opening were 7p.m.-10p.m., Monday to Saturday. In Merthyr, a library was opened at the beginning of December 1846; six months later it had 614 volumes.

Quite apart from these, Mrs Rose Mary Crawshay was eventually responsible for the setting up of no fewer than seven libraries in the Georgetown and Cefn Coed areas, for the use of Cyfarthfa workmen and their families, while in 1850 Tremenheere could report 'excellent lending libraries are now also attached to nearly all the best schools'. At Dowlais, not only did the schools have a library to supplement the work-men's one, but Lady Guest endeavoured to ensure that books on sale in the area were of a good standard. She recorded in her diary that Sir John:

...found the hawkers in the Dowlais market selling such trash that it occurred to us that we might be able to lead them to circulate something more solid and useful. For this purpose, I have determined to put several volumes into their hands, and entrust them for sale, giving them the benefit of a large commission. The object further was to collect books of good tendency and of a popular description, it being quite certain that if a class of literature should take with the people, the hawkers would in future learn to supply themselves with it.

In hindsight, the 1840s witnessed the inauguration and development of much that was positive as far as working-class education was concerned, although the pitfalls of the economic system, the disastrous cholera epidemic of 1849 and the economic slump of the late 1840s and early 1850s certainly hindered the growing movement towards mass involvement. Despite the major problems which still had to be overcome, by 1850 Merthyr was, in terms of education, a far healthier place than had been the case in 1840. Although it was to take a further twenty years before attending school became the right of everyone, it was in the 1840s that the idea of universal education took root in the town.

11

SEX AND DRUGS AND ROCK 'N' ROLL!

L ife was not all gloom and doom. Hard labour, poor housing, dirt, disease and
poverty there were in abundance, but there were recreational outlets also. These
activities might well include a sexual element, for according to R.R.W. Lingen,
one of the commissioners who produced the notorious 'Blue Books', during the
summer months 'gangs of young men and women are in the habit of carrying drink
into the fields, and of keeping up the most riotous orgies all night long'. This, though,
was the only reference to such nocturnal naughtiness and probably tells us more
about the mindset of the commissioner than about popular sexuality. As far as sex is
concerned, we need to look no further than China, and as the criminal activities of
the rodnies, receivers, smashers, bullies and nymphs have been dealt with elsewhere,
here we will restrict our inquiry to a survey of who the prostitutes and their clients
were.

According to one contemporary, the first 'nymphs of the pave' moved into the
Cellars around 1825, and by the 1840s there were at least sixty girls operating out
of China. Landlords revelled in the high rents the brothels could command. As one
commentator put it: 'They wink at the evil for the sake of the profit'. So who were
these nymphs and why did they take to the streets of Merthyr? Poverty characterised China, and the culture of poverty was certainly a prime cause of prostitution.
Employment opportunities for women were available in Merthyr, it is true; but, as we
have seen, job conditions, security and wages were all highly questionable. Women
were almost exclusively employed as a source of cheap and casual labour around the
furnaces and in the mines. In 1841, for example, women employed as limestone-
breakers received seven shillings a week for a twelve-hour day, seven days a week – a

rate of just one penny an hour. Without further elaboration, it should be recognised that 'A prostitute had to have reached a very degraded level not to be better rewarded than a sweated piece-worker', and a young and pretty girl who turned to prostitution in Merthyr could earn more, by one means or another, in one or two days than a respectable woman earned in months. Poverty also prevented some girls from seeking employment. No one would employ a girl dressed in rags for a job in a shop or in service, for example, while Jane Davies, a China prostitute in 1860, argued that the only reason she'd come to the Cellars in the first place was that 'she had no shoes to wear to work'.

The upbringing of many of the Chinese led directly to prostitution and, given such a background, the morality of the respectable classes can have meant little to the girls of China. Indeed, as one historian of prostitution in the nineteenth century has noted: 'In the hopeless squalor at the base of the social pyramid, prostitution was an accepted occupation that rarely attached any shame to its practitioners'.[10] How could the girls of China, denied access to respectable circles through poverty, be expected to accept the same codes of morality as the respectable? For the same reasons that boys became rodnies, so too did girls take to the streets, and just as the brightest of the boys became in time the professional thieves and bullies of China, so the most intelligent girls turned to theft under the cover of prostitution, while their less quick-fingered sisters became beggars or prostitutes *per se*.

Poverty and the culture of poverty did not explain why *all* the girls of China had taken to prostitution, and the fact remains that outright promiscuity accounted for more than just a few cases. In the isolated, sparsely populated parishes of rural Wales, such behaviour would inevitably draw condemnation and punishment, but in the anonymity of the town the promiscuous woman had opportunities and inducements to prostitute herself that were not to be found in the countryside. Others seem to have turned to prostitution to escape the drabness of respectable working-class life, with its 'dreary routine of work, work, stitch, stitch, church-and-chapel going', a tedium that prostitution offered to replace with fancy clothes, gay living and financial independence. For many girls, the glamour, whether real or illusory, which surrounded the Empire proved a considerable attraction. The lure certainly accounted for the arrival of Margaret Traharn in the spring of 1859, even though her washerwoman sister was said to be heartbroken over her departure from respectability.

If there were many who turned to prostitution voluntarily, so too were there those who retreated to the brothels in desperation. Just how many of China's prostitutes began their careers as rejected wives or daughters or as unmarried mothers is impossible to determine, but in a town where desertion and bastardy cases were all too common, the phenomenon was certainly known. Not only were those deserted in a physical sense apt to turn to prostitution, but also those abandoned in other ways. Ann

Jenkins, for example, told an Anglican missionary in 1860 that her husband had 'gave himself to drink', had refused to support her and 'at times abused her shamefully'. She had consequently left him and, in order to support herself and her child, had become a washerwoman. As such, she had fallen in with 'the wrong sort of company', had herself taken to drink, and eventually to prostitution.

If it was a combination of factors that led girls to become prostitutes, a ready supply was not in itself enough; there had to be a demand for their services, and in mid-nineteenth century Merthyr a number of factors served to provide and maintain such a demand. In the first instance, the industrial base of the town and its demand for immigrants led to a considerable sexual imbalance: there were simply far more adult men than women. Thus single men who sought female company were drawn to the Cellars, and when migrants were beyond the social controls imposed by their rural communities, there was little to impede such visits.

For married men, as well, two important factors led many to the prostitutes. The 'chapel culture' which so characterised respectable Merthyr instilled a belief in the pure woman's asexuality, which prevented couples from abandoning themselves to carnal pleasures – of course, no such restrictions operated in the brothels of China. Furthermore, the total absence of birth control meant that wives were frequently pregnant and unable to perform conjugally. To illustrate the latter, the *Merthyr Guardian* reported the following in December 1860:

> At Dowlais there is a woman still living, only 45 years of age, who is the mother of 33 children. She married at 14, and became a mother at 15. She is the wife of a working man in humble circumstances, and she has given birth twice to 3 children, three times to 4, and six times to twins.

Who were the prostitutes' clients? Court cases, inevitably the result of the girls robbing their visitors, suggest that workers and tradesmen of every description availed themselves of their services. In 1860, Ann Jenkins informed the missionary that China was in decline:

> She said that there are no men going to China now but the vilest of the vile, that some of the clerks of the town and well dressed men used to go there, but now they are never coming nigh. That the standard price is coming down among the girls from 1 shilling to sixpence and from 2 shillings a night to 1/6. That their clients used to vary from 10 years of age to 80 but that the youngest and the oldest are keeping off now...

How many girls were operating in China? It is impossible to give accurate figures, but the evidence which does exist suggests a minimum figure of around sixty in the

1840s and forty-odd in the 1860s. Numbers fluctuated, not surprisingly, with the state of the iron trade, and there were said to be more girls working in the summer than in the winter months.

Turning to drugs, there can be no mistaking the fact that alcohol was the number one drug in Merthyr. In 1847 the 'Blue Books' noted that 'Drunkenness is very prevalent, and beer houses abound to an extent wholly unnecessary for any good purpose...'. Every weekend and every pay day was characterised by an epidemic of drunkenness. Easter and Christmas holidays, weddings, funerals, fairs and St Patrick's Day all witnessed heavy drinking.

In April 1850, the *Morning Chronicle* was horrified by the sheer density of pubs:

> There is one public house or beer shop to every 24½ houses. Out of seven adjoining houses in one of the streets, I counted five public houses and beershops... In Dowlais alone there are not less than 75 of these houses.

Despite the best efforts of the local magistrates and police to enforce regulations concerning opening hours, one could secure a drink at any hour of the day or night, nor were there any age restrictions. As the *Merthyr Guardian* put it in December 1848:

> It is quite painful to enter one of the more popular beer-shops, and see grown up men, with their children – little old men of 12 and 13, drinking beer in plenteous draughts, and smoking their pipes with as much importance as men of larger growth.

As we have seen, what horrified Merthyr's authorities was not so much drunkenness as its consequences, and especially its link with crime.

Drinking also incurred a social cost, as families were torn apart and individuals went under. In September 1840, the *Merthyr Guardian* reported: 'An inquest was held... at the Lamb and Flag... on the body of John White who died from excessive drinking – verdict accordingly'.

When looking at why so many people drank so much, personal, group and institutional factors need consideration. As far as personal factors were concerned, first and foremost alcohol was the only thirst-quencher and as such it had little serious opposition. Even in the countryside, drinking water was unsafe and scarce, and in Merthyr it was positively appalling: 'absolutely in motion with living organisms', as one contemporary put it. As for milk, in towns it was unsafe because watering it down was so commonplace. Its price was never once quoted in the *Merthyr Guardian's* weekly chronicle of market prices between 1833 and 1841, suggesting that it was far from a staple commodity. Tea, coffee and cocoa were sold but they were more expensive than alcohol and not universally available.

The industrial base of the town created ferocious thirsts. Those who laboured at the furnaces often fainted in the summer months, while those who worked in the pits often did so in great heat and always exposed to dust. From the very outset, alcohol played an integral part in the iron-making process. A brewhouse formed an extension to the very first furnace at Dowlais, and when it developed into a proper works around 1800 beerhouses and pubs were opened adjacent to all the main centres of effort. Beer was also widely believed to provide added strength, and so whenever extra effort was called for free drink was distributed to the workers.

Alcohol was also the traditional working-class medicine. Unable to afford the services of the town's few doctors, and wary of quacks, Merthyr's workers turned instead to the bottle and the quart jug. It comforted the sick and the dying, aided childbirth, quietened babies and was the surgeon's anaesthetic. Indeed, if ever there was a panacea, it was alcohol.

Moving from the individual to the group, as well as meeting physical needs alcohol soothed the spirit. At a time when urbanisation and industrialisation were tearing apart familiar customs and relationships, many found solace in the taverns. It gave confidence to migrants overwhelmed by urban life; it restored bodies numbed by the monotony and drudgery of work, and it moderated the harshness of the desperate poverty in which so many people lived.

But the institutional factors which encouraged drinking cannot be overemphasised. In a town deprived of most recreational facilities, the pub or the chapel were the only places to spend what limited leisure time there was. Housing conditions were frequently squalid, and even in the best cottages overcrowding was the norm. The pub had many of the comforts denied the workman's house: light, heat, space, furniture, newspapers, sociability. The price of a drink was their entry fee to comforts they could only enjoy communally. The pub was also the only weatherproof meeting place for workers. It was the newsroom and debating centre of the community, and pubs housed Chartist and trade union lodges, horticultural clubs and friendly societies. Furthermore, a great many pubs and beerhouses were owned by the petty agents or gaffers who the ironmasters contracted to supply the workers they needed. So they became the labour exchanges for the works and the wages offices, too, and – as has already been noted elsewhere – charging workers for providing their wages in coin and encouraging them to drink were sources of considerable resentment.

Pubs were also the only buildings big enough to accommodate the civic functions of the town. At various times they acted as gaols and magistrates courts; inquests like the one held for the unfortunate John White were held in them, and they often acted as makeshift hospitals and mortuaries.

In short, therefore, pubs and alcohol played a central role in mid-nineteenth-century Merthyr, but alcohol and tobacco were not the only drugs resorted to. The fact that some of China's prostitutes used drugs to incapacitate their victims has already been referred to, and we have seen that the doping of infants was widespread, but drugs were also resorted to for pleasure, as is evidenced by the following advert from the *Merthyr Guardian* in February 1841:

Laughing Gas!

Mr. Partridge Begs to announce that he will publicly exhibit, NEXT WEEK ONLY, at a room opposite the Bush Inn, High Street, Merthyr, the astonishing and laughable effects of the NITROUS OXIDE, or, as it is expressively called LAUGHING GAS, when breathed into the lungs.

Admission – Ladies and Gentlemen 1 shilling. Mechanics 6d.

Hours of administering the gas, 7, 8, and 9 o'clock each evening.

So popular was Mr Partridge that he stayed for at least a fortnight...

Merthyr's workers craved amusement and it is not surprising that the immigrants brought their traditional pastimes with them. Later in the century, Henry Murton of Dowlais recalled:

The young men would indulge in games of quails, footracing, hurdle-leaping, tennis and football. Others with the angle rod, and some of the more daring with the net and fowling piece, and some of the more rough would take to dog, and cock fighting. Bull and badger baiting were also of frequent occurance.

Sprinting remained popular, featuring such stars as Thomas Jones, alias 'Milgi-min-y-Mynydd', the 'greyhound of the mountains', and T. Thomas, 'the flying weaver of Caerphilly'. Stakes of £10 were not unknown, though sacks of potatoes were also wagered. Perhaps the most popular form of gambling, however, accompanied the games of 'pitch and toss' which were held throughout the town wherever suitable open spaces could be found, though bare-fist boxing was also a crowd-puller. In 1851, two fights held at Penydarren on a Saturday night were watched by a crowd of between 200 and 300 people, and the second bout, between a China bully and an unnamed opponent, went twenty rounds before the police arrived. Brute strength, stamina, pickled knuckles and courage, rather than any Queensberry rules, were the order of the day.

The opposition of the police and magistrates and the growth of an indigenous urban workforce saw many traditional pursuits fade in favour of new amusements. The theatre opened in 1839 and consistently played to packed audiences, while travelling shows were always well patronised, and particularly the circus. In September 1844, Sands American Circus gave two performances: the first at 2.30p.m. drew a crowd of

1,300, and the second at 7.30p.m. played to an audience of between 2,500 and 3,000.
Wombwell's Royal Menagerie and The Circus Royal were annual visitors. Waxworks
were also popular, as were dioramas. In December 1851, Wigglesworths Diorama
enjoyed huge success. The *Merthyr Guardian* reported that the views of Ispahan, Paris
and other places were excellent and added, 'On the occasion of our visit, the exhibition consisted of scenes in the life of John Wesley, the view of Damascus, and a storm
at sea... We can promise a treat to all who have not yet seen it'.

Merthyr's workers appear to have loved the unusual. In 1841, such was the interest
surrounding the public killing of a bear for its grease (by a barber) that the cadaver
was exhibited in the street for several days before dissection. In the autumn of 1847,
the people witnessed, for the very first time, a hot-air balloon ascent, when, according to the *Merthyr Guardian*, 'an intrepid aviator, Mr. Gypson, hovered over the town,
watched by thousands of people crowded on the tips, and he floated down the valley
to land safely near Quakers Yard'. Freak shows were always well attended, and it was
hardly surprising that Merthyr, of all places, gave 'Monsieur Chylinski' an enthusiastic reception in December 1840, when, accompanied by a blind but 'very talented'
musician, 'The Fire King', as he advertised himself, beat red-hot iron with his bare
hands, poured melted lead into his mouth, bit a piece of red-hot iron from another
larger piece, swallowed boiling butter by the spoonful and, by way of finale, danced a
waltz carrying three men at the same time. Seventeen years later, Tom Thumb made
well-attended appearances in the town, and if the diminutive visitor was a source of
some amazement to the inhabitants, so too must have been the venue for his daily
audiences: the Temperance Hall!

Throughout the period excursions were popular, and in June 1839 the *Merthyr
Guardian* reported:

> It is not true that several large foreign ships cannot come into Swansea, owing to the
> tides being lessened by the quantity of sea water drunk by the Merthyr people. A moder-
> ate quantity for one man per diem being about fifteen half pints.

The coming of the railways increased the opportunities for travel, so that at the time
of the Llandaff Fair in 1846, for example, 'Many hundreds – 26 carriages from Merthyr
alone – have taken advantage of the Taff Vale Railway Company's special "to-and-fro"
tickets to visit the fair'. Similar cheap day excursions took groups of ironworkers,
miners and colliers to London for the Great Exhibition. Closer to home, and much to
the horror of the respectable citizens of Cardiff who petitioned against it, the Taff Vale
Railway organised Sunday excursions from Merthyr to the town.

Public hangings in Swansea, Cardiff and Brecon, relatively rare in the 1840s
and 1850s, were always well patronised by spectators from Merthyr. Considerable

numbers travelled to Cardiff in the summer of 1842 to see the town's own Dick Tamar hung for matricide. In April 1845, when Thomas Thomas was hanged outside Brecon gaol before a crowd of 10,000-15,000, the *Merthyr Guardian* reported on the 'many hundreds' who had journeyed from Merthyr, where 'all available vehicles were in requisition and greedily hired'. Four years later, when James Griffiths was executed at the same venue, the newspaper carried the following:

A SINGULAR FACT – Among the hundreds who went from Merthyr to Brecon to see the hanging on Wednesday last, a blind man from Heolgerrig was the most worthy of note. The young man is blind, and no mistake. He has been blind since he was five years old, there can be, and there is no doubt about it; nevertheless, he went to see the hanging, as he himself phrased it. He started early and was there in good time, and anxiously took his place where a good view of the execution could be commanded. He seemed to hear every movement, and eagerly caught every remark. When all eyes were turned to gaze upon the culprit... the blind man saw him too in his mind's eye, and was as highly excited by the spectacle as any of his seeing neighbours. He is a skillful harpist, and a rare hand at dominoes.

This reference to the harp brings us to the fact that Merthyr loved music of all descriptions. Both the Cyfarthfa and Dowlais works had their own brass bands; every chapel and church had its choir; singing festivals and eisteddfoddau drew large audiences; and no pub was without its harp or fiddle: but 'rock 'n' roll'?

Let us end with another account from the *Merthyr Guardian*, this time from September 1851:

During the past week we have been induced to form one of the numerous group of gapers in the market-square, which, considering the badness of the times, may be said to be almost gay. It contains lots of attractions... Let us stand facing the market house. Right in front... is what is called a flying dragon [a carousel]... On the right of the square are a couple of apple stores... and a little in the background is a gentleman who offers to show the natives how they look, in black, upon a piece of cardboard. On the left is a peep show, wherein are shown views of the Crystal Palace, the Holy Land, and the Kaffir Wars. Above, may be seen in great daubs of paint, fighting ranks of soldiers and barbarians... Close to this is a model of a Cotton Factory, with two pretty locomotives, and a seraphine outside, and a model of the Great Exhibition in the interior. In the centre stands the model gallery, to us the most interesting of the whole... we must place a compliment to the brass band belonging to the 'gallery'. They play every evening to delighted auditors, and play remarkably well...

In the middle of the Market Square, right in the middle of the sex-crazed, drug-riddled bedlam that was Merthyr, we find 'Our friend Pulman, the town crier, singing "Rock, rock, rock again!"'[11]

12

DEPARTURE

Perhaps the ultimate working-class response to the conditions outlined in previous chapters was simply to leave Merthyr, and certainly, of all the developments within the period, few were as dramatic or sustained as that of emigration. Unfortunately, however, because of an almost total lack of statistics, the exact scale of emigration during the 1840s and 1850s is impossible to determine. Having said as much, we know that the period 1846–1855 saw the biggest exodus from the British Isles ever known, and the evidence which has survived for Merthyr – most notably, that contained within the pages of the *Merthyr Guardian* – does provide some indication as to how many people left the town and when.

The first report of the phenomenon occurred in a letter to the Dowlais Company dated February 1833, and concerned emigration to America, while in October 1836 the *Merthyr Guardian* published a letter written by a Merthyr emigrant who had settled in Pittsburgh. Five years later, it informed its readers about arrangements being made to attract workers to New Zealand and ran advertisements regarding emigration to Australia and Canada, but up until the summer of 1841 the impression given by the newspaper was that very few working people were leaving the town. Within the space of a few months, however, it could report:

> A great number of workmen, with their families, took their departure from Merthyr Tydfil last week for America; and many more are making preparations for the same purpose. In fact there appears to be quite a mania in that place for emigrating.

In May 1844, a report mentioning that 'A great many of our fellow countrymen left this town on Monday for the United States' suggests that the movement was still a force but, apart from a few isolated cases, no mention of any considerable emigration occurred again until January 1848, when 'several hundreds of the operatives were said to be preparing to depart for Australia'. Twelve months later, 'large numbers' were reported to be going to America and Australia, while in the spring of 1851 the paper argued: 'this year there are reasons for believing the number of emigrants will be fully as great, if not greater than usual'. By April 1852, 'the tide of emigration which has been flowing for some time, still continues; and scarcely a week passes without witnessing the departure of parties of work men...'. A report five weeks later informed readers that 'no less than 900 houses were vacant in Merthyr and Dowlais', and while a number of reasons for this were cited the newspaper declared adamantly that 'the greatest number of the vacancies must be due to the passion for emigration which now prevails'.

Throughout the summer of 1852, similar reports were published. In September 1853 it seemed that 'The tide of emigration still flows on', and twelve months later the newspaper could declare: 'The passion for emigration seems to be as strong among the industrious artisans of Merthyr as among the peasantry of Western Ireland'. Despite this dubious comparison, there can be no doubting the strength of the movement away from Merthyr, a movement which continued to be reflected by the newspaper right through to 1860.

As regards the reason behind increasing numbers of people leaving the town, economic considerations were of paramount importance and there can be no question whatsoever that the major factor behind emigration were the fluctuating fortunes of the iron industry. The boom of the late 1830s gave way to contraction and depression in the early 1840s and, despite a temporary respite in the middle of that decade, by 1850 the town was rapidly sliding into an unprecedented slump. Though there was a short-lived recovery in 1854 associated with the Crimean War, Merthyr during the 1850s was characterised by stagnation and redundancy, the most striking symbol of which was the complete closure of the Penydarren works in 1859. Whereas the population of Merthyr increased by a staggering 81% between 1831 and 1841, the next two decades were to see this rate decline to 33% and then 19%. That a correlation existed between the state of trade and emigration soon becomes apparent. In February 1842, the *Merthyr Guardian's* report of emigration mania came at a time when wages were falling dramatically and 'distress and misery' were said to be common. In January 1848:

> Large numbers of huge placards have been posted about the town, offering free passages to Australia for from three to four hundred colliers, miners, etc., etc. The alarm into which the recent reduction of wages has thrown the district, has caused these bills to be read with avidity. On every street corner groups of men may frequently be seen reading the announcement, or listening while it is being read to them; and we hear that several hundreds... are likely to accept the offer...

In April 1851 the newspaper noted gloomily: 'The Iron trade still continues in the depressed state, which has now been of such long duration... and the necessary consequence is, that many of our artisans are giving way to despondency, and resolving to seek better livelihoods in more western latitudes'. A year later, the depression was even worse, 'forcing large numbers of persons to leave these districts, and seek to better their fortunes in other lands'.

Quite apart from the massive wage reductions and lay-offs associated with depressions, the cyclical nature of the iron trade ensured that, for all but the most highly skilled ironworkers, there was little job security in Merthyr. Consequently, evidence suggests that just as unemployed workers emigrated, so too did those who, though still in work, wished for greater regularity and security of employment. In some cases this promise of greater security came from the ironmasters themselves, as in March 1842, for example, when:

> 30 miners and 2 blacksmiths left Merthyr on the 3rd instant, for the Island of Cuba, in the employ of Mr. Alderman Thompson. With one or two exceptions they are single men, and their stipulation is for three years, or to be returned to Swansea should the climate not agree with them. They are to work in the Copper mines, the blacksmiths at £9 a month each, and the miners at £6, and to get one-half those wages during their voyage with provisions at the worthy Alderman's expense.

Ten years later, in June 1852, the *Merthyr Guardian* reported on Thompson's directorship of the Port Philip and Colonial Gold Mining Company and told of how one Evan Hopkins, a native of Merthyr who had worked for many years in the silver mines of South America, had successfully recruited miners for Thompson's Australian operations. Evidence also points to similar small-scale migrations from Dowlais to Russia and Spain.

Redundancies, low wages and insecurity were not the only factors prompting emigration. Throughout the 1840s and 1850s, men who deserted their wives and families or who were unwilling to marry pregnant girlfriends often regarded emigration as the surest path to anonymity. Emigration also offered an escape route to those whose political beliefs ruled them outside the law, and the Chartists saw a number of men leave for foreign parts after the Newport rising. For more mundane criminals, too, emigration offered a reprieve from the forces of the law, with perhaps the best example being the departure to America of the 'Emperor and Empress' in September 1852:

> EMIGRATION – The tide of emigration continues to flow, but a recent lot of emigrants demand special notice. One night last week, a grey whiskered pigeon, flush in cash, visited the Celestial Empire, and was plucked of £70 for his pains; with the money

so obtained the natives have had the good sense to meditate a trip across the Atlantic; and accordingly on Monday last, the Empress... Emperor... and several of the female mandarins turned their faces to the far West.

Just as enhanced job opportunities and wages tempted many to leave Merthyr, while others left to avoid responsibilities, persecution and imprisonment or transportation, so too workers may have emigrated to escape the rapidly deteriorating urban environment. Though there is little firm evidence to connect such factors as poor housing and public health provision and the appalling mortality rates with emigration, to deny that such aspects of life played a part in the movement out of the town would be foolish indeed. Merthyr was a pioneer settlement, a hastily developed shanty town which existed solely to produce iron and house the labour force necessary for that production; living conditions were often abysmal and if conditions in North America or Australia were to be little better in many instances, at least the New Worlds held out the promise of a better life, of room to breathe and of a fresh start.

It should also be remembered that Merthyr's inhabitants were no strangers to migration. A great many of her workers were either first- or second-generation immigrants who had left the countryside in search of more work, better jobs, higher pay and better living standards. Given Merthyr's work-camp status, there can have been little to tie many of these people to the town during times of depression.

Demographers have long been aware of the fact that, in most cases of emigration, not only are there 'push' factors encouraging people to leave, but also 'pull' factors associated with the recipient country. The movement from Merthyr was no exception. In the first place, emigrants were lured by the promise of employment and – whether or not it was the case in reality – the popular belief was that not only were jobs available but they were highly paid. The Merthyr man who had settled in Pittsburgh, for example, wrote in 1836 telling of how labourers were earning between 75 cents and $1, mechanics from $1.25 to $2, and colliers and moulders $1.50 and $2 a day. In January 1853, the *Merthyr Guardian* published a report concerning the experiences of a recently arrived group of Merthyr emigrants in Australia: 'On landing they found plenty of work, and plenty of money for doing it; wages ranged from 10/- to 30/- a day; a pound a day was offered in a dozen places to the craftsmen of the party...'.

If the temptation induced by such reports was not in itself enough, the bitter depression of the late 1840s and early 1850s coincided with the discovery of gold in both California and Australia, and the prospect of instant prosperity caused many to forgo their misgivings and depart. 'The gold seeking mania has at last invaded the mountains of Wales', wrote the newspaper in January 1849. Three years later, it could report that 'scarcely a week passes without witnessing the departure of working men for the gold fields of Australia and California', while the article cited above concerning the high wages in Australia added that not one of the emigrants had accepted the offers of work, as 'all the Welshmen were going to the diggings'. In August 1852, the newspaper published one of a series of letters from a Joseph Matters, who had been a painter in Merthyr before emigrating to Australia in 1849:

> Geelong,
>
> Port Philip
>
> …As for business here it is nearly suspended for want of labour, everybody is either going to or gone to the gold diggings. I have been once and got about £40 in ten weeks, besides clearing all expenses…There is gold all over the country; I have been over some hundreds of miles, and there is not a spot but you may obtain it…

It was hardly surprising, therefore, that the same month should see the following appear in the newspaper's pages:

> AUSTRALIA – The passion for emigration still continues, and large numbers continue to direct their faces towards the land of gold. Sales of furniture and other effects are very frequent, and valuable articles are sold at nominal prices, in order to convert them into available currency.

It was not only gold which enhanced the appeal of departure; religion also had a part to play. The influence of the Latter Day Saints in Merthyr has already been discussed, and perhaps the most striking feature of their organisation was the emphasis placed on emigration. The Mormon message was welcomed by many, combining as it did 'an apocalyptic assurance of eternal blessedness for believers and an immediate promise of a better life'. In July 1847: 'These spiritual and economic ends were alike consummated when the New Jerusalem was established on the banks of the Great Salt Lake'. In February 1849, when Captain Jones led the first exodus from Wales, the occasion was given considerable coverage by the Swansea-based *Cambrian*:

> This goodly company is under the command of a popular Saint, known as Captain Dan Jones… [They] seem animated only with the most devout feelings and aspirations, which seem to flow from no other source (judging from their conversation) than a sincere belief that the End of the World is at hand; and that their Great Captain of Salvation is soon to visit his *bobl yng ngwlad y Saint* [people in the land of the Saints]… Amongst the number who came here were several aged men varying from 70 to 90 years of age and 'whose hoary locks' made it very improbable they would live to see America. Yet so deluded are the poor and simple Saints that they believe that everyone amongst them,

however infirm and old they may be, will as surely land in California safely, as they started from Wales. Their faith is most extraordinary.

On Wednesday morning, after being addressed by their leader, all repaired on board in admirable order and with extraordinary resignation. Their departure was witnessed by hundreds of spectators, and while the steamer gaily passed down the river, the Saints commenced singing a favourite hymn. On entering the piers, however, they abruptly stopped singing and lustily responded to the cheering with which they were greeted by the inhabitants.

'Among the emigrants', it was said, 'were widows who took with them the clothes of their dead husbands, for they expected to meet them in the millennial city.'

A year later, in February 1850, the *Merthyr Guardian* reported:

DESERET... On Wednesday morning, a body of about 150 persons left this locality, where the sect is flourishing, for the state above named. They started from their head-quarters, the George Inn, under two leaders... whom they have promised to obey in all their commands... the route is through New Orleans...

In February 1854: 'Mormonism still retains its hold on a considerable number of the working men of this place, and large numbers are turning their longing eyes to that holy land which borders the Great Salt Lake...', and in July 1856, a further 703 converts took ship for Utah, again led by Captain Jones. The Welsh Mormons were the first non-English-speaking converts to arrive in Utah, according to Church records Wales contributed some £3,600 to the Mormon Perpetual Emigration Fund, and such was the strength of the movement that 'a competent observer, Sir Charles Dilke, has estimated that of every ten immigrant Mormons, two were Welsh'.

The *Merthyr Guardian* persistently ridiculed the Mormons and in January 1849, when it reported that 'gold-seeking mania' had prompted emigration to America, it expressed the opinion that:

...the general desire to get suddenly rich has been well applied in the service of religious fanaticism. In consequence large numbers of the operatives of this district are preparing to visit California for the double purpose of obtaining gold in abundance, and of settling in the Canaan of the Mormon prophet...

Though no evidence exists to suggest that disillusioned Mormons returned to Wales, in other cases, emigrants attracted by promises of high wages and enhanced living standards found them to be misleading. In March 1843, for example, the *Merthyr Guardian* told of how people who had sailed for the United States in 1842 were returning to Merthyr, and that such was the poverty over there that friends and relatives in Wales were collecting for the return fares for those still in America. In 1845, the newspaper reported that several people who had emigrated some years before had returned, 'declaring that in no country was it possible for an honest and industrious man to live so happily and merrily' as in Wales.

When Joseph Matters emigrated to Australia in 1849, his first port of call was Port Adelaide, where he spent three weeks: 'I was on shore nearly every day, but the heat was almost unsupportable...What with the sand blowing above and the heat, I would not live there for a fortune'. At Port Philip:

> ...after some trouble [I] managed to get a house with only two rooms in it, for which I have to pay 7/- a week... I work every day from five in the morning till seven at night... From what information I have been able to collect, these colonies are far too highly coloured in England. It is not labour that is wanted so much as capital. A man with a few hundred pounds... would do better here than in England, but a mechanic, with nothing but his labour to depend on, had better stay at home, if he can live at all...

Even the prospect of instant wealth at the Australian gold diggings was not enough to conquer the misgivings of certain immigrants, whose comments were published by the *Merthyr Guardian* in January 1853. Lodgings were '2/6d. a night for the privilege of lying on the floor with 50 or 60 others, and glad to get it'. Full board and lodging could cost as much as £2 10s a week, while beer was '2/- a quart, and not half as good as we used to have with Mr. Miller at the Lamb, for 4 pence...'.

Despite the return of some emigrants, and such letters from Australia, the movement away from Merthyr continued to gain momentum. The town's fame as an iron-making centre led its workers to enjoy considerable prestige in the manufacturing markets of the world, and its managers, engineers and skilled workers emigrated to other industrial centres. A newspaper report in 1845 noted that James Davis, son of the late landlord of the Bell Inn, Merthyr, and who had been for some time the principal engineer of an ironworks near Evreaux in France, had been appointed the sole director of another French ironworks. Similarly, in 1844, the paper reported on the drowning near St Petersburg of the eldest son of Thomas John Beynon, 'chain and cable master'. Most famously, Merthyr's John Hughes was invited by the Russian government in April 1869 to establish an ironworks and further develop its railways. Twelve months later, skilled men from Merthyr travelled to Hughes' works in the Donetsk Basin in the Ukraine to provide the nucleus of the workforce, and within six years Yuzovka, or 'Hughesovka', was the largest iron centre in Russia.

Throughout the period, the *Merthyr Guardian* spotlighted the departure of members of the labour aristocracy. In April 1851, for example, it told of how 'from time to time many of the best workmen have been seduced to leave these districts', and in September 1853 it continued to express its sadness over 'many of the steadier and more provident class of working men... are still going away'. However, it would be a mistake to assume that only the skilled or semi-skilled left. During the depression of 1842, for example, when the *Cambrian* reported on crowds which assembled weekly at the vestry room, and on the great numbers who were being returned every week to their parishes of origin, Merthyr's guardians, in their desperation, resorted to paying paupers to emigrate. Later, in their attempts to attract settlers, those in charge of Britain's colonial policy seemed willing to accept almost anyone, as the following report of 1849 suggests:

Inducements are being held out for persons to emigrate to Australia; and we learn that considerable numbers are preparing to go. We do not know the terms on which men are taken; but we should infer that passage is offered on easy terms, for many of the parties who apply... do not appear to have basked for any length of time in the sunshine of prosperity. Many of these are natives of the Emerald Isle, who, during the late calamities of that unfortunate country, sought a refuge from poverty and famine amid these o'er hanging cinder tips.

Just as the reasons for departure differed, so too did the methods of emigration. That some emigrants were sponsored by the masters has already been noted, as has the role of the guardians, but these only affected a small minority of emigrants, and most went either through the auspices of the various colonial movements or paid their own way. Regarding the former, Merthyr had its resident emigration agents and also visiting recruiting personnel from the various companies. In June 1841, for example, 'an agent of the New Zealand Company' was reported to be active in the town, while in July the following advertisement appeared in the *Merthyr Guardian*:

EMIGRATION

TO

AUSTRALIA AND CANADA

DAVID JONES JNR WATCHMAKER

HIGH STREET MERTHYR

Begs to inform the Public and Persons desirous of Emigrating to the above Colonies that he has been appointed EMIGRATION AGENT FOR MERTHYR and its neighbourhood.

Though attracted by the promise of free passage, in fact those who went under this category were carefully screened by the colonial companies. No family would be accepted with more than two children under seven, and the parents could not be older than forty. Good character was indispensable, and 'decisive certificates' of this were required. They had to be vaccinated against smallpox. Single women under eighteen without their parents were not admissible, unless they were engaged as domestic servants to ladies going out as cabin passengers in the same ship. Single men could not be allowed, except in a number not exceeding that of the single women in the same ship.

National statistics show that far more emigrants went to the USA than to British colonies, and consequently had to pay for their passages. Costs were low, however, as the rising volume of US-British trade led to increasing competition between ships. Thus whereas in 1816 a passage cost somewhere in the region of £16, in the 1840s it was very rarely more than £3 10s.

No matter who paid for the passages or the ultimate destination of the emigrants, one common factor was the appalling conditions on board the emigrant ships. Those vessels which transported convicts to Australia were registered as 2nd class at Lloyds, which meant 'they were unfit for carrying dry cargoes, but perfectly fit for the conveyance, on any voyage, of cargoes not in their nature subject to sea damage'. On the other hand, emigrant ships were registered as 3rd class, which meant that they were fit only for short voyages and were not suitable for journeys outside Europe. Emigrants were often crammed into any available space, disease posed a constant threat and passengers were often abused by the ships' crews. Though the introduction of larger American ships on the transatlantic routes after 1847 improved conditions, those emigrating to Australia had to endure long and often hazardous voyages, under conditions which some observers argued were worse than those experienced in slave ships, where at least the crews had a monetary interest in their cargoes.

Joseph Matters wrote: 'After a tedious voyage of 141 days, I am glad to inform you that we arrived here on Monday last, all in good health'. Despite this, however, the remainder of his first letter provides more than a few clues as to the arduous nature of the journey:

> Betsy was very sea sick for the first two months... and suffered greatly; the boys and myself got over it easily. Betsy was confined of a fine boy on the 1st November. We had no deaths and two births on the voyage. One vessel I went on board of off the Cape of Good Hope, had had 13 deaths, and one, the *Douglas*, that came into Port Adelaide... had 26 deaths on the voyage, so that we were extremely fortunate on the whole, although we were at first cheated sadly out of our allowance of provisions...

In January 1853, the *Merthyr Guardian* reported on the experiences of another party of Merthyr emigrants to Australia in the following terms: 'they went by the *Surrey*, were 25 weeks on the voyage, and were several days on short allowances; lost two masts, and were much shaken and knocked about'.

Of all Merthyr's emigrants, it was perhaps the Mormons who endured the most debilitating journey. Those who left Merthyr in 1849, for example, sailed on the *Troubadour* from Swansea to Liverpool, where 249 Mormons sailed aboard the *Buena Vista* for New Orleans. On-board conditions were very cramped, and their discomfort was made worse by a series of severe storms during the two-month voyage. At New Orleans they boarded the river steamer *Highland Mary* for the 800-mile journey up the Mississippi to St Louis, followed by a further 500-mile passage along the Missouri, during which the intense heat of the mid-west was blamed for causing an outbreak of cholera and the deaths of some sixty passengers. At Council Bluffs the survivors disembarked and Captain Jones divided the group into two sections. The first remained where they were, 'to establish a linguistic staging post for monoglot Welsh who would be following'. The second formed a wagon train of twenty-five covered wagons for the final 600-mile overland trek to Utah. This last stage saw the able-bodied going on foot; progress was painfully slow and it was to be many weeks before their epic journey was completed.

Having attempted to discover how many people left Merthyr, when and why they emigrated, and how, some attention should be devoted to where they settled. Although the *Merthyr Guardian* reported on people leaving for New Zealand, Australia, Canada, Cuba, Russia, Spain and South America, the statistics for the movement nationally and the reports of the newspaper itself point to the great majority of emigrants going to the USA. In fact, of the 2,740,000 British emigrants between 1846 and 1855, only 430,000 – less than 16% – went to Australia, New Zealand and South Africa; more than 2,300,000 went to North America, and of these 80% went to the United States. Once there:

> The inducements held out by American employers of higher wages and better conditions of work brought thousands of Welsh pouring into centres like Pittsburgh, Scranton, Wilkes Barre, and Carbondale, names which were as familiar in Wales as those of Merthyr, Tredegar or Aberdare.

In 1850, approximately 96% of Welsh emigrants were living in the northern states and 93% of these were concentrated in New York, Pennsylvania, Ohio and Wisconsin. Here, in the industrial heartland of America, and especially in the mines and foundries, 'the Welsh remained for long the elite of the labour force, the prima donnas of the payroll'. Because of this high regard for their expertise, it is not surprising that the great majority of Welsh settlers were drawn to these areas rather than further west. Only in two states could they be described as pioneers: in Utah, as a result of the Mormon exodus, and California, where following the discovery of gold in 1848 and 'seemingly in the belief that where there was a hole in the ground there should be a Welshman at the bottom of it', they flocked to the diggings from the eastern states as well as from Wales itself.

By no means all who left went abroad. During times of hardship, many people simply returned to their original homes, while colliers and miners abandoned Merthyr for the rapidly developing sale-coal pits of the Taff, Cynon and lower Rhondda valleys. Ironworkers journeyed to the iron centres of the north of England and Scotland where, around Middlesborough and the Cleveland iron field, for example: 'So many were the iron workers who migrated…from south Wales that Welsh communities, worshipping in their own tongue, came into being by the waters of the Tees'. Finally, at the end of May 1859, when 1,600 underground workers were thrown out of work by the closure of the Penydarren works, the *Merthyr Guardian* reported that for the last few weeks the Army 'and now the Navy' had been recruiting – and recruiting well – in the town, despite having had little success in previous campaigns.

In conclusion, what effect did this movement away have on those who remained in the town? Emigration undoubtedly eased the strain on the town's housing supply and consequently led to an improvement, albeit marginal, in the standard of public health. Furthermore, the exodus meant there was less competition for jobs, and thus greater security for those who remained. There is also some evidence to suggest that Merthyr became a more settled, peaceful community in the 1860s, when it had lost its boom-town reputation and character along with many of the elements that image had attracted. Conversely, emigration was seen by contemporaries, and especially the *Merthyr Guardian*, as constituting a sad and expensive blow both socially and economically. In April 1851, it reported on the great number of emigrants whose 'skill and labour now come into competition with those of their countrymen and former fellow-workmen'. Twelve months later, it expressed its frustration in the following terms: '…year after year are we sending our skilled workmen into other districts and countries to form rival manufactures, compete with us in the markets of the World, and to render still worse the condition of those who remain behind'. It is certainly true that within a generation the ironworks of America, founded on the skill of immigrant workmen, were to threaten the very existence of Merthyr's industry.

The social costs of Merthyr's economic decline were exacerbated by the very character of the emigrants themselves. As the *Merthyr Guardian* noted in April 1851: 'what makes the matter worse [is] those who leave are the young and lusty men who ought to be the support of the declining generation'. In April 1860, the *Merthyr Telegraph* put it well:

> One by one, grey hair after grey hair, furrow after furrow, we trace the indication of Merthyr's decline.

CONCLUSION & POSTSCRIPT

In March 1850, the *Morning Chronicle* expressed the opinion:

> If our coal and iron form the substantial basis of our national opulence and power, he by whose skill and labour these minerals are produced ought at least to be well clothed and well fed, to have the means afforded him of educating and advancing his children, and of providing for his old age out of the produce of his labour whilst he is capable of work.

Yet almost everything the newspaper found in Merthyr represented the opposite. Two years later, E.F. Roberts wrote in amazement:

> There is much ignorance, much poverty, dire privation, and on the whole an indescribable state of things existing in Merthyr Tydfil, side by side with the means and facilities for rendering the people the happiest, cleanest, healthiest, and wealthiest among any associated number of working men.

As far as Commissioner Lingen was concerned, the responsibility lay firmly with the masters:

> I regard their degraded condition as entirely the fault of their employers, who give them far less tendance and care than they bestow upon their cattle, and who, with a few exceptions, use and regard them as so much brute force instrumental to wealth, but as nowise involving claims on human sympathy.

Despite the claims that housing conditions were far worse in rural Wales, that hours of work were longer on the farms, that wages were lower in the countryside and diets there were monotonous and inadequate, there can be no escaping the fact that, for many of Merthyr's workers, life was a constant struggle to eke out a living in appalling conditions, while their employers hobnobbed with royalty and built their mock-gothic castles, or bought country estates in Dorsetshire costing £335,000. Meliorists argue that one cannot blame the ironmasters for the admitted evils of the age, as they were simply a part of the general order of things. However, it was the ironmasters who brought the wage-economy to Merthyr in the first place; they were the ones who benefited most from its rigid application; and they fought a vigorous and sustained defensive action against its erosion by 'bureaucrats', 'meddlers' and 'revolutionaries'. Even John Josiah Guest, who owned and presided over the greatest ironworks in the world and whose paternalism was much lauded both by contemporaries and more recent writers, had to accept the 1850 Cholera Commission's indictment that Dowlais was perhaps the dirtiest, most insanitary settlement in Britain. It also helps to explain why Robert Thompson Crawshay chose 'God Forgive Me' as the epitaph on his huge gravestone in Vaynor churchyard.

And what of the town's fortunes since the 1860s? The population continued to grow throughout the nineteenth century, although by 1871 it lost its pre-eminence to the faster-growing towns of Cardiff, Swansea and the Rhondda. People continued to arrive, however, mostly from rural Wales, although in the wake of the Irish came other groups of economic migrants, most notably from the Basque region of northern Spain. Merthyr's population peaked at 80,000 in 1901, since when it has fallen to today's figure of 55,000.

In hindsight, the short-lived boom in the iron trade associated with the second period of railway mania in the mid-1840s probably marked the zenith of the industry in south Wales. In Merthyr, the exhaustion of local iron ores and the simultaneous switch to steel crippled all but Dowlais and Cyfarthfa. The Plymouth works struggled on until 1880, and in 1891 a large part of the Dowlais plant was transferred to Cardiff. Cyfarthfa closed for several bitter years in the 1870s, but then reopened and produced steel until 1910. The First World War saw it being recommissioned, in 1915, to produce steel for shells, but it closed completely in 1919. Dowlais managed to survive the 1920s, but the main part of the plant closed in 1930 and some six years later all steel production ended.

In the second half of the nineteenth century, up until 1914, what prosperity there was came largely from the burgeoning coal industry. As early as 1841, almost 10,000 tons of sale-coal had been sent from Merthyr to the London market; by 1851 that figure had more than trebled and from 1859 the Dowlais Company began to mine coal for its own sake. Pits which had once supplied the ironworks now looked to the coal markets of the world, and new and deeper mines were opened as the south Wales coalfield became the engine house for imperial expansion. In this, the central valleys proved crucial, for here it was that the steam-coal lay in abundance. It was, after all, pronounced the Royal Navy, the best coal in the world, because it lit quickly, gave off great heat, left little ash and was almost smokeless – a factor which, in an age prior to radar, made it the nineteenth century's naval equivalent of stealth technology.

So it was largely coal which sustained the town until the end of the First World War. Then came the Great Depression and the collapse in the demand for both steel and coal, when, by any measure, Merthyr suffered an economic and social catastrophe. Unemployment, in 1935 as high as 62% (in Dowlais it actually hit 80%), gave Merthyr the dubious distinction of being second only to Jarrow in the British unemployment league. Poverty, malnutrition and disease rates soared and the population haemorrhaged. Between 1921 and 1939, an average of over 1,000 people a year left the town, which was increasingly shoddy and derelict, and eventually bankrupt as well. Indeed, so complete was the collapse and so moribund was the government's response that, in 1939, a Parliamentary Report recommended that the town be completely abandoned and the remainder of its people moved in full to either the coast or the Usk valley. What had once been the greatest iron-manufacturing centre on earth was condemned to be flooded to make a reservoir.

It was the Second World War, and the interventionist stance of post-war governments, which saved the town, bringing new industries like Hoover, O.P. Chocolates, Triang and Thorn, as well as renewed investment in coal and steel. The vicissitudes of the trade cycle, however, and the industrial policies of the Thatcher government, meant that Triang ceased production in the 1970s and all mining and steel-making finally ended in the 1980s, while Thorn Lighting closed in 1991.

Following the slow introduction of public health and town planning legislation, many of the slums which had disfigured Merthyr were eventually swept away. Nevertheless, most of the housing stock was Victorian and remained so until well into the twentieth century. This meant that even as late as 1971, 17% of Merthyr's houses still lacked hot water, 29% had no bath and over 32% had no inside toilet. The 1960s and 1970s saw a major programme of redevelopment which swept away this sub-standard housing, but the pity is that many of the houses which disappeared were basically sound. Urged on by the council, whole swathes of Merthyr were flattened by developers in favour of more modern housing. Many of the councillors had been scarred in their youth by the Depression and seemed to loathe everything that represented the town's past. Others wanted to be seen to be taking an active part in the modernisation of the area, and many were convinced this would give people a much better life – aspirations which, in hindsight, have not always materialised. Merthyr's redevelopment not only demolished slums but also destroyed valuable historic buildings and seriously weakened what had been strong and vibrant communities. The pity was that the 'envelope' schemes of refurbishment and modernisation, financed by the European Union, did not appear until the 1980s.

As far as mortality rates are concerned, in 1901 the town's Medical Officer of Health reported that the death rate from measles, scarlet fever, whooping cough, diphtheria, enteric fever, diarrhoea and smallpox was half as high again in Merthyr as the average for England and Wales. While the national infant mortality rate then stood at 151 deaths per 1,000 births, in Merthyr it was 261. Even today, Merthyr is still classified as the unhealthiest place in England and Wales. It is also, along with the other valley communities of south Wales, one of the poorest communities in western Europe.

As for politics, just as the town led the way in 1868 with the triumphant election of the Liberal nonconformist Henry Richard, so it was the first town in Britain to elect a Labour MP, Keir Hardie, in 1900. Apart from the period 1918–22, when it was again represented by a Liberal, it has been a Labour bastion ever since. Indeed, until recently the standing joke was that at elections they didn't count the Labour vote so much as weigh it.

Nonconformity continued to grow in importance and influence until the First World War. Thereafter, its influence was to wane. At first the decline appeared to be a gradual one, but with the coming of the car and television it accelerated dramatically and now, throughout urban south Wales, where they haven't been demolished completely or converted into flats or shops or workplaces, abandoned and derelict chapels stand as silent monuments to a largely forgotten past. Some people continue to attend the churches and chapels, though, and Merthyr still has its Catholic, Mormon and Jewish communities, joined today by a small number of Hindus and Muslims.

As for the benefit societies, they continued to grow, especially the Oddfellows. Indeed, the latter eventually protected so many people that in 1911, when the Liberal government was setting up its National Insurance Act, it used their actuarial tables to calculate the level of contribution and payment required. Similarly, after the Second World War the state poached many of the Oddfellows' key administrators to run the fledgling welfare state and National Health Service. Ironically, National Insurance and a welfare state meant that there was no longer any financial need for benefit societies; they declined rapidly, and the Oddfellows are no longer active in the town. The Freemasons remain, however.

When it comes to sex, Britain, sadly, has the highest rate of teenage pregnancy in Europe and Merthyr has the highest rate in Britain. In the 1970s, when I began my research, the town still had more betting shops per head than anywhere else in Britain, and the tradition remains strong. So too does the town's fascination with boxing endure, with national and international champions like Eddie Thomas, Howard Winstone and Johnny Owen bringing great pride. More alcohol is consumed per person than anywhere else in Wales and underage drinking is a particular problem as, unfortunately, is drug abuse and associated crime.

On the other hand, there is much to recommend about modern Merthyr. The industrial waste and dereliction which scarred the town for so long has now finally been swept away and there has been a glorious re-greening of the valley. Hoover and O.P. Chocolates are still going strong and new factories have been established, providing work for local people as well as the very latest economic immigrants, this time from Portugal and Brazil. A new Tesco has opened in the centre of town and a retail park is being built. Aided by European funding, new transport links have been established, and urban regeneration is ongoing, with the lower High Street now looking better than it has done for years.

There is a great resilience about the people of Merthyr Tydfil. Maybe the pride and dignity of the skilled ironworkers who made the town is indelibly stamped on their DNA. Perhaps it stems from the legacy of so many years of struggle and hardship, but, whatever the cause, there is a renewed sense of optimism for the future.

NOTES

1   J.P. Addis, *The Crawshay Dynasty*, Cardiff, 1957, p.16.

2   H. Carter and S. Wheatley, *Merthyr Tydfil in 1851: A Study of the Spatial Structure of a Welsh Industrial Town*, Cardiff, 1982.

3   G.A. Williams, *The Merthyr Rising*, London, 1978, p.28.

4   D.W. Howell, *Land and People in Nineteenth Century Wales*, London, 1977, p.97.

5   A.H. John, *The Industrial Development of South Wales, 1750-1850*, Cardiff, 1950, p.66.

6   I.G. Jones, 'Politics in Merthyr Tydfil,' in *Glamorgan Historian*, Vol. 10, p.53.

7   M.P.L., *Report on the Sanitary Condition of Merthyr Tydfil drawn up at the request of the Local Board of Health*, William Kay – Temporary Officer of Health, 1854, p.8.

8   Richard Howard, surgeon to the Royal Infirmary and Manchester Workhouse, quoted by George Rosen, 'Disease, debility and death', in H.J. Dyos & M. Wolff (eds), *The Victorian City*, Vol. 2, London, 1973, p.626.

9   A.D. Gilbert, *Religion and Society in Industrial England*, London, 1976, p.89.

10   Eric Trudgill, 'Prostitution and Pater Familias', in J.J. Dyos & M. Wolff (eds), *The Victorian City*, Vol. 2, London, 1973, pp.700-701.

11   *Cardiff & Merthyr Guardian*, 6 September 1851.

LIST OF ILLUSTRATIONS

FURTHER READING

John P. Addis, *The Crawshay Dynasty*, Cardiff, 1957.

H. Carter & S. Wheatley, *Merthyr Tydfil in 1851: A Study of the Spatial Structure of a Welsh Industrial Town*, Cardiff, 1982.

Andy Croll, *Civilising the Urban,* Cardiff, 2000.

M.J. Daunton, 'The Dowlais Iron Company in the Iron Industry', *Welsh History Review*, VI (1972), pp.16-48.

John Davies, *The Making of Wales*, Cadw, 1996.

Chris Evans, *The Labyrinth of Flames: Work and social conflict in early industrial Merthyr Tydfil*, Cardiff, 1993.

Trevor Herbert & Gareth Elwyn Jones (eds), *People & Protest: Wales 1815-1880,* Cardiff, 1988.

Angela John, 'The Chartist Endurance: Industrial South Wales, 1840-1860', *Morgannwg*, XV, 1971.

D.J.V. Jones, *Before Rebecca: Popular Protest in Wales 1793-1835*, London, 1973.

—, *Crime in Nineteenth-Century Wales*, Cardiff, 1992.

I.G. Jones, *Explorations and Explanations. Essays in the Social History of Victorian Wales*, Llandysul, 1981.

—, *Health, Wealth and Politics in Victorian Wales*, Swansea, 1979.

Merthyr Tydfil Historical Society, *Merthyr Historian*, Vols 1-15.

Glanmor Williams (ed.), *Merthyr Politics: the making of a working-class tradition*, Cardiff, 1966.

Gwyn A. Williams, *The Merthyr Rising*, Cardiff, 1988.

INDEX

TEMPUS – REVEALING HISTORY

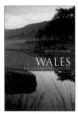

Wales: An Illustrated History
PRYS MORGAN (ED.)

'Masterly... this well-illustrated narrative of Wales from prehistory to the present day can be strongly recommended'
BBC History Magazine
£17.99
0 7524 2970 1

Welsh Kings: Warriors, Warlords and Princes
KARI MAUND
'A must for all lovers of Welsh history'
South Wales Argus
£10.99
0 7524 2973 6

Merthyr Tydfil:
Iron Metropolis – Life in a Welsh Industrial Town
KEITH STRANGE
£17.99
0 7524 3451 9

The Welsh Wars of Independence
DAVID MOORE
'Beautifully written, subtle and remarkably perceptive... a major re-examination of a thousand years of Welsh history'
John Davies
£25
0 7524 3321 0

FORTHCOMING WELSH HISTORY FROM TEMPUS

Tudor Wales
From Owain Glyn Dwr to the Spanish Armada
MATTHEW GRIFFITHS

Welsh Witches and Wizards
A History of Magic and Witchcraft in Wales
RICHARD SUGGETT

The Renaissance in Wales
NIA POWELL

The Welsh Bible
ERYN WHITE

Wales at War
The Experience of the Second World War in Wales
STUART BROOMFIELD

Music in Wales: A History
LYNN DAVIES

If you are interested in purchasing other books published by Tempus, or in case you have difficulty finding any Tempus books in your local bookshop, you can also place orders directly through our website

www.tempus-publishing.com